PRAISE FOR **BUILDING CULTURE**

"Julian Rose builds a compelling and optimistic argument for museums as rare remaining sites for architectural creativity amid a world of optimized sameness. Layered within these striking interviews is a story about the human element of museums: the architects, artists, and publics—as well as engineers, artisans, curators, mayors, funders, and more—who bring to life these hotly debated cathedrals of culture."

—**MELANIE KRESS**, SENIOR CURATOR, PUBLIC ART FUND

"Julian Rose's *Building Culture* takes as its premise the question of how museum architects make meaning—and how architecture impacts one of the most fundamental experiences of museum-going: the ever-changing cultural, historical, and political relationships between subject and object."

—**CAITLIN MURRAY**, DIRECTOR OF THE CHINATI FOUNDATION/ LA FUNDACIÓN CHINATI

"*Building Culture* by Julian Rose offers a luminous and profound analysis of the limitations and potentials that architecture—as a collaborative practice—maintains in the present. Undoubtedly a book museum professionals and enthusiasts alike should read."

—**MANUEL BORJA-VILLEL**, FORMER DIRECTOR OF MUSEO REINA SOFÍA

"Julian Rose's *Building Culture* offers unprecedented accounts from some of our time's most defining voices and invites rigorous reflection at the intersection of visual culture, architecture, and museum studies. *Building Culture* is also a potent reminder of the essential role of oral history in providing us with more nuanced understandings from the perspectives of the makers and thinkers behind the spaces we share."

—**DAISY DESROSIERS**, DAVID AND FRANCIE HORVITZ FAMILY FOUNDATION DIRECTOR AND CHIEF CURATOR, THE GUND AT KENYON COLLEGE

JULIAN ROSE

PA PRESS

PRINCETON ARCHITECTURAL PRESS · NEW YORK

BUILDING

Sixteen Architects on
How Museums Are Shaping
the Future of Art,
Architecture, and Public Space

CULTURE

Published by
Princeton Architectural Press
A division of Chronicle Books LLC
70 West 36th Street
New York, NY 10018
papress.com

Editor: Sara Stemen
Designer: Paul Wagner

Library of Congress Cataloging-in-
Publication Data
Names: Rose, Julian, 1984– interviewer.
Title: Building culture : Sixteen architects
    on how museums are shaping the future
    of art, architecture, and public space /
    Julian Rose.
Description: First edition. | New York :
    Princeton Architectural Press, [2024] |
    Summary: "Sixteen of the world's
    preeminent architects offer insiders'
    views of how museums are designed and
    how they shape our experience of art"
    —Provided by publisher.
Identifiers: LCCN 2023054924 |
    ISBN 9781797223681 (hardcover) | ISBN
    9781797227139 (ebook)
Subjects: LCSH: Museum architecture—
    Social aspects. | Architects—Interviews.
Classification: LCC NA6690 .R66 2024 |
    DDC 727/.6—dc23/eng/20231206
LC record available at https://lccn.loc.
    gov/2023054924

Versions of the following interviews were
previously published in *Artforum*:
Pages 44–61 : © *Artforum*, October 2017,
    "Living Spaces: Julian Rose interviews
    David Adjaye."
Pages 84–105: © *Artforum*, November 2017,
    "Machine Age: Julian Rose interviews
    Elizabeth Diller."
Pages 106–25: © *Artforum*, May 2018,
    "Tectonic Arts: Julian Rose interviews
    Frank Gehry."

Pages 154–69: © *Artforum*, March 2018,
    "Significant Difference: Julian Rose
    interviews Jacques Herzog."
Pages 230–43: © *Artforum*, Summer 2018,
    "Light Houses: Julian Rose interviews
    Renzo Piano."
Pages 264–77: © *Artforum*, April 2018, "Into
    the Light: Julian Rose interviews Kazuyo
    Sejima."

To Helena and Cosima

Contents

Foreword

Yve-Alain Bois

In 1923 the French writer Paul Valéry published a strange little essay beginning with these words: "I don't like museums much. Many are admirable, none are delightful. Delight has little to do with the principles of classification, conservation, and public utility, clear and reasonable though these may be."

He was not the first to disapprove of museums—ever since the birth of the modern museum, in the late eighteenth century, contrarian voices had been raised against it. In 1796, as Napoleon filled the Louvre with artworks looted from Italy by his armies, the French architect, politician, and historian of architecture Quatremère de Quincy composed his pamphlet *Letters to Miranda*, condemning the displacement of artworks not only in moral terms but also for purely aesthetic reasons. His polemic was that the decontextualization of art objects by the museum was sapping the very life out of them and transforming them into mere merchandise, "seen as jewels or diamonds that we enjoy merely for their monetary value."

Valéry's tone was different: rather than denouncing the decontextualization of artworks per se, he condemned the act of collecting itself, the gathering together of artworks in the museum where they would compete with and even cancel each other by their sheer vicinity, overwhelming the viewer in a chaotic and vertiginous accumulation that he deemed "a necessarily unusable excess of capital." Attempting to diagnose his malaise when confronted with this haphazard mix of objects, he abruptly concluded that in the museum, Painting and Sculpture have been orphaned: "Their mother, Architecture, is dead. As long as she lived, she gave them their place, their function, their discipline. They had no freedom to stray. They had their allotted space, their given light, their subjects, their alliances. As long as Architecture lived, they knew what they wanted."

Valéry's peculiar distaste is probably incomprehensible to most of today's museumgoers: we tend to like these institutions precisely for

9

the mélanges and surprises that he dreaded. It is also difficult to figure out exactly what he had in mind when he stated that architecture was dead—after all, he was a close friend of the pioneering Auguste Perret, and he devoted hundreds of pages of his voluminous writings to this art. But what is undeniably striking is that he considered architecture's passing as the main cause of the museum's problems. Could one envision a reverse proposal: a living architecture for the museum, which would ensure a full appreciation of the art it contains?

Such is, in a few words, the question that Julian Rose asks the architects he interviewed for this volume. Their answers are, predictably, affirmative; less predictably, he shares their optimism.

Less predictably, because he begins where Valéry left off: Rose too finds that architecture has died, or rather most of it. The French writer had no culprit to indict—presumably he felt that its death had resulted from sheer exhaustion—but for Rose, architecture was killed by the demon of economy.

His introduction to the topic is dire: "Countless construction projects around the globe proceed without any input from architects at all. When architects are involved, their ineffable contributions tend to be concentrated at the top end of the market, where they can add a signature flourish to a building whose underlying parameters have already been mostly dictated by more concrete constraints or more heavily vested interests." Reading Rose's description of the long list of requirements that any architect has to fulfill in their design process—from building the maximum possible area on a site to squeezing its occupants into the minimum allowable floor-to-floor height—all of which inevitably lead to standardized solutions, one is bound to despair. A building today "is not so much designed… as optimized, in the sense that it provides the greatest quantity of the most profitable space possible in a given context," Rose concludes, a judgment that is, despite its severity, actually seconded by many of the architects he interrogated.

But then comes a coup de théâtre, from which stems his hopefulness: the same architects, whatever their position on other topics, all see the museum as the single building type able to escape the economic mandate imposed on architecture. This explains why they all jump at any opportunity to design one (all of them have made museums one of their specialties, and several have built a dozen or more) and are willing to devote so much of their time to entering ruthless competitions, but it does not explain why the museum, as type, should be such an exception. This is where Rose's framing of the issue is particularly helpful: the museum as a building is exceptional, he proposes, because it cannot be optimized, which, in turn, explains why it can come in so many different shapes. It is not that museum architecture is exempted from financial constraints (its budgets are generally more generous than those of other buildings but never a free-for-all), or that it plays no economic role in the context in which it intervenes. That is, museums do produce value, albeit only indirectly (mass tourism, gentrification, boosting of the art market, et cetera: everything that goes under the umbrella of "the Bilbao effect," which most architects interviewed by Rose wish to dissociate from—though not the one from whose building this phrase was coined). To be more precise, let's say that the value that museum architecture produces directly is not quantifiable, because it rests on unquantifiable capital—the "necessarily unusable excess of capital" mentioned by Valéry. Yet today this capital is based not so much in the objects the museum holds, suggests Rose, but in their aura, which it sets out to amplify.

One of the most interesting aperçus provided by Rose in his synthesis of the extremely diverse responses he received to his inquiries is a comparison between the historical development of the department store and that of the museum. Contrary to the fear of a Quatremère, he notes that "the museum never really turned the artwork into a commodity. Instead, it commodified the experience of viewing." Defying the expectations of numerous Cassandras, the museum did not turn into a department store; rather it is the department store that is currently trying to survive the assault of digital commerce by adopting an art museum model. Despite the well-known prediction by Walter Benjamin that the aura of the work of art was doomed by the proliferation of new mass media, it is solely that aura, on which museums now have a quasi-monopoly, that attracts a mass of visitors to them today. Ironically, their visits are often encouraged by the latest evolutions in media technology. And so the department store is slowly dying, while museums, which have become a favored setting for selfies, are proliferating.

The reasons for this proliferation are brilliantly analyzed by Rose, as well as those for the accelerating growth of the museum's public, even though the architects he asks about those phenomena do not always have ready answers to his probing questions. One growing concern is circulation, surely the most specifically architectural puzzle confronting any museum builder today. Indeed, it is more urgent than ever, thanks to the much-celebrated (and also much-decried) ballooning of the audience for art in the twenty-first century. Somewhat surprisingly, most architects questioned for this volume tend to be vague about how they tackle the problem—perhaps it is because, contra Rose, the flux of visitors is the one feature of museum architecture that does need to be optimized, and with regard to which the architect's creative freedom is thus more constricted? Architects, after all, rarely write their own brief, and architectural questions inevitably shade into institutional concerns.

As a questioner, Rose is persistent. He states at the outset that "the essential program of a museum is, after, all, deceptively simple: it is a place for visitors to encounter works of art. But what is the best way to encounter a work of art?" This leads his subjects to speak about their own relationship to art—which is more often than not what led them, indirectly, to architecture. There is something reassuring in this shared hallmark of their responses, in thinking that what unites such a diverse group of builders is their unabashed love for art. Perhaps this is where lies the kernel of the museum's exceptionality as a building type: above all, it offers architects the chance to think of their own most transformative encounters with art, and how to replicate and even improve these experiences.

Preface

In 2012, I was charged with expanding coverage of architecture at *Artforum*, where I had just been hired as a senior editor, focusing on the increasingly visible interactions between art and architecture that seemed to be both more intense and more varied than at any previous point in the magazine's fifty-year history. Over the next few years, I was able to cover these interdisciplinary exchanges from various angles: new buildings produced by ambitious collaborations between artists and architects; artists expanding the definition of public art to encompass freestanding, inhabitable structures; architects experimenting with forms traditionally reserved for artists, from installation to performance. But I found myself continually circling around one topic: the art museum.

By that point there could be little doubt that art museums were playing an expanded role in society. The "Bilbao effect" was already a decade and a half old. New museums had become a cornerstone of urban development around the world, and these buildings were increasingly shaping both how culture was made and how it was experienced. But what struck me most powerfully was the way in which this topic seemed to have an almost universal appeal across the magazine's readership. Everyone, I realized, had something at stake in the museum: artists and architects, of course, but also curators and collectors, scholars and critics, planners and politicians, not to mention architecture fans, art lovers, regular museumgoers, and the general public.

This diversity of interests and perspectives could make it hard to know how to approach the museum. But I was also struck by the recurring presence of one voice in many conversations about museums: the architect's. Architects weren't necessarily the central character in a given museum project—that role might be played by a powerful patron, a visionary curator, or an important artist—but they were consistently the most unifying force. In the course of designing a new museum, after all, an architect ends up talking to nearly all of the different stakeholders in the project—from the board of directors to the museum's staff, from the museum's members to the local city council, from the artists whose work the museum will exhibit to the contractors who will build it. Above all, it is the architect who must mediate among all these different points of view, coalescing them into a coherent vision and then translating that vision into a concrete form.

And so I decided to undertake a series of interviews with architects about the design of art museums. I began looking around the world for the architects who had done the most to shape the current state of the art museum and those who seemed poised to have the greatest impact on its future. Encouraged by a positive response from readers, as well as by the enthusiasm of my interlocutors themselves, I continued to expand the series. By the time I moved on from *Artforum*, I had completed six interviews with some of the world's leading architects, but I knew that the topic still deserved sustained attention, and the idea for this book was born.

The more I reflected on my experiences both in the art world and in the field of architecture, the richer the topic of museum design seemed. In parallel with my work as a writer and editor, I had received a professional degree in architecture, and by the time I began conceptualizing this book I had spent more than a decade working in a wide range of practices, from large corporate offices to small design-build firms, as well as cofounding my own design studio. All this had given me a firsthand sense of how hard it is to make meaningful architecture in the face of the intense pressures—above all, economic—facing architects today. In this context, the museum came to seem like an almost miraculous exception—in the attention these buildings gained, in the creativity their architects were allowed to exercise, in the very breadth of their significance.

The project continued to develop over the next seven years, eventually growing to sixteen conversations. Midway through, a global pandemic closed museums and, briefly, introduced acute uncertainty about their future. At the time I was grateful that these conversations could be continued virtually, although I was also conscious of a certain irony, given that most of the architects I spoke with emphasized the importance of in-person experience—an emphasis that seemed justified when museums eventually reopened and audiences flooded back.

During that same time, in the spring and summer of 2020, the largest social-justice movement in decades swept through the United States, spurring museums, along with many other cultural institutions, to rethink their role in society, bringing questions of access and equity to the fore. Over the past several years, too, conversations about the relationship between politics and culture have become more highly charged as new armed conflicts have erupted around the globe. None of these developments have diminished the importance of art museums or the role architects play in their design, but they all have introduced new pressures and opened new perspectives that have caused the nature and purpose of the museum to evolve.

Meanwhile, the professional landscape of architecture has continued to shift. Prizes have been awarded, competitions have been won, new buildings have been completed, and others have broken ground. Tracking these developments prompted me to add several new voices to the book, as well as requiring second or even third follow-up conversations with some of the architects already included. It also presented difficult decisions. In the summer of 2023, as the book was being edited, three women came forward to journalists at the *Financial Times* to accuse David Adjaye of sexual assault, which he denied. I had interviewed Adjaye as part of my original *Artforum* series in 2017 and had followed up with him about several more recent projects in 2021. After extensive deliberation, I decided to keep my conversation with Adjaye in the book. Even as these accusations are extremely serious and have prompted important conversations about power and exploitation in the architectural profession, Adjaye's built work—particularly his design for the National Museum of African American History and Culture, completed in 2016—has already altered the course of museum design in the twenty-first century. And his thinking about how museums can confront—and eventually undo—the legacy of colonialism resonates beyond his individual practice, helping to address questions currently facing the entire field of architecture and reverberating across politics and culture around the world.

More broadly, I envision this book as creating space for a new kind of conversation about architecture, both more collective and more comprehensive. While several of the architects in these pages are part of the very generation for whom the moniker *starchitect* was coined, all sixteen reject that label and emphasize the collaborative nature of their practice. (Note, too, the "we" that inevitably creeps into their answers to my questions about their work.) And while many of these figures are frequently in the news, most of the media attention they receive is heavily promotional, whether advertising a new project or simply feeding the cult of celebrity that's a perennially reliable performer in our economy of attention. I would propose, in fact, that a defining characteristic of architectural practice today is that architects have little time for intense reflection or deep conversation. Much has changed, both for better and for worse, since Le Corbusier famously listed "Homme de Lettres" on the "profession" line of his French ID card, but it's certainly true that the dream that architecture itself might constitute a vital form of intellectual discourse has been largely abandoned. My hope is that this book can go some small way toward restoring architecture's discursive dimension; surely there is no better subject to start with than the art museum, since the design of these buildings is vital to the future not only of art and architecture but of culture at large.

Like a building, a book is inherently collaborative, even if both are held by long tradition to be the work of a singular author. A project of such extended gestation could not have been realized without the support and participation of innumerable people. I would like to thank first the architects themselves, as well as their associates, for their generous participation. My deep thanks are also due to Michelle Kuo, my brilliant and generous editor in chief at *Artforum,* who first supported this project, as well as to my expert, eagle-eyed editor at Princeton Architectural Press, Sara Stemen, and her entire team, who were essential to its realization. I would like to thank Hal Foster for providing key encouragement in the early stages of the project, and for crucial input on its evolving scope and form. I'm grateful to Yve-Alain Bois not only for a superb forward but for twenty years of intellectual guidance and friendship. Thanks to Naomi Falk for her invaluable help securing images, as well as to Iwan Baan for providing so many of his fantastic photographs of the buildings discussed in these pages. Harry Cooper kindly shared insights gained from many years of curatorial work. Leo Henke was always ready to share his unparalleled expertise in all matters concerning building technology and construction. Guy Nordenson provided pivotal advice and assistance at several stages of the project. Don McMahon offered an incisive reading of my introduction as well as invaluable advice from beginning to end. Sarah Oppenheimer kindly offered thoughts and advice throughout the process, and her work and conversation have shaped my thinking on art, architecture, and museums for over a decade. Sheena Wagstaff graciously shared her unique perspective on the relationship between contemporary art and the museum. Simon Wu generously offered his thoughts on museums and media. The support, advice, and judicious criticism of two fellow writers whom I deeply admire, Ian Volner and Isabel Flower, were indispensable throughout the project. Finally, I wish to thank Helena Anrather, my most trusted— and most patient—reader, and Cosima Rose, whose imminent arrival into the world proved to be just the right motivation to finally finish this book.

Olafur Eliasson, *The Weather Project*, 2003 , installed at Tate Modern, London

18

Introduction

What is it, exactly, that architects do? The intuitively obvious answer—that they make buildings—doesn't withstand more than a few moments of reflection. The real business of putting buildings together, after all, falls to contractors, laborers, and practitioners of the various construction trades; an entire economic sector, the construction industry, has arisen to provide this service. Architects, meanwhile, work at a remove, their efforts mediated by the various forms of representation—models, drawings, renderings—that are the actual products of their occupation. So is their contribution a higher-order one, requiring us to take a step back for it to come into focus? Architects make plans, architects design things. Perhaps, then, it is their thinking that shapes the built environment; perhaps they are the ones responsible for the texture of our cities and the character of our interventions in the landscape.

But this idea, too, collapses under scrutiny. Today, most cities and landscapes are shaped by forces much larger than the vision of an architect—by politics, by the real estate market, above all, by the imperatives of industrial and economic development. In this broader domain, architects vie with clients, investors, regulators, bureaucrats, project managers, technical consultants, and a host of other interested parties, while countless construction projects around the globe proceed without any input from architects at all. When architects are involved, their ineffable contributions tend to be concentrated at the top end of the market, where they can add a signature flourish to a building whose underlying parameters have already been mostly dictated by more concrete constraints or more heavily vested interests. The real answer, then, seems to be that today's architects are creators of exceptional spaces in an all-too-literal sense: narrow specialists engaged primarily in high-profile projects, routinely enlisted for place making and brand building but largely alienated from the physical fabric of everyday life.

Their arrival at this point has not been sudden; it is rooted in architecture's tangled relationship to modernity as it has unfolded across more than a century. Modern architecture promised to draw out the best from the revolutionary forces of modernity—the radical technological innovations, the rapid growth of new cities, the reshuffling of entrenched social orders—to build a better world from the ground up. In doing so, it simultaneously promised to ameliorate many of modernity's worst aspects—the urban poverty, the environmental devastation, the social alienation—claiming the power to engender social progress through spatial means. But this brave new world failed to materialize, while the forces of modernization only accelerated, continually reshaping physical reality—along with its underlying social, economic, and political systems—in ways that rendered architecture's inefficacy ever more apparent.

Prescient observers have long understood this trajectory. Manfredo Tafuri was among the twentieth century's most precise elucidators of the relationship between buildings and societies that produce them. Over fifty years ago, in his book *Architecture and Utopia*, Tafuri set out to write a comprehensive study of the relationship between modern architecture and modern economic systems, undertaking what he called "the precise identification of those tasks which capitalist development has taken away from architecture." He concluded that by the final decades of the twentieth century, architecture had been reduced "to form without utopia; in the best cases, to sublime uselessness."

At first glance, the art museum would seem to be the apotheosis of this progression. Of all the new buildings constructed around the world in recent decades, museums have tended to be the most iconic, designed by the most celebrated architects. One of the primary functions of a new museum building is, in a sense, to simply look new and exciting, generating interest and gaining attention through expressive architecture and aesthetic innovation. And so the museum has earned a reputation as the most sculptural of buildings, a place for architects—unhindered by the practical constraints that might bog down more pedestrian building types—to give their creativity full reign. Tafuri was no optimist, but it seems unlikely that even he could have predicted the extent to which this particular brand of sublime uselessness would be smoothly instrumentalized by the ascendant and globalized capitalism of the late twentieth and early twenty-first centuries, with museums regularly conscripted to drive urban regeneration, attract tourism, and stimulate economic growth.

And yet the core premise of this book is that art museums are significant for an entirely different reason: rather than being symptomatic of the plight of architects today, these buildings offer one of the few remaining opportunities for architects to realize the full potential of their calling. Over more than half a century, the sixteen architects interviewed here have designed dozens of museums across five continents. These include any number of undeniably paradigm-shifting projects: among them Renzo Piano's Pompidou Centre in Paris, completed in 1977, which radically reinvented the social function of the museum in the wake of the upheavals of May 1968; Frank Gehry's Guggenheim Museum in Bilbao, completed in 1997, which catalyzed such a dramatic regeneration of its urban context that the eponymous "Bilbao effect" was coined to describe the transformative economic potential of high-profile architecture for new cultural institutions; Kazuyo Sejima's 21st Century Museum of Contemporary Art in Kanazawa, completed in 2004, which deployed pioneering techniques of glass construction to explore new immersive effects, rethinking how museum architecture might shape the experience of art in the new century; and David Adjaye's Museum of West African Art, currently under construction in Benin City, which not only breaks with the historical legacy of the European museum but also seeks to actively undo it, reimagining the art museum as a vital piece of cultural infrastructure in a post-colonial society.

Several of the sixteen architects included in this book were already working when Tafuri delivered his bleak diagnosis; a few had their first museum projects underway. All have wrestled, in one way or another, with the conditions he identified. Many were taught or mentored by the generation of pioneering modernists who had dreamed first of using architecture to catalyze social change in the cataclysmic decades leading up to the Second World War, then of rebuilding a better world through architecture in the era after. They came of age acutely aware of the vacuum left by the failure of those aspirations—the loss of purpose that followed from modern architecture's inability to deliver on its promises. Even those who began their practices later, at the turn of the twenty-first century, were deeply affected by the subsequent failure of any definitive version of a postmodern architecture to take root, by the field's ongoing inability to produce a cohesive movement that offered a body of thought about not just how architecture should look but also the role it should play in society. And all acknowledge grappling with the increasing commercial pressures on their work, their struggles to create meaningful architecture in the face of the economic forces that are more and more brazenly dictating the patterns of growth and development. Yet all, too, describe museums as a vital exception to these conditions. Each of them has made museum design a cornerstone of their practice, and each describes crucial ways in which the museum occupies an anomalous status in the field of contemporary architecture, offering opportunities for reflection and experimentation not viable in other areas of their work.

What makes these buildings so different from others today? Collectively, the conversations in these pages present one fundamental answer, profound in its simplicity: the museum cannot be optimized. At its most banal, this means merely that there is no one "best" way to design an art museum. But, more specifically, it means that the art museum does not present a problem that can be "solved" in terms of the parameters that developers are so fond of. Both the real estate market and the construction industry prioritize efficiency, seeking to eliminate risk, minimize costs, and maximize returns. This, in turn, overwhelmingly incentivizes predetermined, standardized solutions that benefit from economies of scale. Particularly on large projects, architects—and, for that matter, contractors, engineers, and the host of other consultants involved in today's complex construction projects—speak less of "design" or even "construction" than of the "building procurement process," a neologism encompassing the multinational supply chains, worldwide networks of labor and material, and dozens of specialized subfields that must be properly administered to produce a building in the current global economy. An architect planning, say, a new office tower or apartment complex might, in consultation with a developer and a contractor, weigh labor costs in the local market against availability and shipping costs of primary structural materials. The architect checks these against basic programmatic requirements such as the maximum buildable area or the minimum allowable floor-to-floor height. Then they factor in a few client preferences that might be tailored to a specific market—perhaps luxury finishes in the lobby or an iconic silhouette on the skyline. Finally, the results of this calculus are crystallized into a physical configuration that is not so much *designed*—in the sense that it is the result of creative deliberation on the nature of the project, the opportunities it presents, or the needs it might serve—as *optimized*, in the sense that it provides the greatest quantity of the most profitable space possible in a given context. No wonder, then, that, as several architects lament in the following pages, buildings and cities tend to look the same around the world today. Contemporary architecture, like most products of globalization, is shaped far more by the process of its origin than by the place of its destination, reflecting the general conditions under which it is produced rather than the specific context in which it will be experienced.

Museums certainly enjoy a privileged status within this ecology of development; usually big-budget, high-status buildings, they are not subject to the same ruthless value engineering as typical architectural projects. But the crucial distinction between museums and other buildings is not one of degree but of kind. It is not simply that more money tends to be available for museum architecture, but that museum architecture creates value in a fundamentally different way. A museum succeeds according to a nebulous convergence of prestige, cultural capital, and soft power; its purpose is not easily reducible to the blunt dollars-per-square-foot commodification of space that drives most architectural production. This irreducibility, in turn, leaves the door open to an almost infinite variety of architectural propositions. The essential program of a museum is, after all, deceptively simple: it is a place for visitors to encounter works of art. But what is the best way to encounter a work of art?

Each of the architects interviewed here has a different answer. In fact, not only does each have a different vision of what an art museum should be, each has also invented a different method to create it. One works primarily in plan because they insist on the primary importance of circulation, arguing that it is the visitor's trajectory through the museum that sets the tone of their experience. A second prefers to work in section, arguing that the varied proportions of the gallery spaces in relation to the works they contain are all-important. Another eschews drawings altogether for physical models, believing that the ethereal interactions between sunlight and natural materials are what produce a superlative exhibition space. Yet another contends that encounters with works of art are meaningful only when framed by other forms of activation and engagement, emphasizing the role played in their design process by conversations with members of the various communities a museum will serve.

Inevitably, no matter which approach is chosen, finite resources must be allocated and tough decisions must be made. These decisions are inherently subjective, based on the architect's consideration of a shifting cloud of variables that ranges from the building's context to its collection, its intended audience to its mission and identity. These are not decisions that can be guided by objective metrics like floor area ratio, and one architect's solution for a museum in a given context cannot be easily compared to another's somewhere else. This form of decision-making prioritizes the expertise of the architect because it demands solutions that are resolutely architectural.

Museums are by no means the most complex buildings confronting architects today—airports, hospitals, and any number of urban infrastructure projects come to mind—but their complexity is surely the most deeply architectural, in the sense that it plays out at human scale, in terms of space and material, light and movement, in the densely intricate choreography of physical encounters between bodies and works of art. Here, the success of a design might hinge on the way sunlight glances off a vaulted ceiling; how a well-placed corner first obscures, then reveals, an adjacent room; the subtle resonance that emerges between a gallery's stone floor and the materiality of the artifacts within; or in a delicate interweaving of circulation and exhibition space, subtly reminding viewers that their visit to the museum is both an aesthetic and social experience.

It bears emphasis that none of this has much to do with the Tafurian caricature of the architect-as-sculptor, the monumental form maker whose main role is to serve as a kind of urban decorator, even if that version of architectural authorship has long been associated with museum design. The working processes described in this book are intensely collaborative and profoundly synthetic. They are rooted in the architects' broad base of technical and cultural knowledge, which allows them to engage meaningfully with the full range of participants in the long and complex process of conceiving and constructing a new museum, from artists to engineers, contractors to curators; they highlight the architects' ability to consolidate a vast array of inputs and constraints into a singular solution. Ultimately, the conversations unfolding in these pages reveal less about the creative genius of the architect than about the stubborn agency of architecture itself, its ability to articulate material and spatial configurations that frame our perceptions, shape our interactions, and establish the horizons of our experience.

This is a mode of architectural authorship much better suited to the twenty-first century. By now it is clear that the Bilbao effect was not just an economic and cultural phenomenon, but also a historical one. It was rooted not only in the shift from industrial to postindustrial economies in developed nations, but also in an emergent post–Cold War world order dominated by a new Europe and an apparently unchallenged United States, and it was underpinned by certain glib and boosterish assumptions about the nature of both culture and political power as well as the relationship between them. A quarter of the way through the twenty-first century, these assumptions have been challenged by both a global recession and a global pandemic, as well as a host of other political and environmental crises. These shifts have led to shrinking budgets for culture as well as soul-searching within many institutions now reevaluating their roles in society. In some circles, rumblings have begun about a "post-Bilbao" era, as extravagant architecture has come to seem troubling—at best, quietly complicit, uncritically serving to reinforce existing power structures; at worst, actively exclusive, serving to intimidate and alienate broad swaths of the public.

And yet, as this volume amply demonstrates, the pace of museum construction has continued to accelerate worldwide. Part of the explanation for the continued growth of museums is simply that these rumblings come mainly from the regions where the Bilbao effect originated and has now run its course; its transformative magic is still fervently sought by other nations in other regions in other phases of economic and political development. (Tellingly, Gehry's next Guggenheim franchise is under construction in Abu Dhabi, set to open twenty-eight years after his building in Bilbao.)

But even in areas where monumental architecture is no longer quite the thing, museums continue to renovate, expand, and rebuild at a brisk pace. The reason is twofold. On the one hand, new build-ings remain the most efficient way for institutions to extract wealth from their donors. The twenty-first century has seen a massive redistribution of wealth across the globe, creating a turbocharged donor class. Museum directors and development offices know that the surest way to draw large sums from deep pockets is to offer a building or a wing or a new gallery to which a prospective patron can affix their name. Meanwhile, as museums become more closely intertwined with financial networks and so more corporate in their operations, they become more beholden to capitalist mantras like *grow or die*. Nor is the flow of benefits from donors to museums unidirectional. As the global art market surges in sync with the increased concentration of wealth in the hands of major collectors, there is a constant threat that booms will swell into bubbles and investment will teeter into speculation, particularly for contemporary art that does not yet have an established historical pedigree. But by hanging an artwork on its walls, a museum offers tangible proof of its worth. In return for investment from art collectors, then, museums stabilize the value of the very goods their patrons collect, serving as something like the central banks of the art market.

On the other hand, as more and more museums come under political pressure from various constituencies—artists, activists, the public, even their own staff—to expand, reorganize, and reframe their collections in order to present new narratives about culture and history, these reconfigurations will inevitably create new spatial requirements for their galleries. Similarly, as museums increasingly seek to engage new audiences in new ways, they will inevitably require new physical spaces for this expanded social programming.

Although these various economic and cultural forces all drive growth, they do so in sometimes violently contradictory ways. Yet paradoxically, the more voices that seek to shape the future of museums, the more complex the conversations about their design and purpose, the more centrally important the role of the architect becomes. It is the architect who is responsible for mediating among the many different stakeholders in a given museum, and ultimately it is the architect who must translate their manifold and occasionally opposed ideas into a coherent physical form.

Even in a post-Bilbao era, architecture seems likely to remain central to the evolving identity of the art museum because important questions about who and what these buildings are for will always require architectural answers. The art museum, in other words, is grounded in the two alchemical translations, recursive and omnidirectional, that lie at the heart of architectural praxis: from the conceptual to the actual—the instantiation of ideas and aspirations in concrete form—and from the spatial to the social—the complex feedback between the physical configuration of a building and the modes of inhabitation and interaction that unfold within it.

And yet the fact that architecture is important for museums does not in itself explain why museum construction has continued to boom around the world or why people are flocking to these new buildings in ever-increasing numbers. It was not necessarily a given, after all, that museums would continue to grow and evolve in response to the challenges presented by the opening decades of the twenty-first century. They could just as easily have gone extinct, particularly in the face of the profound technological transformations that are reshaping not only culture itself but also all forms of media and entertainment, habits of work and leisure, patterns of consumption, and the very rhythms of quotidian existence. In the digital age, the museum seems deeply anachronistic in its stubborn persistence as a physical destination, its continued grounding in embodied experience. Surely today there is something incongruous, even quaint, about so many people traveling in person to the same place to do the same thing during the same set period of time—particularly when that thing is encountering works of visual art.

Here it might be instructive to look back at the visual arts' last brush with anachronism, at the height of the machine age. Walter Benjamin was one of the modern era's most insightful theorists of the mutual inflection of technology, capitalism, and culture, and he devoted one of his most widely read essays, "The Work of Art in the Age of Mechanical Reproduction," first published in 1936, to studying this problem. He argued that the aura of the traditional artwork—"the here and now of the work of art—its unique existence in a particular place," in his memorable formulation—was terminally threatened by new forms of mass media such as photography and film, which could be produced and distributed at a previously unimaginable scale and with theretofore inconceivable rapidity. Eventually, he believed, these new media would reshape not just the tastes of the public but also their very habits of perception, with the numinous authority of painting and sculpture losing out to the more immediate and assimilable engagement offered by the cinema, the newsreel, and the illustrated magazine. He proposed that the twentieth century, as it progressed, would see an irreversible "decay of the aura" of the work of art.

Almost a century later, it is undeniable that aura, in Benjamin's sense of it, has been largely vacated from daily life. But this hasn't made aura obsolete; on the contrary, by the simple logic of supply and demand, it has dramatically increased the value of what little aura survives. Paradoxically, then, even what Benjamin saw as art's most mysterious, ineffable, and entrancing quality proved subject to the common law of the market. In the early twenty-first century, the art museum enjoys a unique concentration of this precious quality. Visual art is currently one of the few forms of cultural production that cannot be, wholly, or wholly satisfactorily, digitally mediated and distributed to be streamed, scrolled, and consumed on demand—anytime, anywhere, and via any number of devices. And as more and more of lived experience migrates into virtual space, the more appealing the museum's good old-fashioned encounters with bona fide originals in real space seem to be.

It certainly helps that aura has become not just a cultural value rooted in centuries of tradition and ritual, as Benjamin argued, but an economic asset as well, underpinning an art market that has grown exponentially since the time of his writing. Even visitors who may not feel a spiritual or aesthetic connection to a work of art can partake in the undeniable thrill of being close enough to touch a "priceless" original. So crucial is aura to the valuation of artworks that the market has successfully assimilated any number of mass media—even digital video—ruthlessly imposing artificial scarcity as needed via numbered editions, artist's proofs, and certificates of authenticity. ("From a photographic plate…one can make any number of prints; to ask for the 'authentic' print makes no sense," Benjamin wrote. But try telling that to a curator in MOMA's photography department, one of the primary sites of the transformation of photography into a fine art over the course of the twentieth century.) Small wonder, then, that in recent decades art museums have seen steadily rising and consistently record-breaking attendance, holding their own with concerts, amusement parks, and sporting events as one of the most popular forms of live experience. Today's art museums effectively enjoy a monopoly on aura, offering direct physical encounters with authenticity in ways that almost no other platforms or institutions can.

Benjamin was no stranger to nostalgia, and he might not have been entirely surprised by the persistent potency of aura in the digital age. But he surely could not have foreseen that media technologies themselves would evolve in ways that further reinforced the museum's appeal. With his characteristic mix of Marxism and messianism, Benjamin believed that the mass media of his time might eventually awaken new forms of politically potent community. But despite its name, the social media of the present day has proven more conducive to solipsism than collectivity, and screens have shrunk along with audiences to the point that most media today is experienced in a state of algorithmically atomized individuality. In this context, the visitor's experience in the museum is doubly exceptional; it offers not only the aura of the individual work of art but also the opportunity to join a collective audience, to participate in a shared experience, perhaps even to gain a sense of belonging.

If there seems to be something paradoxical in this mix, a closer look at Benjamin's argument shows us that it is actually the museum's architecture that makes the combination possible. Benjamin felt that architecture, despite its obdurate physicality, was the proper starting point for any history of media. Citing the example of the cathedral, used to indoctrinate and acculturate the European populace centuries before the advent of mass literacy (let alone broadcast technology), he pointed out that architecture's ability to transmit ideas and ideologies to a large audience makes it the prototypical mass medium—what he called the original "object of simultaneous collective reception."

An often-repeated truism is that museums are the cathedrals of our time. This is usually meant as a glib expression of the fact that they are among the most important structures erected today, enjoying pride of place in our cities and absorbing more time, resources, and attention than other buildings. But Benjamin reminds us that this analogy holds on a deeper structural level as well. Hanging on the walls of a museum, the easel painting originally intended for the private salon of a wealthy patron becomes something very like the figures carved in stone above a cathedral's doorway or illuminated in its stained-glass windows. In other words, once fused with the primordial technology of the museum's architectural frame, even a unique and original work of art becomes a kind of mass media and, by extension, an object of simultaneous collective reception.

If this sounds far-fetched, consider the *Mona Lisa*, by all accounts the most visited painting in the world. Even after a dip in attendance caused by the COVID-19 pandemic, the Louvre receives close to ten million visitors a year, and the museum estimates that some 80 percent of them see the *Mona Lisa* during their visit. This means that this year nearly eight million people will pay for the privilege of seeing the painting in the flesh. If the *Mona Lisa* were a song, that would make it multiplatinum many times over, comfortably among the best-selling singles of the year.

As anyone who has braved the crowds for a glimpse of a painting like the *Mona Lisa* can attest, the museum's transformation of an easel painting into an object of simultaneous collective reception is not a natural one, often resulting in something of an awkward fit. Contemporary art, on the other hand, has had the opportunity to evolve in tandem with the architecture of the museum and has developed a much more symbiotic relationship with it. In recent years, any number of commentators have noted that art is getting bigger, as is the audience for large-scale, site-specific installations, two key developments propelling the construction of ever-growing galleries for contemporary art in museums worldwide. Some critics bemoan this trend as the spectacularization of visual art. This complaint suggests that art's expanding size is mainly a ploy for attention, as if the best way to lure increasingly distracted visitors through the museum's doors is simply to make larger and more sensational works. It also suggests a kind of degradation of the individual viewer's experience, as if deliberate and thoughtful contemplation had given way to more involuntary and superficial absorption.

But this trend is actually indicative of a much more profound paradigm shift: today, visual art is increasingly a collective form. Much contemporary art, in other words, is made with the museum in mind, and is intended to be seen in a crowd. This is a distinct break from long-established traditions of modern art. Despite the thread of utopian social ambitions running through the avant-garde movements of the nineteenth and twentieth centuries, the bulk of modernist cultural production actually consisted of autonomous artworks, by and large intended for individual contemplation. It was perhaps inevitable that the modernist artwork would be primarily targeted at an individual audience, since the emergence of l'art pour l'art was itself enabled by a new economic model based on individual collectors: the rise of an acquisitive bourgeoisie offered an alternative to the official patronage of church or state and allowed artists to connect to a broad base of individuals with widely variegated taste, some of whom supported and encouraged radical aesthetic innovation. There was thus a period when the upper-middle-class audience for modern art was largely coincident with its base of economic support. In recent years, the audience for art has radically expanded, while its base of support has radically contracted. As in the Renaissance, when most art for plebeian consumption—the statue in a town square, the frescoes in a church—was commissioned by the ruling elite and their institutions, today's unprecedented concentration of wealth in the hands of ultrarich donors means that support for new art now increasingly falls to museums—and to the networks of corporations and oligarchs in which they are embedded.

Meanwhile, the scope of artists' ambitions has changed. Contemporary artists have begun to abandon the idea of creating works for the aesthetic contemplation of individual viewers, seeking to more directly address social and political concerns through an increasingly diverse range of artistic practices. This development has dovetailed perfectly with museums' efforts to broaden the scope of their relevance and expand the range of their audience, making them particularly inclined to support such new approaches. While some of this work falls under established art historical rubrics such as participatory art or relational aesthetics, it is too wide-ranging to gather into a single movement or genre. Nonetheless, many of the most prominent artists of recent decades have shared a common desire to directly engage with the social, the political, the material— with the fabric of reality itself—a desire that has, in turn, drawn many of them into intense collaborations with architects, including those interviewed in this book. The collaborations described in the following pages, which span from the 1970s to the present, include an array of pioneering figures such as Joseph Beuys, Louise Bourgeois, Jenny Holzer, Olafur Eliasson, Rirkrit Tiravanija, Ai Weiwei, and Theaster Gates. Whatever their differences, all of these artists fundamentally have sought new forms of participation and engagement with their audience, and all have played critical roles in reshaping the museum into a collective space.

Museum architecture has both enabled and amplified this fundamental shift, and several spaces created by the architects who appear in the following pages have had a decisive effect. Most notably, Turbine Hall, the vast space designed by Jacques Herzog for Tate Modern in London, was explicitly conceived as a provocation to artists and has now housed more than two decades' worth of immensely popular and staggeringly ambitious commissions. Other spaces point to the continuing acceleration of the trend: Elizabeth Diller describes her design for the Shed, in New York City, as a "machine for making art," an attempt to offer artists of the future the necessary infrastructure to create yet-unimagined art forms; in buildings like his Faena Forum in Miami or Audrey Irmas Pavilion in Los Angeles, Shohei Shigematsu is pioneering a new evolution of the museum typology into a kind of hybrid social/exhibition space that blurs distinctions between artwork and event.

Historically, the museum was often assumed to be opposed to the avant-garde; its original role of collecting and preserving artifacts from the past made it seemingly incompatible with the dynamic progress of contemporary culture. "You can be a museum, or you can be modern, but you can't be both," Gertrude Stein famously quipped to Alfred H. Barr Jr., the founding director of MOMA. A parallel assumption was that the museum was essentially a neutral institution, its role to safeguard cultural developments taking place beyond its walls and establish a definitive historical record of the evolution of art. But as MOMA approaches its hundredth anniversary and museums of modern and contemporary art have proliferated around the world, it is clear that museums are by no means incompatible with the art of the present, and anyone still claiming that museums are neutral is either deeply cynical or deeply misinformed. As these institutions have expanded their role from collecting to commissioning and from merely exhibiting work to helping to produce it, they have become indispensable not only for connecting contemporary art to a broad audience but also for the very genesis of contemporary art itself. If the *Mona Lisa* needs the Louvre to reach a mass audience, *The Weather Project*, the immersive installation by Eliasson that drew unprecedented audiences to Tate Modern in 2003 and 2004, could not exist without a venue like Turbine Hall. Another crucial reason that museums are thriving in the twenty-first century, then, is that they have expanded beyond their role of recording history to become primary sites of contemporary cultural production.

But the most powerful indication of art museums' vitality comes from comparing the kinds of cultural consumption that take place within them to the current state of consumer culture at large. For most of the twentieth century, the museum was haunted by that other great modern space invented for the accumulation of objects: the department store. Depending on your point of view, the concern was either that the museum would never be able to compete with the department store's popularity because the contemplative appreciation of the work of art could not possibly hold a candle to the phantasmagoric appeal of the commodity fetish, or simply that the art museum would itself become a kind of department store, with works of art reduced to yet another category of commodity objects.

"Is the department store a museum?" pioneering American museum director John Cotton Dana was already fretting in 1917. In *The Arcades Project*, his monumental study of consumer culture, Benjamin noted that "there are relations between department store and museum...the amassing of artworks in the museum brings them into communication with commodities." In the 1960s, Andy Warhol, who made a career out of reducing the line between artwork and commodity to a razor's edge, was fond of scandalizing his admirers by telling them that his two favorite places to visit in any city were its department store and its art museum. In the 1980s and 1990s, all an art or architecture critic had to do to damn a new museum was compare it to a shopping mall.

Today such comparisons would have no bite, simply because the department store and the mall are largely extinct, while the art museum is a fixture of any city or region with a modicum of wealth and ambition. The fact that the museum has outlasted these major retail typologies suggests that concerns about the commercialization of the museum fundamentally misunderstood the nature and direction of influence between museums and commercial spaces. Despite decades of hand-wringing, the museum never really turned the artwork into a commodity. Instead, it commodified *the experience of viewing* the artwork, and this has turned out to be a crucial distinction. In the twenty-first century, most shopping transactions have shifted into digital space, as sector after sector of the retail market has found this to be a far more efficient medium than the brick-and-mortar store. As a result, today's shopping is by and large no longer a live, in-person experience (or, for that matter, a collective one, as it famously was in the golden age of the downtown department store). In this brave new world—what some are calling a "retail apocalypse"—businesses that remain invested in the survival of physical stores, particularly in the luxury sector, have essentially adopted an art museum model. Consumers are encouraged to visit a flagship retail location not to acquire products but to look at and interact with them, whether via a "styling appointment" or an "immersive brand experience." Often the curated goods purchased in these spaces will be shipped to the customer after the visit rather than change hands on-site. In other words, historical fears that the museum was threatened by commercial spaces were misplaced; to the contrary, commercial spaces have turned to the museum as a model for success in the experience economy of the twenty-first century.

Another powerful benefit of the museum experience is that it lends itself to hybridization in ways that play well in that other pillar of contemporary consumer capitalism: the image economy. The rise of digital media technologies has allowed images to circulate with historically unprecedented speed and ease, and images have become central for building brand identity, engaging with audiences, and driving sales. For all their investment in creating aura, museums function extremely well in this milieu. This is because the physical act of visiting a museum building has been positioned as a central node in the broader network of experiences and platforms—a virtual archive, say, or a streaming video channel—that constitutes the institution at large. The physical experience is not opposed to the virtual; museums function stunningly well as backdrops for social media posts and are also ideal testing grounds for various kinds of augmented reality, from audio guides to interactive gallery maps.

It is ironic, too, that as the widespread use of smartphones and social media platforms has democratized the creation and distribution of images, the flattening of old hierarchies and the elimination of traditional gatekeepers—however laudable in the abstract—have brought acute new pressures to bear on the public. Democratization also means a glut of undifferentiated content, which makes the museum's traditional role of curation—one could even say arbitration—all the more valuable. The spread of social media has recast consumers as content producers (*prosumers*, in marketing parlance), which means that broadcasting taste and status is more important than ever, because everyone is now playing to their own public audience. For social media users promoting a personal brand, signaling a certain lifestyle, or simply trying to get noticed, an art museum is a godsend: a physical space packed with highly curated visual content, it provides the ideal setting for creating virtual images to circulate in an online media environment that is itself heavily weighted toward visual content. If Pierre Bourdieu already saw museums as an important element in the theory of cultural capital that he formulated to explain the stratification of late twentieth-century society, these institutions promise to be more crucial than ever for accumulating cultural capital in the twenty-first century.

Ultimately, it is the mutability of the experience offered by the museum—its paradoxical delivery of aura to a mass audience, its seamless blending of the real and the virtual—that likely ensures its survival. Studies at major museums, typically based on data from security camera footage in combination with tracking from the cellular phones of visitors who sign into the institution's Wi-Fi network, consistently find that the average time a visitor spends looking at a painting is less than thirty seconds. It would be hard to compress an opera, or for that matter a novel, into that interval (although, coincidentally, it is about the same length as the average TikTok video), which helps to explain why museums continue to thrive while so many other bastions of highbrow culture go gently into that good night. And once again, it is the museum's architectural framework that proves decisive: as Benjamin pointed out, architecture provides the prototype not only of the object of collective reception but also for a collective experience "received in a state of distraction."

———

The good news, then, is that not only do museums provide crucial opportunities for architects, but also they have proven to be remarkably resilient and relevant institutions, likely to play a central role in shaping culture for the foreseeable future. This means, too, that a defense of the art museum today need not be couched in the lofty and impassioned terms of appeals to civic ideals, shared values, or the public good, which is just as well, given that ideals, values, and the common good do not seem to be faring particularly well in the first decades of the twenty-first century. The bad news is that, as should be obvious by now, the forces ensuring the museum's ongoing robustness and relevance are not necessarily pushing the museum toward becoming the best version of itself.

This is where the definitive importance of architecture emerges. Architects cannot necessarily be called on to directly critique the vagaries of the art market, subvert the dictates of consumer culture, or resist the inexorable development of new technologies. But then again, neither do these forces act directly on museums in their raw form; they must be mediated by the architecture that shapes these institutions, which means that architecture provides points and counterpoints of possible inflection. Collectively, the conversations gathered here illuminate three fundamental ways in which architects have exercised decisive agency in defining the museum's current role, and in which they can hope to shape its evolution in the future.

First, museums are among the last experimental spaces available to artists. The history of postwar art is in many ways a story of its coevolution with museum architecture. By the 1950s, the white cube had been firmly established as the preferred exhibition space for modern art. In its reduction of the gallery to a kind of architectural degree zero, the white cube seemed to offer an impassive neutrality that rigidly maintained the core modernist value of the autonomy of the work of art. But artists grew increasingly concerned about the limitations this architectural frame imposed on their practices, and many key developments in the art of the following decades can be seen in part as reactions against the white cube: site-specific installations countered its sitelessness; works based on performance and participation redressed its lifeless neutrality; land art tried to flee it entirely; and pop art tried to reintroduce the commercial elements and lowbrow cultural references that had been banished from its pristine abstraction. By the time the artist Brian O'Doherty permanently enshrined the phrase in the art world lexicon with his widely influential 1976 *Artforum* series "Inside the White Cube," this form of gallery architecture had become a favorite object of critique.

Today, these complaints seem quaint. Nine years before the publication of O'Doherty's polemic, the world's first commercial art fair debuted in Cologne. As the art market was supercharged in the 1980s, beginning its transformation into the current era of art investment funds and billion-dollar auctions, art fairs proliferated, and now several hundred occur annually around the world, with a huge portion of art sales to both private collectors and museums taking place at these events. The white cube, in other words, is now the least of artists' problems: it is the *white cubicle* of the art fair that has become the Procrustean bed through which any cultural practice—all manner of images, objects, and ideas—must pass in order to achieve viability as "contemporary art."

This is a problem with which the architects included in this book are deeply familiar. Many of them have designed a wide range of spaces for art, including commercial galleries and temporary structures to house fairs. They have designed their share of white cubes, too, with several arguing that this remains the best format for showing the early and mid-twentieth-century modern art for which it was developed. But all remain steadfastly committed to creating a rich diversity of spaces in their museums. Together, these architects have now provided the formative spaces for several generations of artists, and they continue to design the museums that will shape the art of the foreseeable future—all, too, emphasize the importance museum spaces can play in catalyzing new developments in art. As museums become more active sites of cultural production, artists will have to rely increasingly on the architects of these buildings to supply them with not only a platform or a frame within which to present their work but also a laboratory in which to develop it.

Second, museums offer architects crucial points of contact with art. The architects interviewed here, without exception, have a deep connection to the other arts, and collectively they offer a powerful picture of what art means to architecture today. Sometimes these connections take the form of direct collaborations that would only be possible under the auspices of a cultural institution. Here architects have the opportunity to explore ideas, materials, or techniques outside of their domain or simply to break the rules of architecture—as in Steven Holl's collaboration with Vito Acconci on the facade of the Storefront for Art and Architecture, which is allowed to violate New York City zoning codes because it is technically a work of art.

There are broader connections, too. Museums are places for art and architecture to directly interact but also for architects to digest lessons learned from art and apply them to their own practice. Many of the architects in this book describe drawing on art for important conceptual and methodological realizations that have subsequently guided their museum design. Denise Scott Brown's pioneering interest in pop art helped her to break with modernist orthodoxies in the early years of her practice, while Peter Zumthor's formative encounters with Walter De Maria's works *The Vertical Earth Kilometer* and *The Lightning Field* spurred him to think about space and material at a new level of scale and ambition. These intersections between art and architecture often take place in an expanded field where disciplinary boundaries break down; Walter Hood's outdoor performance spaces in his design for the Oakland Museum of California are inspired in part by his long-held interest in musical improvisation. In a sense, these conversations show that all architecture—not only within the museum's walls but far beyond them—is at its best when in dialogue with art, because artists can help architects imagine a new range of possibilities for their own cultural agency, reclaiming some of the utopian vision that Tafuri mourned in architecture's reduction to a mere ancillary of development.

Third, museums are one of the few viable spaces remaining in a contracting and fragmenting public sphere. As several of the interview subjects point out, the perceived failure of modern architecture in the decades after the Second World War was quickly followed by the rise of neoliberalism in many Western countries, and there was a corresponding reduction in public investment in architecture. By the 1970s, the building projects that were in many ways the backbone of the modernist movement—social housing, universities, civic centers—became increasingly rare, and architects had to turn to other programs to sustain their practices. In this context, museums—often privately funded even when intended for a public audience—remain one of the only public-facing programs available to architects today.

And artists, too, rely on the museum for their connection to the public. The modernist avant-gardes of the early twentieth century—futurism, constructivism, and de Stijl, among others—were distinguished in part by the idea that art could directly enact social change. (To a greater or lesser degree, all sought to reimagine architecture, too, as part of their transformative project.) Adherents of these movements believed that utopian art would eventually lead to a utopian society in a more or less unbroken line. As the course of the twentieth century proved this to be emphatically untrue, many artists retrenched within the museum. From the institutional critique of the 1960s and 1970s to the relational aesthetics of the 1990s and the first decade of the twenty-first century, to the amorphous rubric of so-called social practice art today, contemporary art has been marked by the persistent sense that a utopian artwork might at least transform the museum, and that the transformed museum, in turn, might provide a model for a future better society. In a poignant irony, then, the less impact both art and architecture seem to have in the world beyond the museum, the higher the stakes of their experiments within it become. This microcosmic quality of the museum has lent it an increasingly important place in public discourse. In the past decade, museums have become flash points for activism and protest, with controversy erupting over everything from their sources of funding to the diversity of their audience to their actual impact on their communities, leading some commentators to describe the museum as in crisis. But this is by no means an existential crisis, the kind—caused by dwindling attendance, diminished relevance, or commitment to an unsustainable economic model—facing many other cultural institutions today. Instead, it is a measure of the museum's centrality and vitality, of its crucial function as the place where the present is historicized, the past is reimagined, and where collective narratives about society are literally embodied.

This "crisis," too, is largely focused in Europe and America. Taking it as universally indicative of the status of museums risks losing sight of the fact that the art museum is a truly global phenomenon. The museum is certainly a European invention, insofar as the first examples of institutions performing what we would recognize as the function of an art museum—buildings designed specifically to house art, whether renovated for this purpose or constructed from the ground up, and mandated to be open to the general public— appeared there in the late eighteenth and early nineteenth centuries. This means, too, that the museum's origins are inextricably tied to both the ideals of the Enlightenment and the legacy of European colonialism and imperialism. But to characterize the art museum as a Western institution today doesn't make any more sense than characterizing capitalism itself as a Western phenomenon simply because of its historical and geographical origins.

The conversations in this book evince both global networks of influence and connection and a thrilling range of variation. For his Long Museum, which opened on the West Bund in Shanghai in 2014, Liu Yichun drew inspiration for the concrete vaults of his building from Louis Kahn's 1972 Kimbell Museum in Fort Worth. The institution, in turn, was part of a larger urban development project explicitly modeled on London's South Bank, where Herzog's Tate Modern had catalyzed such transformative effects in the early 2000s. Yet Yichun emphasizes that one of the most important dimensions of the museum is a function unique to China: the privately owned museum provides a robust public space not directly under state control, a relatively rare thing in contemporary Shanghai. For his Museum of West African Art in Benin City, Adjaye looked to West African building traditions for his architectural vocabulary and to Pedro Ramírez Vázquez's 1964 Museo Nacional de Antropología in Mexico City for an example of a museum that explored and elevated a precolonial past in a postcolonial city. For his simultaneous redesign of the Northwest Coast Hall at the American Museum of Natural History and the Michael C. Rockefeller Wing of the arts of sub-Saharan Africa, Oceania, and the Americas at the Metropolitan Museum of Art, both in New York, Kulapat Yantrasast researched the history of anthropological and non-Western art collections in US and European museums and conducted fieldwork with Indigenous communities in the Pacific Northwest. Such projects emphasize both the continued evolution of the museum and the opportunities inherent in this evolution, as new museums emerge in new places and existing museums reinvent themselves in new ways.

At its best, the art museum is a space in which both artists and architects can push their work to reverberate with many possible futures, where new collective and cultural forms can take root. This book is envisioned as something like a manual for all those who wish to understand these opportunities, and perhaps to seize them.

DAVID

ADJAYE

JULIAN ROSE – More than any other architect working today, you have your roots in the art world. Many cutting-edge architects have defined themselves by using art as a model, but in your case the connection seems more social and intellectual than aesthetic. Le Corbusier borrowed ideas about composition from Picasso, Zaha Hadid was famously inspired by the geometric language of constructivism, and Jacques Herzog and Pierre de Meuron have cited early encounters with Donald Judd's work as formative for their own minimalist style—but you went to school with artists; you were part of the same scene in 1990s London. How did those early contacts influence your conception of architecture?

DAVID ADJAYE – The thinking I encountered in the art world became the bedrock of my practice, because it helped inform my position on why I wanted to work in the built environment. I was not interested in architecture until I went to art school. It was the generation of artists that I met while I was studying at the Royal College of Art—both my classmates there and students at other London schools like Goldsmiths—the theory books we were reading and the debates that we were having about practice and what it meant to make contemporary things, that helped me realize working in architecture could give me a certain kind of agency. I loved painting, but it didn't fulfill me as a way of working. And in the end I rejected painting not because it doesn't have any edifying possibilities but because I wanted an art form that was in service to the public and invested in the idea that we make knowledge collectively to move our civilization forward. Architecture seemed to be one of those profound arts that has the potential for that kind of direct impact; I had absolutely no doubt that architecture was the tool that I was most excited to work with.

JR – It's interesting that you were drawn into these debates about artistic practice, because many of the first projects you became known for were, in fact, working spaces for artists: Chris Ofili's home and studio [1999], or the Dirty House for Tim Noble and Sue Webster [2002]. You were working with a generation that was

Adjaye Associates, Dirty House, London, UK, 2002

challenging assumptions about what it meant to be an artist and what it meant to make art—even about what should be considered art in the first place. How do you approach the problem of designing an artist's studio when their working process is so open-ended?

DA – It was an experiment. No one just said, "Give me a beautiful cube with north light." What was interesting for me was that a lot of the artists I was engaging with were in a live/work situation, which was something very particular to London at that time—the way artists were inhabiting the city, the way neighborhoods were changing. My job became about negotiating the relationship between the studio and the home, because the default at the time was to just make them one.

JR – Sure, that's the model of the industrial loft, where you simply throw everything together in one big, flexible space.

DA – Instead, I wanted to define an internal space for creativity, distinct from the space of daily life. For me to understand how to construct the crucible for the work that artists wanted to perform,

I needed to be in a dialogue where they articulated their processes. Each project required a very high level of intellectual clarity and communication before any architectural form-making could begin. And so, because of the artists I was coming into contact with, I was learning about all these different modes of artistic production that were emerging at the beginning of this century—as a result of having to make their workspaces. Rachel Whiteread had a totally different practice from Chris, Tim and Sue had a totally different practice from either of them, and so on. For me, that was the most exciting part of the beginning of my career. I became addicted to that dialogue.

JR – How has that experience continued to inform your design of exhibition spaces? I imagine, in particular, there would be a direct translation into your design for the Studio Museum in Harlem [in New York], given that an artists' residency is one of its core programs.

DA – Absolutely. That project grew out of the dialogues I had at the beginning of my career, but now the building is scaled up into an institution. The idea is to reinscribe the presence of the artist into the visitor's experience of the museum, to oscillate between the large exhibition spaces that a museum needs and the sense of intimacy and the visceral encounters that artists have with their work. This expands the reach of the studio program. For almost fifty years, the residency has been an incubator, allowing and cultivating art practice. Now, it has birthed a very powerful educational program that brings young kids right into the institution and shows them the force that drives art and puts them into conversations about how art making happens and how art is displayed. The museum creates an opportunity to work between education, practice, and experience that's different from that of MOMA, different from the Whitney, different from the New Museum. It's an alternative model. It's not about creating an archival space or a contemporary space; it's about creating an experience where a vital relationship between art making and art presentation can somehow erupt.

JR – The Studio Museum is a special case, but I wonder if much of what you're saying applies to the design of contemporary art museums more generally. They pose a problem that's similar to the one raised by the studios you designed earlier in your career: contemporary art is a moving target. Perhaps one solution is to look beyond the exhibition space to other kinds of programming and activation—in a sense, to foreground the architecture.

DA – I think the prototype that started to map out a relationship between the institutional space and what I learned from those early studio projects was the Museum of Contemporary Art Denver [2007]. That project is very important to understanding my approach to making art spaces. When we won the competition, we realized that all the other architects had designed a version of what I call the Pompidou Centre model: a large, technical, flexible box with a minimal circulation system. Instead, we made a sort of laborious circulation system, which took you through a series of specifically designed chambers that activated various relationships between ground, sky, and building. Our idea was that different lighting experiences—clerestory, window, skylight—would give different kinds of agency to the art. If you look at the development of art over the twentieth century, artists always talked about the different relationships that their work had to light. The notion of a contemporary experience or contemporary condition was often defined through lighting, or the lack thereof. Even when you get to the birth of performance art—something like Yves Klein's black box is another lighting condition, right? So, in a way, the game was to take the kunsthalle, which is normally just about flexibility, and redesign it to become about this mix of experiences of luminescence and contemporariness. Architecturally, this added up to a lot of circulation space, which no one else wanted to propose because there was a sense that it somehow distracted from the exhibition space. But we argued that the circulation was the heart of the experience of the new museum. It would be a very carefully defined space that would create the journey to the artwork.

Adjaye Associates, Museum of Contemporary Art Denver, Colorado, 2007

JR – Flexibility does seem to be the default thinking in museum design today. But there is a thin line between the flexible and the merely generic.

DA – Exactly. Many contemporary museums fall flat because they end up with something generic—they become dead spaces. Spending time to think through the specifics of the space also helps give the institution a kind of agency within the city—through the people coming in, through the activities happening within the building.

JR – One of the few things we *do* know about contemporary art is that it is increasingly propelled by the market. As we expand our understanding of the museum—to encompass a broader role for the institution within the city or a wider range of visitor experiences—are there some limits that are important to preserve? In New York we have seen any number of commercial galleries that aspire to the status of small museums, and there is also the paradox of the growing number of private museums ostensibly aimed at a public audience. How do you negotiate distinctions between public and private and commercial and institutional in such projects? I'm thinking of your building for the Aïshti Foundation, completed in Beirut in 2015, where you have retail and exhibition programs combined under one roof.

DA – There is certainly an ultimate question of ownership and accountability to the public that differentiates museums from other buildings. But for me, all my buildings, whether public or private, must engage with the urban fabric and the urban condition in the widest sense. There is always a broader responsibility—no matter how commercial or private a project, it still has to engage with the city and its context. So, my approach to one project is not necessarily distinct from my approach to the other. I believe what are needed most are spaces for art that are about inviting people in, about dialogue and discussion, and about engaging with different ways of collecting and different ways of seeing the world. Commercial spaces can actually facilitate this. In the case of Aïshti, merging the worlds of commerce and art ignited new dialogues and fresh expectations for the mode of engagement that I found very compelling. But a very important aspect of that project was also the construction of a seaside promenade that is fully accessible to the public. It is a balance and always a case of looking for ways to create generosity, regardless of the project's nature.

JR – You've described the museum as a space of intense engagement between art and architecture, and we seem to be at a moment of especially active interchange between the two fields. I wonder, though, if it's possible that some artists' practices are almost too engaged with architecture, to the point that collaboration becomes difficult. I'm thinking of some of the artists you've worked with: Olafur Eliasson, whose installations often become freestanding structures, or Theaster Gates, who, in the Stony Island Arts Bank in Chicago, has created an entire cultural institution, architecture and all. Do conflicts arise when artists start to take over the traditional role of the architect?

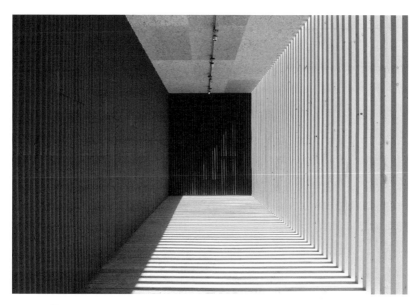

Adjaye Associates and Olafur Eliasson, *Your black horizon*, Venice, Italy, 2005

DA – It's a new field. People like Theaster, Olafur, even Sterling Ruby—all of them produce work that blurs lines in an exciting way. A lot of artists are following a path that was laid out in the 1960s by the minimalists, who wanted to be able to control the frame or the enclosure that produces the viewer's experience of a work of art. In a sense, I see these contemporary artists as seeking to gain more control over the work and gain more autonomy from the curator. But because of the complexity that some of their projects are achieving, even someone like Theaster, whom I do think capable of making beautiful architecture himself, still requires an architect to help soothe the making of the building. But he doesn't need an architect who's just producing a structure; he needs an architect as a viable intellectual partner who can help produce criticality.

JR – So you still see a continued role for the architect, one that goes far beyond physical building?

DA – Of course. If I were simply working for an artist as a producer, there's nothing there. Some artists do just buy the infrastructure, literally, of an architectural office and use it to produce their own artwork as both architecture and installation. And that's fine. But there's also a new condition, which I think is much more interesting, that emerges from artists and architects working collaboratively to create a new ground for experience, expanding the notion of making artwork. The Secession Building in Vienna [1898] was intended to be a space where the artist and the architect came together to create a perfect place for the production and appreciation of art—maybe, a hundred and twenty-five years later, there is finally a coalescence in our culture that is bringing similar forces together. For me, the most exciting thing about the explosion of these new projects is that we architects actually get to do what we do even better than before, and so do artists. It's less about the Enlightenment idea of the museum as a container for art and more about coming together to find ways of allowing the public to experience the power of art, to get a sense of what art can do in society.

JR – And, of course, questions about public experience extend beyond art museums to other kinds of institutions. The National Museum of African American History and Culture [NMAAHC], which opened in Washington, DC, in 2016, is an extraordinary project in part because it seems to push the social and cultural roles of both museum and architect to their limits. Civic and institutional buildings are often asked to play a dual role—on the one hand, their architecture is a potent cultural symbol, charged with representing history and defining identity, and on the other, they act as a kind of social catalyst, a gathering space with the potential to create new forms of community. I've heard you discuss this as a kind of form/content problem in relation to NMAAHC. But in a sense this project seems even more complex, because there is also the narrative created by the objects in the collection, which you had to consider when constructing *both* the spatial narrative of the building and its symbolism. How did you use the architecture—its organization, material, form, et cetera—to negotiate these different registers of meaning and experience?

Adjaye Associates, National Museum of African American History
and Culture, Washington, DC, 2016

DA – The central narrative for this project became an exploration
of the meaning of *American*. I intentionally layered different kinds
of architectural references that offered various ways for the public
to begin to understand the project—materials that mirror the
Washington Monument, a facade motif that draws from Black
ironworkers of the American South, a form derived from Yoruban
art—to show how African influences are fundamental to America.
This is a nation that was literally built on the backs of Africans, and
one cannot fully understand the country without acknowledging
this heritage. Through my design for the museum, I tried to represent African American history in a global context and to situate it in
relation to the beginning of modernism and, more broadly, in
relation to the trajectory of America's cultural engagement with the
world. In that sense, NMAAHC stands both with and against the other
buildings on the Mall: it, too, is a museum of American history;
it, too, is American.

JR – I'm particularly interested in your use of the inverted stepped pyramid, derived from the carved capitals on veranda posts in Yoruban architecture. You've taken that geometry as the organizing principle of the facade and massing of NMAAHC, and in a way this move is analogous to the way the so-called orders were used in neoclassical architecture, where a Greek or Roman column became the basis of an architectural grammar that regulated the proportions and geometry of an entire building. Neoclassicism was the primary language of museum design for centuries. Not coincidentally, neoclassicism was also the language of colonial architecture all over the world: both the Enlightenment museum and the colonial capital were about projecting the superiority of one—Western—cultural tradition. Is part of your project here to begin building an alternative architectural language that references a different cultural legacy?

DA – Yes—and it's a very conscious effort. I'm establishing an alternative knowledge base for contemporary architecture in the twenty-first century—that has been my agenda from day one. But when I started making architecture I was very guarded about it because I was building my own awareness, trying to understand how I could cross-pollinate the systems of technical knowledge you need to produce buildings today with new sources of cultural intelligence and history. Now, twenty-five years into my practice, I can be clear about what I am trying to do. I feel like I am part of the tip of the spear of a generation of African architects imagining what it means to build on the African continent and thinking about how the buildings we produce there will contribute to world architecture.

JR – I imagine that your Museum of West African Art [MOWAA] in Benin City, Nigeria, is a central part of these efforts. Did that project grow out of your work on NMAAHC?

DA – You could say that my research for NMAAHC started me on a journey into understanding the significance of West African art and its contribution to world culture. And it turned out that the Benin Dialogue Group—which is a multilateral working group that includes representatives from Western museums, the Nigerian

Adjaye Associates, rendering of Museum of West African Art,
Benin City, Nigeria, anticipated completion 2030

government, and the Royal Court of Benin—had initiated a conversation about repatriating the Benin Bronzes and other cultural artifacts at around the same time I had started working on NMAAHC. That dialogue was slowly coming to my attention and had been unfolding for about a decade when I was invited to participate in a conference organized by the group at the British Museum in 2019.

JR – How did your involvement change the dialogue, given that it had already been in progress for ten years? Repatriation raises a whole range of complex questions—from the legal and economic to the political and cultural—and I'm interested in the specific role you see for an architectural perspective in these conversations. Was it a matter of finally giving a concrete form to the group's ambitions, of literally creating a space for the artifacts to be returned to?

DA – Actually, I think what was most important was looking *beyond* the building. When I spoke at the conference, I made clear that I felt that we didn't just need a new museum for the Benin Bronzes, as beautiful as that idea might be. What was necessary was a radical thinking of what it means to create a museum in West Africa.

JR – The process of repatriation is not as simple as designing a nice new building and returning the bronzes, in other words.

DA – It's insensible to think that after one hundred years, or two hundred years, or three hundred years, or four hundred years you can just hand objects back, because the cultures that created those objects are gone. The shrines that housed those objects are gone. So, you're not exactly restituting. We are in a modern world, and the objects have taken on a new provenance. And that provenance was developed in the West, so how does it relate to somebody in West Africa?

JR – Right, it wasn't just that the objects were looted; they underwent a kind of ontological transformation, too. They were essentially turned into works of art in a very Western, and very modern, sense—they were treated as if they had a kind of aesthetic autonomy, independent of context. That's why they could be put on the wall in a museum, or lent from one institution to another, or sold at auction to go into a collector's house. It seems like one paradox you're confronting is that on a fundamental level the museum is a machine for deracination. That was part of its original mission, given that the first public museums to emerge in the eighteenth and nineteenth centuries—whether the British Museum or the Louvre or any number of other examples—served in part to house the spoils of empire.

DA – Yes, and the critical issue that must be addressed is the impact of colonialism on African cultures. The continent has been made to feel inferior to the world—it's been excavated not only of its natural resources but also of its cultural richness. There's an assumption that Africans know their own heritage, but that's not necessarily true. Colonialism has cut off the past. In fact, the structural legacies of colonialism have led to the continued demonization of local religions and, to an extent, the local culture and history. You can imagine the magnitude of recontextualization necessary to allow people to understand that these objects are part of an incredibly rich culture and great history of the continent. We have to build an empathy with the past, and that means our project is a very different thing from the typical process of building a museum. It's a narrative of teaching, of empowerment—a social justice program rather than a program of empire and conquest.

JR – Your description of this task reminds me of a powerful line in Frantz Fanon's *The Wretched of the Earth*: "The citizen must appropriate the bridge." He's writing about the importance of physical infrastructure in nation building but arguing that it can't result just from a process of top-down modernization; construction of new infrastructure has to be part of a transformative process of raising consciousness. In a sense, you're describing a subsequent phase of postcolonial development: the construction of a cultural infrastructure. And it sounds like an analogous process—"The citizen must appropriate the museum."

DA – Beautifully said. We have to think about both training a workforce—museum professionals, experts in heritage and preservation—and creating a culture. In the first decades of the twenty-first century, there has been tremendous growth in the physical infrastructure of the continent. Partly this is due to China's relationship to Africa, and of course some people are critical of that. But the fact is that the gross domestic products of many African countries have doubled, and in some cases even tripled, which has started to build a middle class. And then the critical question is: Why should they stay? You have to create a place where people will want to live their lives, where there is a sense of community and culture and history. Otherwise, you get a brain drain. This issue is not unique to Nigeria. My office is privileged to have discussions with leaders of many nations across the continent, and this has become a very important question everywhere: How do you build the right cultural infrastructure for the new Africa?

JR – It's an enormously complex task, but I'm curious to hear how you see your design for MOWAA starting to take it on in concrete architectural terms.

DA – Rather than think in terms of a grand storehouse for objects, why not start with the urban situation and create multiple sites: the main museum building within a landscaped compound, a separate center that's primarily for research and training, a contemporary art gallery, a whole cultural district? The thrust of that large-scale vision then informs what we do within the galleries of the main building. Our idea is to build out from these cultural fragments, beginning with the artifacts themselves, and actually reconstruct at a one-to-one scale some of the spatial relationships that can demonstrate their significance in the organization of the Edo culture that produced these objects. We have a series of rooms, and each takes on one type of artifact—from the bronzes to the ivory to the wood carvings—and we try to explain both the spatial and contextual relationships between these objects and their place within the broader cultural form. Our goal is not in any way a "complete" reconstruction—these are not didactic spaces—we're just trying to restore the dignity of these objects as much as we can.

JR – I imagine there's a tremendous amount of research involved in setting up these exhibitions, as well as ongoing conservation efforts and so on. That's also part of where your idea of cultural infrastructure comes into play?

DA – One goal is to turn the museum into a scholarly machine. That way it's doing much more than simply providing exhibition space; it's creating a new class of professionals who will be part of a very long-term effort. We're building spaces for the objects, but we're also building conservation labs and offices for the museum staff and the curatorial teams as well as state-of-the-art training facilities in all these related fields. The museum's site is also part of ongoing archaeological excavations, which will link the museum to a network of other sites throughout the city.

JR – Link it in what sense?

DA – MOWAA has evolved beyond the singular museum. Its mandate to establish, or really revive, a cultural district in Benin City involves the resurrection of the extraordinary network of walls that were constructed throughout the city and the surrounding region. These were the largest man-made earthworks in the world—a system of construction that stretched for thousands of kilometers and was built up over centuries, on the scale of the Great Wall of China—and has been almost entirely wiped out.

JR – On top of all this, you're also including spaces for contemporary art at MOWAA. We were speaking earlier about the fact that contemporary art is always a moving target, which makes it a challenge for museum design. Was there ever a point when, given the extraordinary complexity of this museum's historical mission, you thought that including contemporary art might be too much? That you just couldn't add another unknown to the program?

DA – Not at all! I always laugh when people are purists about combining historical and contemporary art—as if history isn't itself this overlapping and relational thing. We are including a large contemporary art space precisely to enable cultural and historical exchange. The idea is to establish this part of Nigeria as a cultural destination. This is already happening in Lagos—there's a great art fair that has a major international reach. There's also already a huge artistic community in Benin, but they do not have state-of-the-art exhibition space that is commensurate with the quality of the work being produced. If you think about it, the mechanical services and all the other infrastructure we're putting in to preserve historical artifacts are also perfect for exhibiting contemporary art. Why not combine them? Especially since the cultural history we're presenting is the foundation, the crucible, of a lot of the great art coming from this region now. So, yes, it's a historical museum and a contemporary art museum at the same time, which is fantastic. But what I really hope it will be is a place for the transfer of knowledge across generations and a place where a creative community finds sustenance. For me, the typology of the museum in the twenty-first century has to become a new social center.

JR – Given how radically you're transforming this typology, what is at stake for you in continuing to call MOWAA a museum?

I can't help but wonder if the very idea of the museum is ultimately inseparable from the legacies of colonialism and violence and exploitation that your project seeks to redress. Take the British Museum as an example; in some ways an event like the looting of the Benin Bronzes by British forces in 1897 is so egregious that it distracts from more fundamental questions about the nature of the institution itself. There's a sense that if the museum gives back certain objects that were unjustly acquired then it can just go about the rest of its business. But recent scholarship on the origins of this museum is unequivocal: most of the wealth of Hans Sloane, the museum's founder, came from sugar plantations in Jamaica, which means that much of the original collection was built directly through the exploitation of enslaved people. To its credit, the current staff of the British Museum is trying to reckon with this legacy, just as it is participating in discussions about repatriating the Benin Bronzes. But when you have the opportunity to build a new institution in a new place, does it make sense to break with that legacy—to say, that's what the museum was then, and now we're creating something different?

DA – That's a very important question because when you say *museum*, you're thinking immediately of the Western Enlightenment project, the colonial project—there is a trauma there. But I think the process of change has to be dialectical. No institutions are eternal; they have to be remade continually. It is a bit of an illusion that just retooling the word can let you escape from the past. Yes, the museum comes from this problematic legacy, but that doesn't mean we can't remake it; in fact, we have to, because as we create our new project we are continually learning from the typology of the museum as it has evolved across the past centuries. Our building has many of the tropes that you would expect from a Western museum today: it has galleries, it has a theater, it has an education center. But it also has things like an active archaeological site embedded in it, a living social and cultural dimension. In a way, I see us as completing the museum—I think the West built one half of the museum, and it's up to the Global South to build the other half. One of my favorite museums in the world is the National Museum of Anthropology [Museo Nacional de Antropología] in Mexico City. After you visit, you are left with no doubt that the Spanish conquistadors, the whole colonial and postcolonial development of that city, are layers of an incredibly deep and rich history. That is profoundly inspirational to me, and I think of it as part of the genesis of this other half of the museum, the twin to the Western institution. So, it's important to me that we use the word *museum* because we're remaking that word now.

JR – So your project is to recontextualize the institution itself, along with the objects it contains; the museum has a legacy that must be addressed.

DA – Engaging with that trajectory is the only thing that makes sense. You can't just erase history. Many people have tried, and we know that erasure doesn't work.

DAVID

CHIPPERFIELD

JULIAN ROSE – Your museums are often praised as both subtle and restrained, and those are not words I would typically connect with your alma mater, the Architectural Association [AA]. The school was famous—particularly when you studied there, in the late seventies—for fostering all kinds of exuberant formal experimentation. How did you escape that influence and forge your own more understated approach to architecture?

DAVID CHIPPERFIELD – Well, I went to the Kingston School of Art first, and I spent two important years there. I knew I wanted to study architecture, but I went to Kingston because my exam results weren't very good and I couldn't get into a university, or at least not a good one. In those days, in the UK, you had an alternative route to study architecture, which was to go to a school of art, where the grade requirements were lower. Coming from a rather provincial West Country background, I found art school extremely exciting, because it was this slightly anarchic institution where architecture was mixed in with sculpture, painting, graphic design, and fashion. But the content of the courses was fairly traditional, and I began to take a rather conceptual approach to my work. My tutors took notice, and I owe a particular debt to one of them, David Dunster, who was an influential teacher for many of his students. He said that Kingston was too conservative for me, and he really pushed me to apply to the AA. I managed to get in, and my father agreed to pay the difference in the school fees. But on arriving at the AA, I found it all much too conceptual, and I became rather conservative.

JR – It sounds like you have something of a contrarian streak, which perhaps helps to explain why you've always resisted creating iconic museum buildings, even when they have been in high demand.

DC – I think in the conservative school, I felt the desire to distinguish myself by being radical, but at the radical school I began to see the value in a conservative approach. The AA was based on a unit system, which means that small groups of professors taught together, each group more or less independent from the others. I came under the tutelage of David Shalev, Patrick Hodgkinson, and Su Rogers, because they were interested in teaching how you actually put together a building. Their unit was fairly calm and rational within a sea of much more experimental ones, where people like David Greene from Archigram were doing inflatables and light-weight structures and things like that. But of course I benefited from what was going on in other groups as well. That was the condition of being an AA student in those years—you were surrounded by every imaginable approach to architecture. It was a chocolate box full of different flavors, and you sort of dipped in and took whatever you wanted.

JR – Would you say there was any underlying culture unifying the school during this period, or were the different units simply too eclectic?

DC – It was a time of enormous change, and I think what everyone was responding to in one way or another was the collapse of the modern movement. There was a total loss of confidence in modernism, and that created a vacuum that was being filled by various kinds of postmodernism.

JR – It strikes me that the collapse of modernism wasn't just an aesthetic problem, a matter of finding the next new architectural style. There was also a loss of confidence in the utopian social aspirations of the modern movement, and this was correlated to broader cultural and political changes as well; for example, Margaret Thatcher took office in 1979, the year before you graduated from the AA. How were your architectural ambitions affected by the shifts that British society was undergoing during this time? I imagine that if you had graduated twenty years earlier, you would have gone on to build social housing or university campuses. But those kinds of archetypal public projects, which had in many ways been at the core of modernism, were no longer available to an architect of your generation.

DC – They were not. The generation that taught me had made their careers building universities and housing projects and the whole postwar welfare state. My generation finished our education in a time of recession—the economy was poor, there weren't many competitions, and the state was not building anything. We were sort of the children of the Thatcher years, which were also the Charles years, in a way.

JR – You're referring to then-Prince Charles's notorious antipathy to modernism and his very public advocacy for neoclassical architecture?

DC – Yes, precisely. As the profession was attacking itself intellectually, it was also being attacked from outside, socially. As you say, there was a loss of confidence not only in the aesthetic dimensions of modern architecture but more profoundly in the social aspirations that it had promoted. By that time, the big postwar planning projects, like housing estates and rebuilt city centers, had become unpopular. And so the kind of architect that had produced those plans—the grand, bow-tied, respected professional—was disappearing, too. I think my peers and I came out of university at a time that was not only intellectually confused, in terms of the vacuum left by the demise of the modern movement, but professionally confused, because that role played by the modern architect in society was no longer really viable.

JR – It all sounds fairly bleak! Were you ever tempted to reconsider your career path?

DC – Well, you have to understand that in some ways the instability was also quite exciting. I think two positive things came out of this period. Postmodernism in architecture was disappointing in its results, in terms of the buildings it produced, because in most cases the protagonists just followed what was still a basically modernist approach and then merely applied a pastiche of historical forms. But, in intellectual terms, I think postmodernism had a positive and lasting effect by reawakening an interest in architectural history. As a young architect, all of a sudden it felt like I had a new diet, a wider range of references. And then, in professional terms, the demise of the old bow-tied modernist had cleared the way for a new figure: the pink-shirted high-tech vanguardist, personified by people like Richard Rogers and Norman Foster. They had both spent time in the States in the sixties, and I would say that they were both tremendously excited by corporate America.

JR – I'm fascinated to hear that, because many historians look at high-tech architecture as a kind of pop style. There's a tendency to see it as having a slightly ironic, largely iconographic relationship to technology—almost as if high-tech architects took the same attitude as the postmodern architects, say Robert Venturi and Denise Scott Brown, who pioneered a kind of pop historicism and simply turned it toward the future rather than the past. But you're suggesting that there was a more earnest side to the high-tech movement, a kind of ingenuousness about the application of technology to architecture and perhaps also a kind of faith in a technocratic, corporatized approach to the social problems left by the perceived failure of the welfare state.

DC – You've got to think about what America felt like for these English students at the time. It was progress. Especially Norman— a boy from Manchester who ends up on a fellowship to Yale and spends his formative years there during a rather exciting moment in American architectural history. It's difficult today to imagine corporate architecture as being energetic, but if you think of the buildings of SOM [Skidmore, Owings & Merrill] or other firms at the time, there are some thrilling projects—huge corporate campuses, super-tall towers. I think Norman continues to be inspired by that excitement.

JR – I know you worked for both Foster and Rogers, but I'm especially curious to hear about your experience with the latter because the Pompidou Centre was still in progress while you were a student. When did you start working for Rogers? Did you get to see the building under construction?

DC – I didn't work for him until after I graduated, but I got to know Richard while I was a student. My girlfriend at the time was a member of the extended Rogers family, and we used to go to Paris and stay with Richard and Ruthie, his wife, in their flat in rue de Sévigné. Richard did take me around the Pompidou while it was being built, and I met his collaborators Renzo Piano and Peter Rice, the engineer. It was the most exciting thing I had ever seen in my life. It was just extraordinary to see these young people running such a huge project—they had won the competition while they were all in their thirties. I mean, as a student that was the sexiest version of being an architect you could possibly imagine. This was architecture at a very high level. Whether one liked the results or not, it was impossible not to respect the sheer ambition. And I'm too close to it, still, to be anything other than totally in love with it. It was the last radical project. I can't think of one since, not truly radical. Frank Gehry's Guggenheim Bilbao is radical in formal terms, but Pompidou was radical in institutional terms and in social terms; it wanted to change the relationship between architecture and society.

JR – I agree with you completely about the radical nature of the project, but I'm curious to know how that radicality was already apparent while the building was under construction. Was it the scale of the urban intervention—this huge plaza and the hulking structure rising from one side? I imagine it must have been incredible to see the interiors in progress—could you get a sense of the vast open spaces that were being created? In architectural terms, what stood out to you?

DC – Well, it wasn't the interiors. I was sort of an angry young student at the time, and I was even a little bit irritated by Richard's obsession with flexibility. I remember him explaining in great detail the structural principle of how the trusses are held up by the gerberettes, which in turn are cantilevered out to one side and pulled down by tension rods, and how that combination allowed them to create this enormous span—it's almost 50 meters [164 feet]. And the whole time I was just thinking, what's wrong with a column in the middle of the room? It wouldn't make any difference at all.

JR – That's so funny—that column-free span has gone down in history as one of the signature achievements of the building! But you mentioned earlier that you developed a contrarian, slightly conservative attitude at the AA.

DC – Well, the problem of the high-tech school was always that it turned architecture into structural performance. But I would say the saving grace of those early projects is that they were highly motivated by social ideas. You could criticize Pompidou for being technically obsessed, but at the same time there was an undeniable 1968-inspired, antiauthoritarian dimension to the project. In reality, of course, it was a building sponsored by the state, but it was still extraordinary to see these young architects creating a new kind of space within the city.

JR – Would you say, then, that you found the ideology and the ambitions of the project were more inspiring than the architecture?

DC – Not entirely, because the building also gave me a new appreciation for the process of construction. I think there's a tendency, especially as a student, to think architecture is just drawings and sketches, and here I saw that architecture was made of highly articulated pieces that were controlled down to the millimeter. I still find it fascinating to think about architecture as large-scale product design, where structure and services are efficiently engineered and integrated.

My office just spent the last several years restoring Mies van der Rohe's Neue Nationalgalerie in Berlin. That building is also, in a way, an expression of structural clarity and order. But as we started to take it apart, we were shocked to find that the services, like air handling and plumbing, were just squeezed in as if the building was some sort of postwar Soviet housing estate. There was absolutely no

David Chipperfield Architects, Neue Nationalgalerie refurbishment,
Berlin, Germany, 2021

integration of building systems whatsoever. And when we repaired
Mies's building, we realized that the plan was a sort of sacred thing.

JR – You're talking about the iconic reflected ceiling plan of the
main exhibition hall, showing the scalar relationships between all the
different structural elements—a grid within a grid within a gird.

DC – Exactly. That plan encapsulates the idea of the building.
It's perfectly balanced, nearly like a Mondrian painting. So we
realized that we actually couldn't change the plan at all, because we
weren't just protecting the building, we were protecting the idea of
the building. There's an order in the building that is quite virtual
and conceptual, and largely two-dimensional, but it's profoundly
important. I think Rogers and Foster, on the other hand, took great
pride in seeing a building as a totally three-dimensional, optimized
object. I remember, in their offices, it was the drawings of the
integrated building systems—the details and the axonometrics—
that were terribly important, in the same way that Mies's plan
was for him.

JR – That's a wonderfully succinct account of the core achievement of high-tech, and a good argument for further distinguishing it from both other forms of postmodernism and from modernism itself. So much of the rhetoric of modernism was about functionalism and efficiency, but, as you point out, modernist buildings often offer more of an image of efficiency than an actual embodiment of it. And again, since many historians have looked at high-tech through the lens of pop, there's a tendency to see it as a kind of surface-based style. Reyner Banham famously referred to buildings like the Pompidou as "serviced sheds," playing on the concept of the "decorated shed" introduced by Venturi and Scott Brown. He was suggesting that the service systems had migrated to the exterior and simply replaced more traditional forms of neoclassical decoration—the air shaft replaces the column. But you're making a convincing case that, at its best, high-tech was a genuine attempt to rethink the design and production of architecture.

DC – The danger is that it does tend to become just a style, because it's a hell of a lot of work to do it properly. From the beginning of the project, you need everybody at the table. And I would say that the most important thing that I learned from working in those offices is how to integrate consultants as a fundamental part of the design process.

JR – That's a good segue to your renovation of the Neues Museum in Berlin. That was a paradigm-shifting project, in part because you collaborated with a small army of specialists to seamlessly integrate newly designed elements into an exhaustive restoration of the original nineteenth-century building, which had been heavily damaged in the Second World War. Today—thanks in no small degree to the enormous success of the Neues Museum—it's become more common to approach museum design as an exercise in adaptive reuse or historic preservation, but at that time it was quite unexpected. The competition was held in 1997, and the other finalist was Gehry, whose museum in Bilbao opened that same year. I can't imagine he was especially concerned with maintaining the

David Chipperfield Architects, Neues Museum, Berlin, Germany, 2009

historical structure, and it's interesting to think about how different subsequent trends in museum design might have been if the Neues Museum had become another Bilbao-style sculptural icon. Why do you think your approach prevailed, and—perhaps more importantly—where did that approach come from?

DC – That's a good question. I suppose it was a convergence of a whole series of factors, going back to the beginning of my practice in 1985. As I said, there were no architectural competitions in the UK at that time. We had rejected the European welfare state and gone with a very Anglo-Saxon neoliberalism, and therefore it was the private sector that was commissioning buildings. And the private sector doesn't really commission thirty-two-year-old architects with no experience.

JR – So where did you find work?

DC – I ended up doing lots of shops. The first one was for Issey Miyake on Sloane Street in London, and then he invited me to Japan to do a series of shops for him there. And I ended up working in Japan for about five years, going back and forth from London every month. And, frankly, I was doing rather mediocre shops, but the experience allowed me to develop a connection to Japanese architecture. I became good friends with people like Arata Isozaki and Tadao Ando, and I think I learned a sort of Japanese attitude of making everything important, taking every detail seriously. Especially as a young architect, when most of the projects I was doing were small anyway, that resonated with me. The idea that I could take something very small and simple, like a stair or an entryway, and make an important project out of it.

And, in a funny way, having that steady work in Japan allowed me to start making connections in Europe. Because the whole time, I was running a little office in London, trying to look like an architect without really having an architectural practice there. I believe the American expression is "all hat and no cattle."

JR – Well, it's hard to make it as a young architect without at least a little of that. But you were also using your London office to build an intellectual community—you ran 9H Gallery out of your office, right?

DC – I gave half my office space to the gallery. That's what I mean about starting to build connections in Europe. 9H started in 1980 as a magazine run by a group of students at the Bartlett School of Architecture, including Ricky Burdett, Wilfried Wang, José Paulo dos Santos, and Rosamund Diamond. The idea was that, in this sort of postmodern vacuum, they wanted to promote the work of European architects who were not really known in the UK. So in 1985, when I started my office, we began organizing shows of the work of people like Rafael Moneo and Álvaro Siza. We would invite them over, they would bring drawings, and we'd make a show out of it. And it was a fantastic opportunity to encounter new approaches. These people were thinking very seriously about how architecture could connect to the history of a place, but their work wasn't just more postmodernism.

JR – In the eighties there were several American art galleries, most notably Max Protetch's gallery in New York, that dabbled in the exhibition and sale of architectural drawings. This could be seen not just as a foray into interdisciplinarity, but also as a self-conscious attempt to elevate architecture to a higher level of cultural production, to put the architectural drawing on par with the work of art. Was that part of your mission at 9H?

DC – No. 9H was purely about architectural debate. The only time we veered into architecture as art was when we showed Isozaki's competition entry for Tokyo City Hall. He didn't win, but he did beautiful silkscreens for his submission, and we thought, Why don't we try to sell them? Maybe that could help us fund the gallery. But it didn't work. We couldn't find anyone who wanted to buy them.

JR – Honestly, I think that's why the trend didn't last in America, either. Even when they're done by hand, architectural representations always occupy an awkward in-between status. They're notational, always referring to something beyond themselves—the architectural project itself—so in some ways they're more like a musical score or a recipe than a work of art. That's hard to sell to a collector who's used to the aura of "originals." But I didn't mean to get us off track. Did your intellectual exchanges with Europe through 9H lead to work in Europe, too? Was that the thread that eventually led you to the Neues Museum competition?

DC – Yes, but later. First, we did a lot of competitions in Italy in the early nineties. It was a period of anti-corruption reform—it was called *mani pulite* [clean hands]—where the Italian government was trying to be more transparent. They organized a number of significant competitions for public buildings and encouraged international firms to enter. And I think we won four in a row: the San Michele Cemetery in Venice, the Museo delle Culture [MUDEC] in Milan, the Palace of Justice in Salerno, and the Natural History Museum in Verona. Some of them proved to be difficult projects—I mean, decades later we're still working on Salerno, and the Natural History Museum in Verona was never realized—but these competitions were a great opportunity to step up. And, working in Italy, we got more familiar with issues of conservation and thinking about history. So that was another factor that played into the Neues Museum story.

And then eventually we got one building in Germany, a housing project that we managed to win a competition for. Through that, by chance, someone introduced me to the senator who was organizing the competition for the renovation of the Neues Museum. It was an incredible coincidence: I happened to walk into his office one day while he was scratching his head, looking for one more architect to put onto the list for the invited competition. So we were put in slightly as a wild card, which was very nice of him.

JR – **What an incredible opportunity. And his hunch was a good one, because you went on to win.**

DC – Actually, we didn't! There were two competitions. This was the first one, in 1994, and we got second place. Giorgio Grassi won it. But the museum director was furious because the whole competition had been set up for Gehry to win. There was a huge fight, and the jury rebelled, but the director was a very powerful person. Instead of giving in, he sulked for three years, refusing to work with Grassi. It became like an unconsummated marriage. So finally the director could say, Look, our relationship doesn't work; I want to redo the competition. And in 1997 he did.

JR – **And this time it came down to you and Gehry?**

DC – Gehry had come fifth in the first competition, so the second competition was among the top five competitors. The joke was that if Gehry had been eighth, it would've been among the top eight. The director made no attempt to hide his preferences. When I presented our project, I had all the drawings pinned on the wall, and I started to talk. After a few minutes the director stood up and said, "This is shit." And he walked out.

JR – **That's unbelievable—I'm impressed that you managed to finish your presentation.**

DC – Well, it slightly put me off my stride. But the jury said, "Carry on." And then shortly after we got the phone call saying, "Good news and bad news: you got through to the final round, but it's going to be just you and Gehry." So we did another three months of work on the proposal and presented again, and the jury chose us.

JR – **You were obviously facing strong headwinds from the director, so what do you think it was about your project that ultimately persuaded the jury?**

DC – I think we didn't win on our design. We won on our philosophy. I suppose this goes back to something that I've always felt is important in architecture: you have to clearly define what the project should be about. Each project needs a purpose. As architects, we love all the visual and tactile elements of our buildings—that's the stuff we work with. But think about a writer's relationship with words. Language is a writer's material, but you don't make a great novel just out of nice descriptions and good grammar and clear sentence structure. You need those things, but you also need a story, an idea that puts them all together. And in architecture, too, I think it's important to ask, What's the story? In what ways is that story relevant beyond this one building?

I think maybe this gets back again to my time working in Japan. I found it very strange to be an unknown British architect doing work outside of the culture I knew. It's a very precarious and pretentious position to be in, and it made me think hard about what I might contribute. What am I bringing to this project that any number of good Japanese architects couldn't do? Much of my work has been outside of England, so I think I've carried that mentality to most of my projects. It's forced me to think very carefully about the cultural relevance of my work in a way that other architects might not. In the case of the Neues Museum, I think Gehry saw it primarily as an architectural opportunity. And it *was* a great architectural opportunity, but I felt that the project also presented the challenge of confronting deep issues in Europe's past.

JR – The structure you were tasked with rebuilding certainly embodied a long and tumultuous span of history. It was originally finished in 1855, before Germany had been united—at the time Berlin was still the capital of the Kingdom of Prussia. Then it was nearly destroyed by Allied bombs during the Second World War, and then it sat in ruins until the nineties because it's located in East Berlin and the German Democratic Republic never had the resources to repair it.

DC – Here was an opportunity to think about how we deal with the war and everything that came with it: German guilt, four decades of Berlin as a divided city and Germany as a divided nation, reunification—all of that. And I felt my challenge was not merely to monumentalize that history, but also to incorporate it into the project in a positive way. I did not think it could be ignored. Modernist architects tend to keep old things at arm's length. The typical approach would be to just leave the old building alone and build a new steel-and-glass thing next to it, as if history is something you can just take or leave as you like. Whereas we took a different approach, asking, Can't we make something out of this story?

JR – I'm interested in hearing more about the model of authorship that developed out of that approach. We were speaking about the importance of integration and coordination on a project like the Pompidou, but the Neues Museum was an even more extreme case. I've seen some of the working drawings for the project, which are now in the collection of the Victoria and Albert Museum, and they're extraordinary palimpsests—layer upon layer upon layer of annotations, some of them printed from AutoCAD and some of them added later by hand. From what I can tell, there must have been at least a dozen different specialists all working on one section of the building at once, each engaged in a different aspect of restoration or new construction, and many of the final design decisions must have been made collaboratively in the field. The drawings evoke an almost premodern way of working. I'm imagining all these different crafts-people, from plasterers to welders to fresco painters, on- site

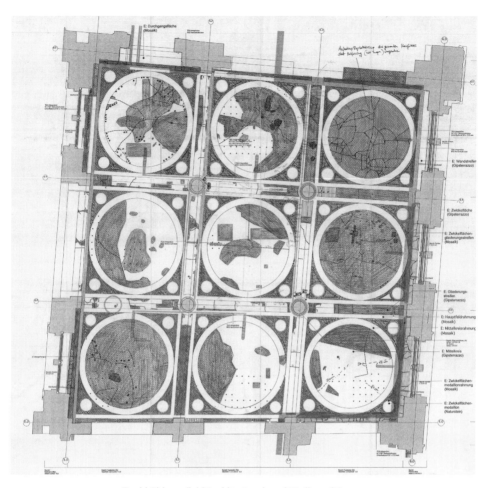

David Chipperfield Architects, plan of Mediaeval Room,
Neues Museum, Berlin, Germany, 2009

together, coordinating their efforts ad hoc. That is profoundly
different from the way most buildings are produced today, when
there's such a ruthless emphasis on preplanning and efficiency.

DC – I think the drawings you saw are in a way the most romantic part of the project. They do encapsulate everything you say, but
you would probably find that on other restoration projects as well.
In other words, when you're working with restorers, there are always
going to be these complex conversations and these delicate questions
of interpretation. But the more interesting questions for us,

intellectually, were, How much do you restore? And why are you restoring it?

When we won the competition, there was already some repair work being done. In fact, there was a restoration in progress on the frieze in the Greek courtyard, which I had to stop. I said, "Why are you doing this? We haven't even finished our design yet." And they said, "We're just putting it back to how it was." And I had to say, "Yeah, but that doesn't make sense, because I'm not necessarily putting the whole building back to how it was." If they put the horns back on the cow in the frieze, they're setting a certain pitch for the whole restoration, and it was important to think about the destination of the project.

The issue with restoration is never, Can you do it? The world is full of very good restorers who can bring anything back to how it was. And they're true craftsmen, so they love to do it. You have to ask, What does it mean if I bring this back? And if I bring this one thing back, what do I have to do with everything else?

JR – That's interesting. The challenge for you as an architect wasn't so much the logistical one of coordinating the restoration work but the philosophical one of establishing a conceptual framework for integrating the restoration into the broader story of the whole project.

DC – Absolutely. So while I love those drawings—because, I agree with you, they embody the delicacy and the physicality and the collaborative nature of restoration—the truth is that the real work came before them. The real work was to agree on the philosophy of the project. And I would say that this is much harder in architecture than it is in other fields, like archaeology or art history. If you have a Greek statue, you don't say, Shame about the arm; we know there was an arm there at some point, so let's make another one and stick it on. There's a fairly straightforward consensus about stabilizing the object, preventing further damage, and letting it be. But that's quite difficult to do with a building. When we came on to the project, the museum was missing parts of its roof. Well, you can't just stabilize the fragments and leave them like that, because it rains. You need people to be able to use the space. And they have to be comfortable, and the objects inside have to be taken care of, so you need to add air conditioning to a building that didn't have it originally. So in a sense, you are adding the arm. You are going to have to complete the building.

And, by the way, this work was not for a private client who's restoring a little country house and making all the decisions themselves. This was for the German state. Every decision had to be approved by multiple people and multiple agencies. So just deciding where an elevator should go, for instance, became incredibly complicated. The heritage department said, "No way can you put an elevator in that part of the building." But then the technical team said, "Well, that's the only place in the building where we can make it work."

JR – It sounds like a coordination nightmare. How did you solve it?

DC – After six months I realized that we were just being bounced around from one meeting to another, hearing different things from everybody. So I just said, "You know what, we're all going to sit in the same room once a month and you are going to tell them what you told me about where you want the elevator. And they're going to tell you what they told me about where they want the elevator, and we're going to sort it." We had to invent a collaborative process to shape the decision-making. And that was an enormously informative experience, both in terms of learning how to collaborate and build a coalition and in terms of establishing a philosophical approach to a project. I would say the Neues Museum was our PhD—it was the training on which we then built an office.

JR – Would you say that this intensely collaborative model of practice has prevented you from developing a signature style of museum design? I can think of any number of your buildings—say, the Turner Contemporary in Margate [2011] and the Museo Jumex in Mexico City [2013]—that look like they could have been designed by entirely different architects. And I'm wondering if that's because your approach is not formal, as you say, but based instead on the conversations that develop around each project.

DC – I think that's true, to an extent, because I think being an architect is about ducking and diving and working out what your opportunities are. Turner Contemporary was a $20 million project—almost nothing for a museum, rather like a big house—and there's no permanent collection and they don't have a big operational budget. So in that case, as we talked to the curators and the director, I thought the best idea would be to make a series of rooms. When you design a museum, the room is a crucial thing. Do you design a big, flexible space that can be subdivided or a series of rooms that can be combined? Those are your two options, and museums oscillate between those two positions. At the Turner I knew it wasn't feasible for them to be constantly subdividing the space and rearranging it in different ways.

For Museo Jumex, our first iterations were quiet boxes. But then we realized that we were working in this visually cacophonous urban site, and these poor little boxes were getting lost. So the silhouette became more important, and the building had to start taking a bit more of a posture—having a bit more of an attitude—in order to establish a civic presence. I think of architecture as a sort of process of extraction. I mean, that's what the Neues Museum is—a museum extracted out of a certain history and a certain site and a certain cultural and political situation.

JR – You're using *extraction* in an almost archaeological sense, and you're describing a deeply collaborative process—of which your museums are certainly exemplary. But I wonder how easy it is to maintain that way of working in more developer-driven projects, where architecture can become extractive in the more exploitative sense of squeezing profits out of the landscape or the city. In a recent lecture you described museum design as offering architects a sanctuary analogous to the Green Zone in Baghdad. That's a very powerful metaphor for evoking both the chaos, perhaps even the violence,

David Chipperfield Architects, Turner Contemporary, Margate, UK, 2011

David Chipperfield Architects, Museo Jumex, Mexico City, Mexico, 2013

of private-sector development and the degree to which prestigious cultural and civic projects are sequestered from those forces. It also strikes me as a fairly ambivalent metaphor, ethically speaking. So I have to ask—do you see this as simply a matter of the privilege enjoyed by a certain caliber of architect working on a certain type of building, or do you see a broader value in the sequestration of museum design? Can architects use museums to test radical ideas that might then be applied to other kinds of projects? You're a very outspoken advocate for the idea that architects should take on more social responsibility, and I'm interested in what role—if any— you see museums playing in that shift.

DC – It's true that museum projects have been a bit of a shelter for a lot of us. But going forward, I'm not sure whether they are going to be as valuable as they have been. I suspect that the hardware costs are going to overload institutions. I worked on the Metropolitan Museum of Art for a while, and it was clear that the hardware was a problem. If you want to fix your roof lights, suddenly it's $100 million or something. That's a lot of money. Now in New York you can probably raise it, and I recognize that institutions of a certain scale like the Met are part of their own financial ecology and will probably survive. But in places like Germany, where the state has historically paid for these cultural spaces, that's going to be much more difficult. And the other thing is that the main purpose of this hardware has been to attract tourists and increase visitor numbers, but we're starting to realize—slightly too late—that tourism is ruining our cities. There are many places where the economy has become overly dependent on tourism, and, really, museums have helped to enable that.

JR – Is the solution to build fewer museums?

DC – Well, it's a serious question. I think, first of all, museums have to refocus on being part of a community and being relevant to that community. So great architecture is wonderful, but you need good programming and good outreach and optimization of resources. I can see the purpose of museums becoming more pointed, and I think that museums are going to concentrate much more on software and probably spend less time and money building extensions. I've got a feeling that the period of great museum building may be over—maybe not all over the world, but in the US and Europe. And I would like to think that this isn't necessarily a bad thing for architects. Yes, we've benefited tremendously from this patronage, but we should be able to get out of the Green Zone. I hope that we can learn to operate more freely in other areas, because that's where the challenges are. I mean, you can't live on museums. You need good housing, you need good schools, you need good infrastructure. And that's where we as architects need to be looking.

ELIZABETH

DILLER

JULIAN ROSE — You went to the Cooper Union in New York, one of the few institutions in this country where an art school and an architecture school coexist in the same building. How did that interdisciplinary environment affect you?

ELIZABETH DILLER – The schools were in the same building, but they did not share anything except the shop. I was studying photography and film in the art school but was drawn to a class called Architectonics from the course offerings in the architecture school. I wondered what it meant, and on a whim I signed up. The first assignment was to build a nine-square, Sol LeWitt–like white grid that would serve as a quarter-inch scale model to do a semester's worth of spatial exercises. My first act in that course was to build this rigorous pedagogical tool and then fur-line it.

JR – LeWitt meets Meret Oppenheim! So from the beginning you were inoculating your formal rigor with a dose of surrealism. Did you enjoy the course?

ED – Unexpectedly, I discovered the third dimension, and my world changed. The school was nothing like I imagined. In contrast to the art school—where there was little discussion about what you did, what it meant, why you did it, and how you positioned yourself in the field—the architecture school had you reflect on the discipline constantly, its history and its intersection with other disciplines. The architecture program was so much more structured than the art school, which gave me something to push against. I had to present my ideas and defend them to the faculty—this allowed me to develop a critical voice. I was ultimately seduced into architecture by John Hejduk, the dean, but I had no interest in being an architect. Hejduk taught me that architecture was about much more than building buildings. In fact, he was rabidly opposed to the profession of architecture. He felt it was intellectually and morally bankrupt.

JR – Do you think that was because he had a sense that architecture had to define itself as more than just a profession— as a legitimate intellectual pursuit?

ED – Absolutely, though the irony was that he was a hardcore intellectual whom no one could quite understand. He tended to speak in indecipherable riddles. He was like a guru who had access to the truth and dispensed it in a kind of encrypted language. But his charisma and sense of irreverence were undeniable. He cultivated a critical ethos in his students and was particularly fond of trouble-makers like me. I was fascinated by him but able to resist his spell at the same time.

JR – It's interesting that you describe Hejduk's primary influence on you in terms of discourse, because he was also known for a very particular aesthetic: a highly formal language that owed a lot to the modernism of Le Corbusier and Mies van der Rohe but also to artistic avant-gardes like de Stijl and cubism. I don't see those influences in your work.

ED – His references at that time were very selective, many of them from twentieth-century literature, film, poetry, painting, and sculpture—all outside of architecture. Over time, his work became less formal and more narrative. His projects were like allegories out of a children's book—earnest, beautiful, and increasingly dark as he became ill toward the end of his life. His approach was idiosyncratic, and his blacklist was deep. Very few architects and educators were invited into his monastery. He was principled to a fault, self-published till the very end, and always suspicious of competing ideologies, fleeting trends, and the practice of architecture in general. He sniffed out hypocrisy and had a very low boiling point when around people he found insincere. Entering Hejduk's universe was liberating but dangerously cultish.

While he opened me up to interdisciplinary thinking from across the twentieth century and around the globe, I was even more drawn to what was happening around the corner in real time. It was the mid-to-late seventies, and artists like Vito Acconci, Gordon Matta-Clark, and Trisha Brown redefined what a spatial practice could be. I ended up drifting away from Hejduk and toward these figures. At Cooper I also met Ric Scofidio, who ended up as my partner in work and life.

JR – And that artistic context is the genesis of works like *Traffic*, the installation you two did in Columbus Circle?

ED – Yes, but *Traffic* was also influenced by artists who were experimenting with repetition and modularity. It was a response to a competition organized by the Institute for Architecture and Urban Studies with a charge to rethink Columbus Circle after the demolition of the New York Coliseum. Most of the proposals tried to unify this chopped-up traffic circle into a spatially coherent European-style public plaza defined by a strong building wall. It was 1981, and postmodernism was taking hold in architecture. Ric and I saw no

Diller + Scofidio, *Traffic*, Columbus Circle,
New York, New York, 1981

reason to apologize for cars, but we also saw room for a different type of unifying strategy. We thought it would be powerful to merge the shards of the circle with a material indigenous to the site: international-orange traffic cones. If we could arrange thousands of these cones on a perfect grid, it would have a unifying effect—like the white blanket of a snowfall, indifferent to cars, trees, and streets.

Our proposal won by votes among the competitors, and we were asked to execute it. Somehow, we convinced the MTA [Metropolitan Transportation Authority] to loan us twenty-five hundred traffic cones. At four in the morning, Ric started to survey the site and prepare it for the installation. The weather that day was shifting from sunny to rainy to foggy, which exuded an international-orange glow into the atmosphere. We collected the traffic cones twenty-four hours later.

JR – That piece was almost anti-architectural—in its ephemerality, in shaping space through the accumulation of found objects rather than actual construction. And I can see how, as you described, it was productive for you to push against the conventions of architecture and urban design. But, at the same time, you did graduate with a degree in architecture. You had a very specific, highly specialized skill set. With *Traffic*, you were critiquing architecture, but you weren't simply making art, either.

ED – I could not help seeing everything through an architectural lens. *Traffic* was our first reflection on the city and its neglected spaces, and our practice continued to be focused on the spatial conventions of cities, buildings, and institutions. Our output included installations and performance works—and not without irony. In 1987, we were invited to collaborate on a theater piece commissioned by the Philadelphia Museum of Art as part of the Marcel Duchamp centennial. I spent a month in the museum with *The Large Glass* [1915–1923] and the Duchamp collection and was very taken by his techniques—the subversion of the conventions of spectatorship, the opposition of flat versus perspectival space, the sublime banality of everyday operational space, the play between verbal and visual languages, the notion of "assisting" familiar objects by simple procedures like displacement.

JR – Duchamp doesn't just turn a commodity into a sculpture but also spatially manipulates the object. When he puts the urinal [*Fountain*, 1917] on the floor, you go from looking at it from the front to looking at it from above—you're essentially shifting from an elevation view to a plan view.

ED – And rotating it completely defamiliarizes it. *The Large Glass* was the starting point for our theater piece *The Rotary Notary and His Hot Plate* [1987]. The stage was split by a rotating wall into a downstage half and an upstage half. A large mirror tilted to forty-five degrees was suspended over the upstage side. The audience saw the downstage performers from a typical frontal perspectival point of view and the upstage performers reflected in plan in the mirror. The characters were sometimes physical, sometimes virtual presences— so you would see the male downstage and the female in an unde- fined floating space above, or vice versa. In one scene, the bachelor's headboard was aligned with the dividing wall and revealed the performer's head punched through to the audience while his body was reflected in plan. The headless body conversed with the bodiless head in a duet. The theatrical potential of these devices came from an architectural sensibility.

JR – And yet many of your projects that were exhibited in galleries and museums could, in fact, be seen as forms of institu- tional critique. I'm thinking of works like *Para-site*. In 1989 you were invited to do something in the Projects room of the Museum of Modern Art [MOMA] in New York, and you turned your installa- tion into an interrogation of the museum's conventions of movement and vision by introducing live video feed from surveillance cameras placed along the threshold of the building. At the Whitney Museum of American Art, you programmed a robotic drill to systematically destroy the gallery walls during your retrospective [*Mural*, 2003]. These projects make your eventual transition into the actual design

Diller + Scofidio, *Para-site*, installed at the
Museum of Modern Art, New York, New York, 1989

of institutional spaces seem like something of a paradox. At the time
of the Whitney show, you were already working on the design of
your first major museum, the Institute of Contemporary Art [ICA] in
Boston. How did you think about building one set of museum walls
even as you were literally attacking another?

ED – From the beginning of our work together, Ric and I were
questioning institutions, especially museums. Our early installations
were conceived for urban spaces on borrowed sites. Context meant
everything. So when we were invited to do a commissioned work for
the Projects series at MOMA, we came in with an intense awareness
of our role in that particular context. We were not just going to put
drawings on a wall or models on bases. We would attack the neutrality of those walls; we would make visitors acknowledge the threshold
between municipal and institutional space; we would have viewers
look at the very act of looking. As I think about it now, *Para-site* was
quite didactic—maybe not our most mature project, but it reflected
our early desire to critique from within in a stealthy way. It no

longer felt like enough to lob grenades at the institution from the outside—it would be more effective to enter through the front door.

JR – Artists love to critique architects as complicit, as instrumentalized, as merely manifesting institutional power. But surely by now we've also seen the limits of art practices based in institutional critique. You mentioned Acconci, and I'm reminded here of something he asked in his statement for the catalog of *Rooms*, the pioneering show at PS1: "Were we trying to find an 'alternative space,' or just trying to keep all the alternatives in the family?" That was in 1976, decades before PS1 merged with MOMA, but I think he already had a sense that the radical practices of his generation were being absorbed by the institutional mainstream. In retrospect, there's almost no avant-garde practice that hasn't been smoothly assimilated by the museum. In other words, physically reshaping the institution does seem like a more effective strategy for actuating real change.

ED – Assimilated can mean co-opted. But something else was happening, too. Museums were becoming more self-aware with a new generation of leaders. When Jill Medvedow asked us to design the ICA in Boston back in 2000, I had a crisis of confidence. Here was our first institutional client, and she was a woman of my generation—a peer with shared values who wanted to make a new kind of museum.

JR – How did that dynamic play out in your design of the space?
ED – I asked myself, In whose voice do I speak when I build the walls of a museum? Ric and I have been on both sides of the museum wall. We've cut up those walls and destroyed them. How can we maintain a critical position as we step inside the institution that was the object of our critique? We sided with the artists who would be inhabiting our galleries. We didn't think they would want to see the architect's hand; we wanted them to be free to newly script the space. At this point Charles Renfro joined our studio, and our mutual dilemma was to produce galleries that were not overdetermined but did not default to generic.

JR – Could you do both? Could you somehow create a white cube that was site specific?

ED – At the time, the debate ignited by the Guggenheim Bilbao was playing out: Should architecture be the protagonist or the background player to the art on its walls? Should architects design an icon for the city or an ideal space in which to view art? We thought that these were false binaries and that architecture could have it both ways. The galleries had to be flexible, well lit, and scalable. But it's the obligation of the museum architect—almost the moral imperative—to add to the culture of architecture through the design of the building. That's the museum's obligation as well. As the museum introduces art to the public, it should do the same for architecture. Since the ICA sat on one of the most photogenic sites in Boston, on the harbor, we chose to make the galleries inwardly focused, while circulation through the building was conceived as a cinematic unfolding, revealing the site in small doses—scanning it, framing, and turning it on and off.

JR – I can certainly see the appeal of a hands-off approach to the galleries in a place like the ICA, which started its permanent collection only relatively recently and is still largely functioning as a kunsthalle. But aren't there times when a more directed approach is called for? You recently designed a major expansion of MOMA, which opened in 2019, and the new version of the museum wasn't just bigger, it also completely rethought the display of the permanent collection. The division into discipline-specific galleries—separate spaces for painting, photography, design, and so on—was gone, as was the chronological (not to say teleological) presentation of modern art as a march of successive "-isms," from postimpressionism to cubism to surrealism to abstract expressionism and so on. I'm curious to hear what role your design played in this reinvention—particularly given that you were working at one of your early sites of institutional critique. As institutions like MOMA try to deconstruct, or even just expand, the canon that they themselves have helped establish, what accompanying architectural shifts need to take place?

Diller Scofidio + Renfro, Institute of Contemporary Art,
Boston, Massachusetts, 2006

ED – We were fortunate to work with a dynamic group of
curators, many of them young and relatively new to the museum.
They wanted more space for the collection, and I wondered, Why
are they so maniacal about expanding? As we worked together,
I realized how much of the collection never saw the light of day.
The curators had a sense of moral obligation to expose more of
it to the public and to explore narratives across disciplines and
geographies that were previously suppressed. We gave MOMA over
30 percent more gallery space that was not media-specific.

JR – But I would argue that it isn't just more space—it's a new
kind of space, and it seems to be cultivating new ways of looking
at art. Historically, the purity of the white cube was geared toward
the viewer's complete absorption in a single, transcendent artwork;
it was about vacating context so that you could have your moment

with a masterpiece. The mode of looking in the new MOMA seems based more on juxtaposition and comparison, which means it's also more mobile and more synthetic. Take the rehang of Pablo Picasso's *Les Demoiselles d'Avignon* catercorner to Faith Ringgold's *American People Series #20: Die*. This is a good example of how expanding the collection has allowed the curators to tell new stories: the Picasso, painted in 1907, has been a cornerstone of the museum's collection since 1939. The Ringgold was painted in 1967 but acquired only in 2016, while your project was well underway. I'm not asking you to weigh in on the art historical merit of this particular juxtaposition— it got quite a bit of attention, with some people saying it was a stroke of genius and others that it was too didactic—but I'm interested in what this kind of curatorial move means for you as an architect when you're designing gallery space.

ED – The galleries we inherited were very fixed: similar in size and connected through a rigid circuit. The purity of the white cube reflected the purity of the discipline and the purity of the historical narrative. The curators were already motivated to lose that purity and break down the walls between departments. And the new galleries also had to accommodate curatorial needs that could not be anticipated; the collection is constantly being redefined by the present, and curators are always rethinking its significance through the lens of contemporary culture. The best we could do was to design large, state-of-the-art galleries that could accommodate all media and could be broken down into spaces of any size. How could a giant, flexible gallery subdivide into thirty-foot rooms? Was there sufficient lighting to cover every square foot of space? How would the new proportions feel? Curators ended up embracing this spatial versatility in ways that have produced the desired cross-contamination. Disciplines and time frames are colliding, and new linkages are emerging.

JR – I agree that these collisions can be tremendously exciting, but I wonder: Are there limits to this approach, simply because artworks from different places and times are often made for very different viewing conditions? William Rubin, the legendary MOMA curator, used to emphasize that modern art "is essentially domestic in scale," by which he meant that it was intended for a fundamentally private mode of viewing. His favorite talking point was that the average Delacroix is larger than the average Pollock; this is contrary to what most people would probably assume, but it makes sense given that modern painting developed in opposition to salon painting, which itself was rooted in a long tradition of the public display of monumental artworks. But as art has continued to evolve, it has become more collective again.

As you pointed out, many radical practices in the sixties and seventies— including your own—developed outside of the gallery, in urban spaces. More recently, as museums have expanded and evolved, quite a bit of contemporary art has been produced with institutional support, which has further pushed art toward a condition of collective reception. All of which is to say that even something as ostensibly simple as showing modern and contemporary art together can turn out to be quite complicated—not only are the works themselves often at different scales, but also they're made for different audiences and, frankly, intended to be experienced in different ways. How do you address that? You can't just supersize the white cube and expect it to work for both.

ED – Once a work enters the museum—whether it was conceived for a living room wall, an exhibition space, or an alternative space—the artist's intentions are inevitably superseded by those of the curators, who add another creative layer. To give maximum freedom, sometimes a one-size-fits-all approach trumps tailoring. But we also split the baby, so to speak, by introducing new typologies of exhibition space into the site previously occupied by the American Folk Art Museum. MOMA had assumed that we would use that space for circulation only to complete the loop between new and existing galleries. We had something else in mind. We carefully carved new vertical circulation space out of MOMA's existing footprint because we wanted to give the entire footprint of the Folk Art Museum over to exhibition space. As this space had not been

Diller Scofidio + Renfro, Museum of Modern Art renovation and expansion, New York, New York, 2019

programmed in the brief, it was a kind of bonus—we called it the "space of exception." We developed a stack of galleries, each with unique attributes—double-height, L-shaped spaces that interlock or overlook one another, a storefront that faces directly onto the street, a daylit gallery open to sunlight, and, for the first time in MOMA's history, a gallery engineered to meet acoustic criteria for performance. The stack completes yet interrupts the circuit of white galleries in a fresh way.

JR – How do these spaces disrupt the smoothness of that primary circuit? Is it a matter of idiosyncrasy versus neutrality?

ED – They create friction and moments of reflection. The performance space, for example, has a window wall onto the street. It can be blacked out, translucent, or transparent, which means that New York City can become the backdrop for a MOMA performance. Back in the 1970s there was a performance work at the Public Theater—I think it was by JoAnne Akalaitis and her company Mabou Mines—where the theater backdrop abruptly disappeared in midperformance, exposing the building's brick wall and punched windows onto the street. We had been sitting in a black box, and we were suddenly plunged into an actual context—an abrupt reminder of the artifice of the theater. That stayed with me; I think there's something important about introducing friction into the museum by refusing to let the space be completely sanitized, reminding the viewer where they are.

JR – I can see the historical connection to experimental theater, but it also feels like a very contemporary move because there's a degree of social awareness that comes with that situated-ness—a consciousness of being in the middle of a city but also part of an audience—that speaks to the collective dimension of so much recent art. While we're on the subject of introducing friction into the museum, though, I have to ask—did you ever think of intervening in the huge atrium at the heart of Yoshio Taniguchi's 2004 MOMA expansion? That was surely the most criticized aspect of his design.

ED – In the context of the 2004 expansion, that space felt shockingly monumental and out of touch. So, sure, at some point I had the thought that it could be cut in half to make a stack of two nicely proportioned galleries. But I realized how, over time, the curators conceived of brilliant ways to use it and artists proved that they could conquer it. At a certain point, I realized its scale provided a challenge for curators and artists that I didn't want to screw up. Our work for the expansion stayed away from grand gestures. It was geared to improving MOMA's main objective: to show art. The expansion was meant to be all muscle and no fat. But there were areas of the museum that were screaming for attention. The lobby was claustrophobic, congested, and disorienting, and it felt like art was a mile away from the front door. We were adamant that if MOMA was going to rethink its institutional paradigm, it had to address not just its galleries but also its unwelcoming urban threshold. We wanted to bring the city into the museum with an open, contiguous layer of public space, where art could be brought to pre-ticketed audiences. For example, we suggested reinstating the Projects room, a free ground-level gallery that had been eliminated from the 2004 renovation (incidentally, the same gallery that hosted *Para-site* in 1989). In a sense, our renovation and expansion of MOMA was speaking in the same, albeit now more mature, critical voice that we originally brought to the museum with *Para-site*.

JR – In parallel with your redesign of MOMA, you were working on the Shed, which also opened in 2019. In a sense, the Shed seems like a radical extension of some of the core ideas of the MOMA project. It's hyperflexible—the structure literally expands to double its space—and it's hyperinterdisciplinary, hosting everything from art exhibitions to orchestral concerts to comedy performances to film premieres to fashion shows. It's probably too early to tell, but it seems like one effect of the Shed's increased flexibility and interdisciplinarity has been to decenter visual art, or at least to undermine certain hierarchies—between high and low culture, between art and commerce—that are still operative at a place like MOMA. How do you think about the relationship between these two institutions?

ED – They're entirely different. As a cultural start-up, the Shed had no collection, no history, and no legacy—in essence, nothing we could destroy. It needed to be defined, while MOMA wanted to be realigned. And while we responded to a brief at MOMA, we more or less wrote the brief for the Shed. The Shed was a response to an RFP [request for proposals] released by New York City in 2008 to fill an open plot at Hudson Yards designated for an as-yet-undetermined cultural use. The city was looking for an idea, whether it was a museum expansion, an alternative theater space, or even a brand-new institution. The economy was tanking. The notion of realizing a new cultural entity seemed totally improbable, so we figured why not go out on a limb? By chance we ran into David Rockwell in Venice and decided to make a proposal together. Our thinking was, New York has plenty of cultural venues: we have museums, we have commercial galleries, we have Broadway venues, we have alternative performance spaces for theater and dance, we have opera houses and concert halls. By conventional wisdom, each of these is supported by a distinct kind of physical space with its own precise technical criteria, especially for sound and light and climate control. If an exhibition space has fluctuations in temperature and humidity standards, for example, other institutions will not loan art to it. If a performance space cannot meet acoustic criteria, visiting orchestras won't come. But what if the criteria for each discipline could be slightly relaxed, and the trade-off would be to engage all art forms at once?

JR – So from the beginning you thought of it as more than a museum.

ED – That's why I wanted to do it. Again, my education was in the seventies, when artistic disciplines were being disrupted. But I was also thinking back to that era because it was such a fertile time in New York for creative production. In a way, I felt that the city had lost its edge, and this was an opportunity to retrieve it. Throughout the nineties and the first decade of the twenty-first century, the city had increasingly become a place of consumption. We still had the world-class institutions, but we had little space for working artists. So I started to think about the Shed as a center of interdisciplinary production. Could it also provide artists' studios? Or rehearsal spaces for peer institutions? Could it commission new work as well as provide exhibit space to other institutions that need overflow? Dan Doctoroff, the pioneering board chair, and Alex Poots, the visionary artistic director, made good on many of those notions and much more. For example, every year the Shed's Open Call initiative supports thirty emerging New York artists.

JR – There's an irony here, because it was the decline of industrial production in urban centers in the 1950s that enabled a subsequent rise in cultural production, largely because there was so much cheap space available for artists to experiment with in the sixties and seventies—the now-legendary lofts of SoHo are a prime example. Then culture became increasingly monetized for leisure and entertainment, and the culture industry pushed out the cultural producers; artists were priced out of these neighborhoods, as were any number of experimental venues. But part of the strength of your concept for the Shed is that it's not simply nostalgic for the good old days. You're very clear-eyed about the nature of the contemporary city, and you included a range of income-generating functions—one could call it a calculated embrace of the culture industry—that help to finance things like the Open Call.

ED – The Shed was conceived during the great recession, and we know that the first things to lose support in a spiraling economy are the arts. So our idea was to make the Shed less dependent on philanthropy and more financially autonomous. Part of the business plan was to generate income by partnering with creative industries and events such as the Frieze art fair and New York Fashion Week. This very large, very well-equipped, and very flexible space was intended to provide the institution with independence and safeguard it from economic fluctuations.

JR – It bears emphasizing that you're describing a paradigm shift in terms of the architect's role, because you responded to the RFP with both a building design and a business plan. You've pointed toward a new paradigm for cultural institutions, too, where the old philanthropic funding model is replaced by a new kind of cultural entrepreneurship. It seems prescient that you were already thinking about this more than a decade ago, because in recent years we've seen any number of scandals involving board members, whether due to the source of their wealth or their political views. Even the Shed hasn't been immune—the real estate developer Stephen Ross had to step down from the board after an uproar over his support for Donald Trump. Do you think the philanthropic model is collapsing? Should the alternatives explored by the Shed be pushed even further?

ED – First, you're right—the role we played was that of both architect and client for the Shed for the first six years. Then Alex became artistic director in 2014. He was suspicious of the entrepreneurship model, but his vision of all newly commissioned work supported by a steady stream of philanthropic funding was utopian.

It was hugely successful in the first year but not sustainable in the long run. Meanwhile, I had my own utopian vision of balancing costs with box office, income from collaborations with creative industries, and maybe just a tiny bit of philanthropy. My model was overly optimistic. There were definitely some uncomfortable conversations about all this. In the end, a successful commissioning institution would require both income generation and sustained philanthropic support. The philanthropic model is unique to US institutions and must continue. But it should be refreshed with the next generation of trustees, and we also need to be less reliant on philanthropy. Compared to its peers, the Shed has tipped the balance between philanthropic support and income generation to the side of self-reliance. The pandemic, which struck barely a year after the Shed's opening, was the first major stress test of this hybrid model. The combination of financial self-sustainability and an on-demand indoor-outdoor infrastructure proved to be a major asset, allowing the Shed to reopen earlier than many other institutions. The Shed is still learning and evolving.

JR – We've been focusing on the program of the Shed, but I want to get deeper into its architecture. The name suggests a particular architectural genealogy. As a typology, the shed—in the sense of a generic, functional, open-span building with an exposed structure—is one of the paradigmatic spaces of modern architecture. I'm thinking of the incalculable influence of a building like the Crystal Palace in London [1851] or the Galerie des Machines in Paris [1889]. But somehow the shed has never quite worked as a museum. The iconic steel-and-glass structure at Mies van der Rohe's Neue Nationalgalerie is a kind of idealized shed, but it rarely houses art, which is typically exhibited in the traditional white-cube galleries buried in the plinth below. The Pompidou Centre by Renzo Piano and Richard Rogers is probably the closest living relative to your building, but when part of that building was converted into the Musée National d'Art Moderne, they brought in Gae Aulenti to subdivide the wide-open space into—again—a warren of white

Diller Scofidio + Renfro, the Shed, New York, New York, 2019

cubes. I know the Shed is still an ongoing experiment, but do you envision its success as coming more from the changes in cultural production that we've been discussing or from your reinterpretation of the shed typology?

ED – Well, probably some combination. The curatorial vision is very strong, and the building is generative rather than generic. When I say "the building," I mean not just the singular large space but also the gallery stack, the black box, and the infrastructure that accommodates just about everything. When we began, there were two interesting models: the Park Avenue Armory in New York, which was just emerging, and the Grand Palais in Paris. They're both used for exhibitions, fashion shows, and festivals, and they generate income unabashedly. But both venues have infrastructural problems; both are very tall spaces that are expensive to rig for large shows and events. The Shed is also very tall, but it's purpose-built for flexibility. The roof of the McCourt—the deployable shell—is a theatrical deck that provides physical access to anywhere on the footprint. You can also use the shell as a gantry to haul heavy loads up into the gallery stack. This "architecture of infrastructure" allows for the agility of the space. It can change on demand. Drop the grid and create a long-span horizontal gallery. Darken the space for film. Flood it with people for a dance performance. The shell is fully climate controlled and infinitely divisible into spaces of different sizes.

JR – So you're providing more than a setting. It's not just a blank wall or an empty room for artists to do what they want; you're giving them a set of tools, a physical infrastructure that can actually help produce their work. The building becomes a collaborator, in a sense.

ED – Yes. Space has always influenced art, whether it's the nineteenth-century salon or the twentieth-century loft. The twenty-first century poses the very distinct challenge of a dwindling supply of urban space for artists operating in a highly volatile cultural, economic, and technological landscape. We felt strongly that we could not predict what artists would be doing in ten years, twenty years, and beyond, and that museums, with their passive and overdetermined white-cube galleries, are ill-adapted for an era of breakneck change. So the question became: How could we design something that speaks to today but does not get in the way of tomorrow? We realized that infrastructure would be the answer. By shifting emphasis from the aesthetics of the architecture to an infrastructure for production, we created a kind of machine for making art. We want artists to feel uninhibited to appropriate this open-ended tool kit. But, more than that, we wanted to give artists the gift of too much space—a daunting, three-dimensional, blank canvas. The measure of the Shed's success will be the extent to which artists and curators use the space in ways that continuously surprise and even shock us.

FRANK

GEHRY

JULIAN ROSE – Not many architects can say they have a cultural phenomenon named after their work. But it's been more than two decades since your Guggenheim Museum Bilbao building opened and people still refer to the "Bilbao effect" to describe the transformative impact that architecture can have on a city. That project unquestionably changed architecture's role on the global stage. Is it also fair to say that museum design has played a key role in your own practice?

FRANK GEHRY – The whole topic of museum design is precarious for me.

JR – Precarious in what sense?

FG – Soon after I finished Bilbao, the director of an LA museum told me he had attended a professional conference where a resolution was passed to not let me do another museum, ever.

JR – It didn't quite succeed, did it?

FG – But I didn't get to build another museum for a long time. The Fondation Louis Vuitton in Paris was the next big one, and that opened in 2014.

JR – I take your point that the Guggenheim Bilbao has been controversial. It's ironic that for all its influence on how museums are understood within culture at large—especially in terms of tourism and development—the building has not become a proto-type of museum architecture. It's also true that museums are not your primary building typology. But I would still argue that your work is marked by an exceptionally close connection to the visual arts. So maybe I should rephrase: Is it fair to say that a connection between art and architecture is at the core of your practice?

FG – I was into art from the beginning, because my mother used to take me to the museum as a child in Toronto. I fell in love with painting at the Art Gallery of Ontario, and then, many years later, I got to do an addition to that building, which was an amazing experience. I used to draw all the time, too. I was a curious kid. On Friday evenings I would go to lectures on music and art at the University of Toronto.

JR – You studied architecture at the University of Southern California [USC] in the early 1950s, almost a decade before many of the artists we associate with the postwar scene in Los Angeles—the "cool school" and so on—became established. After your initial exposure to art history at the museum, how did you develop a relationship with practicing artists?

FG – Well, actually, I ended up in architecture school because of my interest in art. I came out to LA with my family in 1947. We were very poor, so I worked as a delivery-truck driver. I took some night-school classes, including one in ceramics taught by a man named Glen Lukens, who started the ceramics program at USC. We got along, but I think he saw I wasn't going to be a ceramicist. So one day he took me to visit a house he was building for himself with Raphael Soriano, the modernist architect. Soriano was there, and they were in the middle of construction—they had a rig and were moving these big pieces of steel around—and my eyes lit up. Glen must have seen how excited I was, because he insisted I enroll in an architecture class. The art and architecture schools at USC were in the same building, so I spent a lot of time talking to art students. I was always interested in what they were doing.

JR – Next you studied urban planning at Harvard, where Josep Lluís Sert was dean. He was famously an advocate of the so-called synthesis of the arts—also advanced by Le Corbusier and others—wherein architecture would provide a platform for the integration of artistic media. Did you find a fluid interconnection between art and architecture at Harvard like that you'd found in LA?

FG – Sure, we talked about modernist painters a lot: Klee, Kandinsky, Albers—all the Bauhaus guys. While I was there they also had a show of Le Corbusier's paintings in the architecture building.

JR – What did you think?

FG – I had mixed feelings. He had just finished Notre-Dame du Haut, the chapel in Ronchamp [1955]. I love that project, and I could see the beginnings of it in the works in the show. It made me think, Here's an architect who works out his buildings through his paintings. That was interesting. But, at the same time, his paintings weren't great, you know? They were derivative of all those people he hung out with. He wasn't a painter; he was an architect.

JR – **You were intrigued by the idea of using art to think through architectural problems, but you felt that in this case the work was unoriginal?**

FG – I wasn't interested in him as a model. I remember that one of Le Corbusier's assistants who had worked on Ronchamp was enrolled in the architecture school at Harvard at the time. Every building the guy designed looked like Ronchamp. It was fascinating to watch him.

JR – **Also exasperating, I imagine! In retrospect, your frustration at Harvard isn't surprising, because the modernist version of a synthesis of the arts was, in practice, about architecture following the lead of painting and sculpture. I think for people like Sert and Le Corbusier there was a sense that visual artists were the true avant-garde and that architects had the job of translating their aesthetic innovations into built form. It sounds like at USC you had a different experience—developing your work directly in conversation with artists. Was it refreshing to return to LA in the early 1960s as the art scene there was taking off?**

FG – Yes. There was an amazing energy in the city—an openness and a sense that new things were happening. One of my first projects after I got back was the studio I did for the graphic designer Lou Danziger on Melrose Avenue, which was finished in 1965. I remember visiting the construction site one day and there was this funny guy wandering around in the structure. He introduced himself as

Ed Moses, and I was flabbergasted, because I was already a fan. He liked what I was doing for Lou and invited me to remodel his house. I told him my fee was three hundred dollars. He told me there was no way he was going to pay me three hundred dollars for a design, so the building never happened, but we became very close. He was the first guy in that scene who really connected with what I was doing. He gave me love at a time when I needed it. And he also introduced me to Billy Al Bengston, Larry Bell, and Bob Irwin.

JR – It must have been an exciting moment. Many of these artists were trying to push beyond traditional media just as you were looking for new approaches to architecture. I'm curious how your contact with these artists influenced your work when it came to designing spaces for the display of art. In 1983, you designed the Temporary Contemporary for the Museum of Contemporary Art, Los Angeles, to house exhibitions while their new permanent home, designed by Arata Isozaki, was under construction. The design was radically simple: you turned an old warehouse into a museum by essentially cleaning out the interiors and sandblasting some of the concrete. The design became very popular, and now, renamed the Geffen Contemporary at MOCA, the building is a permanent part of the institution. Thanks in part to that project, the minimally renovated industrial space is one of our primary gallery typologies. But in the early 1980s it was a wild idea—leaving the space raw made it closer to an artist's studio than to a gallery. Was this a new kind of exhibition space that came from hanging out with artists?

FG – Yeah. I loved the way they showed their stuff, the way they lived with it. Bengston would always remodel his dining room for a dinner party. It would look one way, and you'd go back a month later and it looked completely different. It still pisses me off that he didn't photograph any of those spaces—nobody did, because they weren't being taken seriously in that way. But I thought of his remodeling as a startling kind of artwork. He was making a still life and we were all living in it.

Gehry Partners, Geffen Contemporary (formerly Temporary Contemporary) at the Museum of Contemporary Art, Los Angeles, California, 1983

JR – It's as if you recognized ideas about architecture in Bengston's work by reading it against the grain. I wonder how that compares to your more direct collaborations with artists. By the mid-1980s, just a few years after you did the Temporary Contemporary, you were working on the Chiat/Day Building [1991], which incorporates a sculpture by Claes Oldenburg and Coosje van Bruggen. How did that come about?

FG – Claes and I were teaching a class at the University of Milan, and we asked the students to design a city on an island in the Venetian Lagoon. He and I were working together on our own version of the project on the side. None of the buildings were ever developed, but he made a series of models and drawings that I loved. My favorite was a small model of a library in the form of a pair of binoculars standing vertically. He gave it to me, and I ended up keeping it in my office in LA. A few years later, I was working on Jay Chiat's building. I had decided on a three-part massing, with the entry in the middle and a block of offices on either side. I had

Gehry Partners, model of the Chiat/Day Building, Los Angeles, California, 1991

figured out what I wanted to do with the offices, but I couldn't decide how to design the center. One day, I had lunch with Jay. We'd had a few drinks and were sitting in front of a model of the building, and he said, "Frank, tell me what's going to be in the middle. I can't wait." I told him I needed more time, but he pushed and pushed. I happened to look across the room and saw the binoculars, and I realized the scale was just right. So I picked them up and put them down right in the center of Jay's building. And he loved it. I called Claes, and he and Coosje came to LA. Over the next few years we worked to develop the binoculars into an actual component of the building. I insisted on only one thing: I told them, "If you're going to be architects, you have to put windows in your design. Otherwise, it's not a building." My office did all the drawings to make it work as architecture, and we got it built.

JR – That's a refreshing contrast to the way architects often deal with the so-called integration of art into urban projects, which is simply to plop a monumental sculpture in front of their building. James Wines infamously described this as the "turd in the plaza" method. But what you're describing also sounds like an intense and time-consuming process. Do you think the kind of collaboration you had with Claes is too complicated to become common?

FG – It's funny, because around the time that building opened, I attended a conference—I think it was organized by UCLA—about the relationship between art and architecture. There was an intense discussion about how art in public spaces becomes an afterthought. There were a lot of big artists there, and most of them complained about feeling like second-class citizens. Richard Serra was upset that architects got to do all the big pieces—the buildings—while artists did only the small pieces—the sculptures in the plazas and so on. I wanted my project with Claes to show that it was possible to collaborate in a deeper way. But it was barely discussed in the architecture world, and the art world completely ignored it. I don't remember any critics writing about it.

JR – In the end, it's something of an uneasy hybrid; it may have windows like a building, but it can still be read as a blown-up sculpture. Do you think that part of the problem is that, as collaborations between artists and architects become more intense, it becomes more difficult to categorize—and so maybe to talk about—the resulting projects?

FG – I have no idea. But to this day, people don't really discuss it.

JR – The Chiat/Day Building raises questions of scale. You mentioned that Serra, too, posed scale as a central problem in the relationship between art and architecture. How do you feel this issue played out in the Guggenheim Bilbao? There has been criticism of the way some art, particularly Serra's, looks in the building. Often the argument boils down to some combination of two points: the building's form competes with the sculptures, and the sculptures are dwarfed by the building's size.

FG – That problem of scale in the galleries was created by Richard himself. The main exhibition space is 430 feet long. In my original design I sectioned that gallery by dividing it along the trusses that run perpendicular to its length. It was supposed to

Gehry Partners, Guggenheim Museum Bilbao, Spain, 1997

be a series of geometric platforms that would allow work to be displayed in different ways. I didn't want white-cube galleries, so the spaces wouldn't be square, but they would still be polygonal. The idea came from an early conversation with Tom Krens [then director of the Solomon R. Guggenheim Foundation in New York]. He told me he wanted rectilinear galleries for the artists who are no longer with us and more inventive galleries for contemporary art, so that living artists could interact with the building. That idea always made sense to me: make the architecture neutral in some places for the artists who can't defend themselves, and give it character in other areas so that working artists will want to engage with it. I had that in mind when I designed the lower-level gallery in Bilbao for temporary commissions, and I have had conversations with artists who really liked the idea of messing around with that space—Sol LeWitt used it very inventively, and so did Anselm Kiefer.

JR – What happened to the subdivisions, then?

FG – Richard wanted his work right in the middle of the space. I had nothing to do with where those sculptures were placed. *Snake* [1994–1997], which was commissioned for the opening, is over one hundred feet long, and once it was there the partition walls became impossible. Tom agreed with Richard—he insisted that a big work needed a big space, and it was important to him that the museum would provide that. But I felt it was counterproductive, because the open span made it impossible to look at anything in the space without also looking at the building's structure. The partition walls were going to follow the trusses, so you wouldn't see them. Now, when you walk into the gallery, you're looking at the four-hundred-plus feet of structure that holds up the roof, and I feel like the structure competes with the artwork. Of course, the fact that the gallery was left wide open also meant that Richard could take it over. I don't think it's a coincidence that in 2005 the museum bought another series of seven of his pieces [*The Matter of Time*, 1994–2005], so now the gallery is completely filled with his sculptures. And I do think that the works themselves are spectacular.

JR – There's an irony here because bigger work does require bigger exhibition spaces. But then artists complain that these expanded spaces overpower their work, and they often respond by making their pieces even larger in turn. Sometimes it feels like artists and architects are locked in an arms race—and that's by no means limited to Bilbao. Do you think it's possible to create a less competitive relationship?

FG – With Richard, it's complicated. We've been friends on and off, and I love his work. But he doesn't think very highly of architecture.

JR – In some ways, though, this notion of art and architecture being in direct competition seems absurd. I've always thought that the idea of a "sculptural building" is a paradox. Constructing a building—especially one as formally complex as Bilbao—is nothing like making a sculpture. While you work like an artist in some ways—sketching and modeling by hand, for example—there is also a highly sophisticated technical side to your practice. In fact, you started an entire company, Gehry Technologies, to produce your buildings, and that company is hired by other architects and contractors around the world. Doesn't your relationship to technology differentiate your practice from that of an artist?

FG – Let's get back to basics: from the beginning, I've been interested in building buildings. I grew up with modernism, right after the Second World War, and technology and construction were a big part of the modernist approach to architecture. But when modernism hit a dead end, it created a crisis.

JR – I never thought about the decline of modernism as disrupting architecture's relationship to technology, but you're right that postmodernism emphasized representation over construction.

FG – Yeah, exactly. Arthur Drexler, who was the director of the MOMA architecture department for many years, organized a show in 1975 called *The Architecture of the École des Beaux-Arts*. It was a staggeringly beautiful exhibition of renderings of Beaux-Arts buildings, and it appeared when contemporary architecture was struggling to find itself. For many, it seemed like a license to retreat into the past, into the world of drawing—and that became postmodernism.

JR – I imagine that did not appeal to you?

FG – I was looking for a way to express feelings without reverting to history, without these nineteenth-century references. I remember thinking a lot about classical sculpture. Why just go back 150 years? I had seen the *Charioteer*, the great Greek bronze at Delphi, when I was in my forties, and it brought tears to my eyes. I keep a picture of that sculpture on my wall as a reminder. Some unknown artist made this thing two thousand years ago, and here I am crying over it. That gave me the idea that maybe you could express feelings with inert materials just by giving them shape, without reverting to a style. You could just do it.

JR – But then the question becomes, How do you build those shapes? I could argue that all the technologies that have developed in architecture since the Renaissance have been geared toward designing, and then building, regular geometries. With very few exceptions, architects haven't tried to construct organic forms.

FG – While working on the Vitra Design Museum [1989], I designed a stairway that had a complex curve. I used descriptive geometry to draw it because that's what I was taught in architecture school. But descriptive geometry failed me in the field. When the contractors built the stair, it had a kink in it.

JR – You're saying there was a mistake in the construction because you had not been able to accurately represent your design in two dimensions?

FG – It wasn't really a mistake. There was just no way to draw it, and the contractors had to figure out how to build it the best they could. After that, I asked one of the young architects working

Gehry Partners, Vitra Design Museum, Weil am Rhein, Germany, 1989

for me if he could find another way. Architects were starting to use AutoCAD, but I knew that was still 2D, so it wouldn't help us. We talked to Dassault, the aerospace company. They had CATIA, this software they were using to build fighter planes, paperless—no drawings. When I saw that, I said, "Holy shit!" I had been trying to figure out how to build this curved stairway, but I realized that the technology had a much bigger application. I know the business of architecture really well, and its norms and methods are, in many cases, archaic. But they still exist, and they result in an enormous waste of materials, time, and effort. I saw a whole new approach— not just to design, but to construction.

JR – When did you begin incorporating that technology?

FG – The first real test was the pavilion I did for the 1992 Summer Olympics in Barcelona. I designed it in the shape of a fish. I was interested in it as an expressive form. I thought of it like the Greek sculptures, but going even further back, before art or architectural history to nature. The contractor said it couldn't be built. He tried six different mock-ups, and they all failed. So I decided we should try this CATIA thing, and we got it done in six months on budget.

JR – And that's when you knew you had to make it a part of your process?

FG – Exactly. We talked to Dassault about adapting CATIA for architecture, but they weren't interested, even though it's a huge market. So we developed Digital Project, which is our own software based on CATIA, and that's what we used for the Guggenheim Bilbao. That building also opened on time and on budget. Over the years, we've approached perfection. The apartment tower we did in New York in 2010 had zero change orders for the curtain wall. Can you imagine? Seventy-six stories high, with a very complicated geometry, and not a single mistake during the construction process. The dream is to go even further. What if you could get the building department to use this software for their reviews? If they weren't looking at drawings, you could get the approval on a huge building in two weeks instead of six months.

JR – There is no question that these technologies have transformed the way buildings can be made. I wonder if they should also be changing the way we understand construction theoretically. Modern architecture, like constructivist sculpture, emphasized transparency. The idea was that the outer form of a building, or an artwork, should follow the inner logic of structure. There's an obvious and almost ethical appeal to this approach—an honesty. Sure enough, some critiques of your architecture focus on the contrast between the exterior form and the interior volumes. This happens in Bilbao, and it's even more extreme in the Fondation Louis Vuitton in Paris, because the museum's outer envelope is glass and the galleries are housed in separate concrete volumes within. That separation only becomes possible, or at least feasible, when you use the kind of design and construction tools you have developed. Would you argue that one of the benefits of digital-design technologies is that they obviate traditional approaches to structure?

Gehry Partners, Fondation Louis Vuitton, Paris, France, 2014

Are you trying to take advantage of the freedom this technology provides and to remind us that interior and exterior no longer have to correspond?

FG – You're overthinking it. With the Louis Vuitton building, I wasn't trying to prove a point. It's simply a matter of circumstance, not intention. Bernard Arnault had acquired the site, which is in the Bois de Boulogne, and there was a strict height restriction on the construction. There had been a bowling alley there, and he was going to knock it down and build the museum in its place. The city said that any new construction couldn't be any taller than that original building. That wasn't going to work for a museum, so Bernard and I met with Bertrand Delanoë, who was then the mayor of Paris. I told him there's a long tradition of building glass structures in parks, conservatory-type buildings. Right in Paris there's the Grand Palais [1900]. We talked about the Crystal Palace in London [1851]. But of course you can't hang paintings on glass, so I envisioned a building with a double skin. I asked the mayor, "If we made a glass shell with the museum inside of it, would that work?" He loved the idea. He said, "Show me what it would look like." So based on that conversation, I designed a building with a double skin, which separates the solid structure—the building itself—from what I think of as the persona of the building—the glass volumes.

JR – But does that create a problematic split between the museum as urban icon and the spaces within? Are you divorcing the galleries from the building's architecture and separating a visitor's experience of the architecture from their experience of the art?

FG – Not at all. It's a hybrid. The idea is to provide many different kinds of space to display art. There are some very traditional galleries, sure, but the building itself can also be used as a platform. One of the things that most excited me about this approach to the design is that it created outdoor spaces between the glass skin and the solid volumes, and I had a feeling that this space would be perfect for sculpture. At first the curators were skeptical, because it was a totally nontraditional space, but I called up Jeff Koons and some other artists I'm close to and talked to them about it. They all thought it would be exciting to bring their work into a site like that. So I made a model where I filled that in-between space with artworks. I was trying to say to both the client and the artists that this is not a precious space. It's supposed to be used; it's supposed to be interactive and collaborative. And artists have shown that they're up for it. Look at what Daniel Buren did in 2016— he put colored panels all over the exterior.

JR – How did you feel about that? Buren has a genius for creating maximally disruptive interventions in buildings and public spaces. Some of his projects could be described as downright hostile. In 1971, the Guggenheim in New York famously removed his *Painting-Sculpture*, which filled Frank Lloyd Wright's atrium, from that year's *International Exhibition*.

FG – Daniel and I have been close friends for years. Sure, when you give him a chance, he'll be overpowering. But I feel that the building is up for that kind of intervention. I'm actually the one who invited him to work on the building. He had already been commissioned to do something for the Fondation Louis Vuitton, but it was going to be a kind of gateway in the park that visitors would pass through as they approached. I saw the proposal and told him he should take on the architecture instead. And then he completely overwhelmed my building with those little colored rectangles. I knew it wasn't going to be easy for me or my building, but I think it's important for artists to do things like that and for architects not to be fussy about it. People talk about it, and artists realize that the building is something they can play with, and I hope others come and do more interesting stuff. I think of it as an extension of the great French Gothic tradition of putting sculpture on a building—Chartres, Notre-Dame.

JR – Do you think that combination of art and architecture broadens the museum's appeal?

FG – I remember that soon after I had finished my own house in 1978, Daniel came to visit me. I think he was with Michael Asher and Benjamin Buchloh, and we got to talking about museums. He asked me what kind of building was best for showing contemporary art. I didn't want to piss anyone off, so I basically gave them the spiel most architects give, even today: museums should be neutral and flexible and should be considered a backdrop for the art, blah-blah-blah. I was shocked by Daniel's response. He said simple and neutral was the worst. He wanted to be shown in an important building. And you know, it's true. The Louvre isn't the ideal place to show a painting—it's an old palace. But it's one of the most important buildings in Paris. If an artist has a show there, he can go home and tell his mother, "Look, I got a painting in the Louvre!" So a museum should stand out. It needs a persona to help define the city's landscape—just like a courthouse, or a church, or a city hall, or a library, or any of the buildings that have historically played an important part in the design of our cities.

JR – That's a convincing argument for powerful architecture, but it might not be incompatible with a desire for simplicity. Couldn't someone argue that a white cube is more honest, or more pure, and therefore more powerful as architecture?

FG – I absolutely don't think being a purist is any more true to the nature of architecture. You're right that some critics look at my buildings and complain that the interior walls don't correspond to the exterior walls. But making a building where the two are perfectly lined up isn't any simpler or any more honest. Let's take the example of a small wood house, like they used to build in the 1950s. You see one of these under construction, with all the wood studs framed up, and it's so beautiful you could die—just a simple timber frame, totally pure, right? I used to see thousands of those tract houses being built when I was driving around Southern California. I loved looking at them. But then what happens? You bring in the plumbers, you bring in the electricians, you bring in the HVAC contractor, and everybody starts drilling holes in the studs and moving things around and then taping it all back together. They totally violate the structure—they torture the purity out of that thing. So, there's a conflict between this idea of an ideal structure and all the things you need to put into a building to make it a building.

JR – So you're saying that the appearance of honesty is itself a kind of fabrication?

FG – Absolutely. And when you try to make a building with a tight skin stretched over the structure, it costs a fortune. Go to Mies van der Rohe's 1929 Barcelona Pavilion and look at the columns intersecting with the roof slab. It's so beautiful, this thin column hitting a roof that's just six or eight inches thick. But then you look at the drawings and you realize that it's not even a structural connection, it's just two things touching! And you start to understand all the structural gymnastics Mies had to go through to make that building look honest. That's why I have always said we should separate the mechanical elements of the building from elements that provide shelter. And if you have a cavity between the exterior and the interior where mechanical systems can go, then they can also be changed without completely taking apart the building. If you're making architecture in the twenty-first century, that seems like a good idea. So we can argue forever about the inner skin and the outer skin and how far apart they should be and how much they can deviate from each other, but at the end of the day the space in between isn't wasted.

JR – It's easy to forget that the relationship between how something looks and how it is made is often profoundly different in architecture, as opposed to art. There's certainly a different relationship between form and structure, and maybe even between appearance and reality.

FG – A lot of ideas about purity and simplicity come from art and don't square with the everyday problems of building. This doesn't mean architecture is any more complicated than art. But you can't take an idea from one and expect it to work in the other.

I also think part of the problem is that we need to update our artistic reference points. When we talk about purity, who are we thinking of? Ad Reinhardt? I love his black paintings, but that's not the only way to make art. I love Kazimir Malevich, too, but painting didn't end after he stripped it down to a square. A lot of artists today— Koons, say—are working more like architects. They're using technology; they're directing fabricators; they're hiring consultants. They're not craftsmen. Why hold architects to this anachronistic standard?

JR – So maybe, in the end, the similarities between art and architecture are just as important to keep in mind as the differences?

FG – We have to remember that historically architecture was always considered one of the arts. Giotto was an artist who became an architect. The same is true of Bernini, Borromini, Brunelleschi, Michelangelo...I could go on. People blame architecture for a lot of things today. They complain that every city looks the same. Well, I agree, but architecture isn't what's building our cities anymore. Our cities look the way they do because of economics, because of politics, because of development. Maybe if we thought about architecture as art again we could start to change that.

RICHARD

GLUCKMAN

JULIAN ROSE – I've always wondered if you were drawn to designing spaces for art in part as a compensatory project. In the late 1960s you went to Syracuse University, where your professors were committed modernists, by which I mean that they believed not only in the aesthetic principles of modernism but in its progressive social aspirations as well. Many of them were busy building civic projects like hospitals, universities, and subsidized housing—in a sense, the architectural embodiment of President Johnson's Great Society. But by 1977, when you started your own office in New York, there had been profound political and economic shifts. The energy crisis had caused a full-blown recession, and the city itself famously had a brush with bankruptcy in 1975. That kind of civic work had evaporated. I can imagine that museums and galleries were some of the only projects available then that allowed you to design spaces for a public audience. Did you see cultural institutions as part of a retrenched public sphere?

RICHARD GLUCKMAN – It wasn't a choice I made consciously at the time. But, looking back, it's true that this period was a critical turning point for architecture in America. I was at Syracuse for six years, from 1965 to 1971, getting both a bachelor's degree and a master's degree. Back then, many architects who taught also practiced. While I was a student, I worked part-time for three of my professors: William Scarbrough, Louis Skoler, and Kermit Lee— all smart, talented, and wonderful teachers. Lee was the first Black graduate of the Syracuse University School of Architecture and an important mentor for me and many other students. The three of them had a partnership and were getting a lot of public work for the New York State Urban Development Corporation [UDC]. I worked on a series of fire stations, public schools, and subsidized housing buildings, all for the City of Syracuse. Ed Logue, the head of the UDC, truly believed that good architecture was a social good. He was responsible for many of the new State University of New York campuses built during that time, and he hired the best architects around—I. M. Pei did the master plan for SUNY Fredonia, which has always been a favorite of mine, in 1968. We all benefited from this level of public investment in architecture. It sustained the offices of a lot of established and midcareer professionals, including my professors and, of course, their fledgling staff. I felt I should be paying for the experience rather than the other way around.

JR – Unlike New York City, the UDC did default in 1975, and Logue resigned shortly after, so in a way he's a perfect bellwether for the shift we're discussing. But since we're talking about the legacy of modernism, too, it's worth mentioning that among the projects Logue commissioned were the Eastwood and Westview apartment complexes on Roosevelt Island, designed by Catalan architect Josep Lluís Sert. After Sert emigrated to the US, he was the longtime dean of Harvard's Graduate School of Design. But prior to that he had worked closely with Le Corbusier in Europe and served as the president of the Congrès Internationaux d'Architecture Moderne for nine years. This was modernism right from the source.

RG – Sert's generation was hugely influential while I was a student, and most of my professors were second-generation modernists who had been educated and greatly influenced in the fifties by Sert and his colleagues at Harvard. My closest connection to modernism was through Werner Seligmann, a Cornell graduate, whom I also worked for while a student at Syracuse. He was teaching at Cornell, and his home and office were in Cortland, New York, south of Syracuse. Two or three days a week, I would drive down there after class or on weekends. Some evenings, Werner would come back to the studio after dinner, and we'd often have the office to ourselves. Depending on how busy he was, he'd ask what I was learning in history. My usual answer of "not much" was occasioned by the departure of our history teacher, who had left Syracuse out of disgust for the student strikes in 1968. Werner was close to Colin Rowe, then a colleague at Cornell and before that at the University of Texas at Austin in the 1950s, where they were both part of the group of crusading young faculty known as the Texas Rangers. Werner would sit at my desk, giving me abridged versions of Rowe's lectures, and while he talked, he sketched diagrams analyzing the work of

Le Corbusier, Mies van der Rohe, and Frank Lloyd Wright. Those impromptu lessons were a welcome part of my education. Those and the opportunity to work on the Typewriter Building [Scattered Site Housing Project, Elm Street, 1973]—a low-rise, high-density housing complex in Ithaca that was another UDC effort—made working for Seligmann one of the best jobs I ever had.

JR – **Did his connection to modernism influence the way design was practiced in his office?**

RG – Absolutely. He taped a small graph of Corb's Modulor to everyone's desk, and we all used it to great effect during the design phase of most projects. He was a true believer—a dedicated modernist and a great teacher.

JR – **It's interesting that you mention Wright as part of your modernist trinity, because, unlike Le Corbusier and Mies, he built a lot in upstate New York. Did you visit any of Wright's buildings?**

RG – I grew up in Buffalo, New York, and regularly went to see the three Wright houses there, in particular the Martin House [1904], semi-trashed then but now impeccably restored. Louis Sullivan's Prudential [now Guaranty] Building— completed in 1896 and among the earliest steel-frame skyscrapers in America—and H. H. Richardson's psychiatric hospital, designed in 1870 but not finished until the 1890s, were part of the huge system of parks and parkways that Frederick Law Olmsted designed for the city in the last decades of the nineteenth century. Olmsted's landscape also embraced the Albright-Knox Art Gallery [1905] by Edward B. Green, brilliantly but perversely complemented by Gordon Bunshaft's addition [1962], a great binary composition. The first modern spaces I truly experienced were Bunshaft's addition, as a weekend art student, and Kleinhans Music Hall [1940], designed by Eliel Saarinen and his son, Eero, which I visited for dances as a thirteen-year-old—even more influential, albeit slightly awkward, experiences. Later concerts in the same building assuaged the earlier trauma.

JR – It sounds like your childhood in Buffalo showed you that modern architecture wasn't only something you had to study in a book; there were homegrown versions, too, right in your backyard. I don't think that's necessarily a common experience for an American. Like modern art, modern architecture is often thought of as something that was born in Europe in the late nineteenth and early twentieth centuries and then migrated to America during and after the Second World War. It may be true that America never quite produced an avant-garde movement like de Stijl or an institution like the Bauhaus, but there's a tremendous amount to be learned from pioneering figures like Sullivan and Wright and Olmsted.

RG – In that regard, Buffalo's industrial buildings were even more fundamental. My grandfather trained as a mechanical engineer but practiced as an architect. He designed three houses in Buffalo before the Great Depression, when he was compelled to find work at the local board of education, where he stayed for the rest of his career. But he taught me how to draw and how to use hand tools. When I was very young, he or my father drove me around the industrial waterfront of Buffalo. The grain silos, the grain elevators (which are the umbilical cords between the lake freighters, the silos, and the railroad cars), the steel mills, and the automobile factories: all were fascinating and ever-present for a nine-year-old. I didn't know it then, but these very same industrial structures were already world-famous—they had been an important inspiration to many European modernists, including Walter Gropius and Le Corbusier. This was the core argument of Reyner Banham's *A Concrete Atlantis: U.S. Industrial Building and European Modern Architecture* [1986], a book that defined "daylight factories" for me when I read it thirty-five years later. These were essentially exposed concrete structures, filled in with transparent glazing to maximize natural light for factory work. I thought of these structures as three-dimensional frames that could be exploited for large-scale artworks—the kind of art supported by the Dia Art Foundation and the Andy Warhol Museum. Thinking about those art typologies and these industrial structures had a powerful impact on my design sensibility and my focus on mutually supporting strategies. Framing art and making frames became my foundation myth.

JR – I didn't realize that you had such a personal connection to industrial architecture, although I shouldn't be surprised, since you've played a huge role in popularizing the conversion of industrial spaces into galleries and museums. Your work with Dia was where all that started. How did you get involved with the foundation?

RG – After graduation, I finished two design/build projects and then worked in Boston for a firm called Stahl Bennett from 1972 to 1975. Most of their work was commercial, and it started to dry up after the oil crisis, so I was already thinking about quitting when a client asked if I'd help him relocate to South Africa on his thirty-foot sailboat. I learned how to use navigation tables at the Cambridge Center for Adult Education and how to use a sextant from an itinerant sailor living on his boat in Winthrop, Massachusetts. My former client and I left Scotland for Cape Town in mid-1975 on a real adventure; neither of us had sailed offshore before. It took three months to get to Cape Town. The next six months were spent mostly on land in southern Africa and South America, including another month sailing from Cape Town to Rio. While I was traveling I had been in touch with Fred Stelle, my college roommate, who encouraged me to come to New York to start a practice partnering on a couple of design/build projects.

JR – Were DIY projects something that you were interested in?

RG – They still are. Drawing, detailing, and putting it all together is a real joy. Seeing the space become framed—literally and figuratively—is very satisfying. While I was in architecture school, my parents gave me a great gift by allowing me, as a third-year student, to design and construct their home. I drew it under the supervision of an architect and did the framing under the direction of a general contractor and a carpenter. Two influences were Dave Sellers's Prickly Mountain houses and Steve Baer's *Dome Cookbook* [1967]. The *Dome Cookbook* led me, after graduation, to Baer's home in Placitas, New Mexico, where I saw his experiments with wind power, Trombe walls made from fifty-five-gallon drums, and aluminum-clad insulated panels that made up the geodesic structure for his house.

JR – Did you go to Drop City, the commune in southern Colorado based in part on his ideas?

RG – I didn't. But I did spend a couple of nights at the New Buffalo Commune west of Taos. A month later, my plan to help a couple of Syracuse faculty build a dome in Oregon was derailed by an unfortunate encounter with a drunk in a pickup truck. I sometimes wonder where I would have landed had I spent the summer of 1972 in Oregon.

JR – Even if you did end up back East, it's fascinating that your modernist education was leavened with a healthy dose of counterculture. And I can see how an interest in that kind of tinkering, hands-on approach would be useful when you were converting lofts into exhibition spaces. But you still haven't explained how you started working for Dia. It was founded in 1974 by Heiner Friedrich, Philippa de Menil, and Helen Winkler—a gallerist, a collector, and an art historian, respectively—so you must have gotten started almost as soon as you arrived back in New York.

RG – Soon after Fred and I partnered, we intended to finish our New York projects and relocate our practice to Maine. He was building his parents' house in upstate New York while working for Edward Larrabee Barnes as his day job. One of his projects for Barnes was the conversion of the Mercer Street Fire Station in SoHo for Heiner Friedrich. That project was never realized, but meanwhile, Heiner knew Fred was going off on his own and asked him to take on the design of a townhouse at 7 East Eighty-Second Street for Philippa de Menil and himself. Fred introduced me to Heiner, and I ended up as the point person for that project.

JR – Was Barnes the go-to architect for art spaces? I would have thought that maybe Pei was the obvious choice at that time.

RG – Pei's East Building for the National Gallery of Art opened in 1978. His Louvre pyramid wasn't finished for another decade. I believe Heiner had visited Barnes's Walker Art Center in Minneapolis, which opened in 1971—a museum with a great diagram: a slow path and a fast path that spiraled through clean exhibition spaces and a simple structural expression. Years later, when I renovated and expanded two Barnes buildings, the Carnegie Museum of Art Scaife Galleries [1974] and the Dallas Museum of Art [1984], I came to appreciate the Walker even more. It needed no adjustment.

JR – Getting back to 7 East Eighty-Second Street—what did Friedrich want you to do with the building?

RG – Interestingly, it was a classic Gilded Age mini-mansion that Heiner basically wanted to turn into a loft. He wanted a clean, minimalist setting for work by Dan Flavin and other Dia artists.

JR – So how did you do that?

RG – Mainly by subtraction—the house had been built in 1906, but it had typical nineteenth-century decorative moldings, which Heiner thought were inappropriate. He would tell me, "No design! Let the space be what it wants to be!" He knew he could tell a young architect what to do and in later years enjoyed telling me that he took me off the street with soap behind my ears.

JR – What do you think he was afraid of when he told you not to design? Did he want to backseat drive and basically design the space himself, or was he worried that a heavy-handed architectural intervention would distract from the art?

RG – To his credit, he wanted the artists to have exactly the space he believed they needed. For Flavin, the relationship between the wall and the floor was critical. That's where many of his early pieces were placed—the fluorescent fixtures were resting on the floor with one edge against the wall. So to install his pieces, we removed the baseboards and added a little quarter-inch gap between the floor and the wall to clean up that crucial corner. Dan's installations were my first encounter with minimalist, site-specific work, and this was an incredibly serendipitous moment in my professional life. I learned a lot about both poetics and pragmatics seeing his work installed in the house.

JR – I want to hear more about that gap. Nowadays we call it a "reveal," and it is ubiquitous in gallery architecture. I'm sure there are exceptions out there, but I can't think of any museum or gallery built in the last thirty years that doesn't use that detail. The funny thing, though, is that it wasn't a part of what we might call the first-generation white cube, by which I mean the museums that were built in a modernist style from, say, the twenties through the sixties. I checked the original detail drawings for Marcel Breuer's Whitney Museum of American Art [1966]—which I know you are deeply familiar with, since you renovated it in the nineties—and there's a dark band at the bottom of the wall. So, the visual effect is similar, but the material is flush with the wall surface—definitely no gap. In Mies's Neue Nationalgalerie in Berlin [1968], the lower-level galleries are classic white cubes—white walls, white ceilings, gray floors—*except* they have very traditional baseboards made of dark wood. Is the reveal something you invented?

RG – You're right about the Whitney. Breuer designed a two-inch dark wood baseboard that created a visual connection between the wall and the dark bluestone floor. Ironically, since it was flush with the rest of the wall, it got painted over immediately. When we worked on the renovation, we peeled off more than one-third inch of white paint—dozens of layers that had been applied for new exhibitions over the years.

But I wouldn't say I invented the reveal—it was the result of both a poetic and a pragmatic need. The poetic necessity was created by the aesthetic innovation of minimalist artists moving out of the center of the room or the center of the wall to engage the space in a different way, fundamentally changing the relationship between the viewer, the art object, and the architectural frame. The pragmatic necessity was that we had to paint the gallery on a regular basis, and I observed that a three-sixteenth-inch sheet of Masonite was often used to protect the floor. The quarter-inch gap between the metal corner bead at the edge of the gypsum board and the floor simplified the task.

JR – I love that pragmatic side—I never thought about sliding a sheet of Masonite into a reveal, but I can see how that would be quite handy to protect the floor. I want to talk more about the reveal's aesthetic aspect, though, because it does have a profound effect of dematerialization or abstraction. It makes the connection between floor and wall into a visual relationship between two planes rather than a tectonic relationship between two material surfaces.

RG – And artists engaging the spatial volume of the gallery, using its architectural surfaces to frame their work, liked it for that reason. Heiner told me I had to run the quarter-inch gap by Dan, and he immediately agreed. Other artists—for example, Richard Serra, with his *Props* and other works—worked with floor and wall, too. Sol LeWitt obliterated the baseboard with his wall drawings. The reveal is very effective for work like that, and we've used it for all the gallery spaces we've designed except for the Galerie St. Etienne [1987], where we wanted a slightly more traditional feeling.

JR – The reveal makes a lot of sense to me in an industrial space, where in a sense you're using it to add a level of refinement to an existing architecture that is already very raw and empty. But it's interesting that in a domestic setting you had to strip away traditional detailing to create it. Did you feel like you were some-how working against the grain of the house?

RG – This gets back to the relationship between Dan's work and the existing architecture, which was not simply a binary opposition. As I said, the house had been built in 1906, and it was badly renovated in 1917. Heiner had directed the removal of the rather heavy rococo detailing in the main rooms of the piano nobile: the crown molding, chair rail, baseboard, and ceiling trim. During demolition, we discovered much finer original detailing under the 1917 intervention. I reported this to Heiner while he was on the phone with Dan, who expressed an interest in preserving the original details and asked if they could be restored. I nodded yes, but Heiner told Dan that the demolition was already complete, telling me afterward to finish the removal. But Dan kept thinking about that original detailing. His reaction was revelatory. The work he installed consisted of three arrays of fluorescent lights: one in the living room, one in the center hall, and one in the dining room. In the living room, triangular arrays of circular fixtures were installed at the corners on the walls, spanning from the floor to the height of the chair rail. In the center hall, two staggered rows of two-foot pink and yellow fluorescent tubes were installed on the ceiling against one wall, mimicking the crown molding. In the dining room, five arrays of two circular fixtures, each mounted on the ceiling diagonally out of the corners (an alcove added an extra corner to the space), reference the crown molding and decorative plaster ceiling medallion.

JR – So it sounds like the work had an almost indexical quality. You're saying that Flavin was intentionally referencing the absent architectural details that you had removed?

RG – Eliminating the conventional decorative trim gave the space a pure, geometric format. But, at the same time, that original detailing had been very carefully calibrated to the scale of the space, and Dan reintroduced those scale-defining details, translated into his own contemporary language.

JR – Was that his only work in the house?

RG – There was a second installation in the four-story stair, which was topped with the original laylight comprising yellow, pink, blue, and green stained glass. At each of the four landings Dan located arrays of four-foot yellow, pink, blue, and green fluorescent tubes, the number of fixtures corresponding to the floor number. The effect was extraordinary. Iconicity and aura—I was hooked.

JR – I'm fascinated to hear how contextually responsive both these pieces were, because I think there's often a sense with Flavin and other minimalists that their work is made for the white cube, or even needs the white cube as a framing device—in other words, that it works best with a kind of zero degree of architectural context, which could be one interpretation of Friedrich's "No design!" But you're offering a powerful example of how interested many of these artists were in responding to an existing space or structure— in making their work truly site specific, in the sense of establishing a collaborative dialogue with its architectural context.

More broadly, though, I have to point out that there's a delicious irony to this story about Friedrich's brownstone: the man who would be king of the downtown scene moves into an uptown enclave and then busies himself trying to make his mansion look like the inside of a factory. But it also encapsulates a profound historical shift. The Museum of Modern Art spent a number of its early years in a nineteenth-century townhouse owned by Abby Aldrich Rockefeller, and in some ways the living room of the wealthy patron was the prototype for all early museums of modern art, because that's the primary space for which most art—even the most radical art—was made in the late nineteenth and early twentieth centuries. The art of that period was shaped by the space of its destination, in other words. But you're describing a very wealthy and powerful patron trying to make his own home look more like the studio spaces that were used by the cutting-edge artists of his time. In the intervening half-century, something was reversed—the art was now being shaped primarily by the space of its origin, and destination (i.e., exhibition) spaces had to change to accommodate that.

RG – Exactly. The seventies was a time when the place of art's presentation was generated by the place of its production. This was an organic evolution, partly related to the economic changes that

Walter De Maria, *The New York Earth Room*, 1977,
installed at 141 Wooster Street, New York , New York

you asked about at the beginning of our conversation. When the
city was going bankrupt, it meant the end of a certain kind of
ambitious, progressive, modernist architecture, but it also opened
up a lot of new opportunities for artists. Businesses were shutting
down, people were leaving the city, and neighborhoods like
SoHo and Tribeca were full of defunct commercial and industrial
space that artists could get cheap. They moved into those big lofts
and exploited the space they had. When gallerists like Heiner
and Paula Cooper became interested in that work, they found
similar venues.

JR – And did you help Friedrich find spaces downtown?

RG – I scouted buildings downtown and uptown, mainly on
the west side of Chelsea. One of them, 548 West Twenty-Second
Street—a perfect "daylight factory"—became Dia's main exhibition
space [Dia Chelsea] in the mid-eighties, and that put me on the
map. But after 7 East Eighty-Second Street, the next thing I did for
Heiner was the renovation of Walter De Maria's *The New York Earth
Room*, installed in 1977 on the second floor of 141 Wooster Street,
the location of his gallery from the early 1970s in SoHo.

JR – The idea was to do a permanent version of an installation De Maria had done at Friedrich's space in Munich, where the gallery floor was completely buried, right?

RG – Yes, but Heiner had me renovate the space *after* twenty-two inches of soil was in place. Protection was put down, sprinklers relocated, wiring concealed, and paint was applied. A low glass partition was installed at the viewing point in the narrow corridor that revealed the depth of the earth: we called it the ant farm. It took three tries to get the glass right, which means there are two *Earth Room* coffee tables somewhere in SoHo. But we weren't done yet, because all the work had tamped down the soil, and the compressed earth needed to be fluffed up. My idea was to use a rototiller, but we learned that under the top few inches of soil small particles of vermiculite were put in the mix.

JR – They had done that to reduce weight? That's clever.

RG – Too clever, because in the end six inches of additional dirt were required and many cubic yards of sterilized soil were ordered. A few weeks later I got a frantic call from Dia: "Go to 141 Wooster immediately, the sheriff has put an injunction on the building!" Someone in the co-op was concerned about the added weight and called the building department, which sent the sheriff to issue a stop work order.

JR – And no one had done any calculations to check that the floor would support the load?

RG – Hence the vermiculite. I don't know what was done initially, as we weren't involved, but rototilling seemed like a reasonable approach that abrogated the need for additional soil.

JR – That's a pretty succinct encapsulation of the difference between an artist and an architect! What did you do?

RG – I called Robert Silman, a brilliant structural engineer known for his work on historic buildings such as the restoration of the cantilevers at Fallingwater. He did the engineering on our Dia projects and was a great mentor. We met on-site with Dia people and co-op people, and he got everyone to agree that the posted loading capacity would be the governing parameter (the only alternative would have been to x-ray every joint in the building). This was a nineteenth-century manufacturing building with an interesting structural system comprising I beams spanned with clay tile arches. He directed us to make a one-cubic-yard plywood box and rent a waste scale from Zelf, a paper and rag storage business down the street, and reconvene a few days later. The box was filled with soil, weighed, and Bob did the math. With perfect aplomb he announced that the floor would not collapse. Everyone breathed a sigh of relief, turned to pack up and leave, and, with perfect timing, Bob declared, "Unless the sprinklers go off."

JR – Oh no—because the soil would get wet! What did you do?

RG – A hose was found; the dirt was soaked. Bob recalculated and just as calmly announced that if the dirt was fully saturated, the floor would collapse. But he then pointed out that it is not mandatory that a building be designed to hold water, and, from a fire perspective, it was likely the safest loft in the city since no one was cooking and no one was smoking in bed. The co-op agreed to let the piece stay, and it helped that Dia eventually bought the ground floor below.

But back to the dirt: sterilized soil was specified, but nature usually wins. Within days, the earth showed signs of life. We had installed a hose bib, and the earth was lightly watered on a regular basis. Watering the first time generated a light green carpet of shoots over much of the surface. These turned white after a few days, and it was incredibly beautiful. The other aspect is olfactory; when one enters the building on watering day, a rich humus smell permeates the stair hall. I like to think that Walter would approve of nature being a quiet presence in the work.

JR – And then you also worked on his piece *The Broken Kilometer*, from 1979?

RG – Yes, that was the last of a series of installations by Dia artists over a period of several years at 393 West Broadway. This was the next chapter in my architectural education—witnessing, sometimes assisting, these projects. Some were straightforward installations of the work: John Chamberlain's wrecks on the floor and Donald Judd's boxes on the wall. Fred Sandback's installation—three string pieces that optically defined three transparent planes—was almost as ephemeral as Flavin's. Andy Warhol lined the perimeter of the space with *Shadows* [1978–1979]: 102 panels, mostly black canvases, placed edge to edge, unwinding like a filmstrip around the room. This was Warhol's reaction to Heiner's insistence that he install paintings; at the time, Warhol was mainly interested in film. The artist's assistants should have asked us for help. We could have made it work the way it was intended: no white gaps between the canvases except door or window openings. We achieved this a few years later when the same panels were installed in the space I designed for the Andy Warhol Museum in Pittsburgh, which opened in 1994.

We had absolutely nothing to do with my favorite installation at 393: Dan Flavin's installation of four arrays of four different colored fluorescent tubes, all facing away from the front windows and all attached to an existing architectural component: the elevator wall, the stair wall, a cast-iron column, and the remnant of an elevator shaft. The effect was transformational. Air became matter. The colors—pink, yellow, blue, and green—stood clear and blended to form multicolored clouds of light. West Broadway on a misty night extended the work beyond the gallery walls, and, on a few magical occasions, the street became a great outdoor public art installation.

JR – So, again, Flavin was responding to specific elements in the existing architecture—there's that same contextual aspect of his work that made such an impression on you in Friedrich's house. What came after the Flavin installation?

RG – The next project was *The Broken Kilometer*, which, like *New York Earth Room*, is still in place. Walter planned to install a kilometer piece on each continent. Two are built: *The Broken Kilometer* in New York and *The Vertical Earth Kilometer*, which was a solid brass rod one kilometer long, two inches in diameter, drilled into the earth in Kassel, Germany, in 1977. The concept for *The Broken Kilometer* is simple—five rows of one hundred polished brass rods, two meters long, two inches in diameter. I worked with Walter and his assistant John Cliett on many of the details of the installation. The windows were sandblasted to give the space a quiet presence. I learned the best way to clean frosted glass is by rubbing a raw potato on it.

JR – That's amazing—not the kind of trick you learned in architecture school, I imagine.

RG – Definitely not. Walter was particular about all the details. A sitting area was roped off to keep people from walking into the field of rods. Walter was very specific that he wanted rope, not cable. A "come along" was installed behind one wall to tension the rope, and we threaded the rope through one of the cast-iron columns, which took a whole day to drill through. Illumination was a challenge. Walter wanted the brightest lights known to man. John looked into aircraft landing lights, but they drew eight thousand volts of direct current, and, if mishandled, they could have turned anyone to dust. Eventually he found superbright metal halide lights used in German television studios, and they were installed.

JR – What about the installation of the rods themselves? Were you involved with that?

RG – Initially Walter installed the rods equally spaced from front to back. When the lights—which were as bright as the sun—were turned on, only about the first two-thirds of the rods reflected the light back; the ones beyond were almost invisible. The viewing angle was too low. So I sketched two options for Walter: install bleachers to increase the viewing angle or space the rods according to an arithmetic progression that started close and got further apart farther away. The bleachers were a nonstarter. The spacing was also

Walter De Maria, *The Broken Kilometer*, 1979,
installed at 393 Broadway, New York, New York

a tough sell. In our previous conversations, Walter had told me that
he imagined the work being installed in the Palace of Versailles,
each rod equally spaced two meters [six and a half feet] apart,
extending throughout the corridors of the palace. He went silent for
a couple of weeks but eventually used the second option, and an
unexpected result is that, because of foreshortening, the rods appear
evenly spaced from front to back even through in reality the spacing
increases dramatically. Another accommodation was necessary to
level the plane of rods. We discovered during the installation of
Warhol's *Shadows* that the floor dropped more than six inches from
the front northwest corner to the back southeast corner, which also
exacerbated the reflection issue. So each rod is carefully installed on
top of two pairs of finishing nails, which gradually increase in height
as the floor slopes. It's a different strategy, but the purpose is similar
to that of the different heights of the stainless-steel rods used in *The
Lightning Field* [1977], which allow the top of the field to be completely level even though they're installed on uneven topography
below. When you look closely at *The Broken Kilometer*, the plane of
brass rods appears to float above the floor.

Working with Walter was a unique, pleasurable, and exhausting experience. I would meet him most evenings after five o'clock to discuss details; after an hour or so, he'd take me to Raoul's for dinner and a bottle of wine. He'd sketch and describe ideas. He was a strong believer in the beauty and utility of the nine-square grid in architecture, and I remember once he suggested that I should use Astroturf as a facade material for one of my buildings. He was an inquisitive, voracious reader, whether it was Eastern philosophy or *Popular Mechanics*. But then I would have to be back at seven the next morning to direct the contractor to implement our discussion from the night before, and that evening our schedule would repeat. This went on for weeks.

JR – Given how closely you worked with De Maria on *The Broken Kilometer*, do you consider that—or your work with Flavin, for that matter—to be a collaboration?

RG – Absolutely not. When working with artists on installations, I referred to myself as an "expediter" or a "facilitator" of the artist's work—it would be utterly presumptuous to call it a collaboration. I would participate when asked, usually to solve a technical problem, occasionally to offer an aesthetic opinion. I have done a few true artist-architect collaborations, but only a few. We worked with Jenny Holzer on a couple of competitions and installations that came to fruition. While we were working on the Watermill Center with Robert Wilson in the late 1990s, we held a two-week workshop there with him one summer that produced two large light installations in the Cultural District of Pittsburgh. And I did a competition with Richard Serra. Working with the Dia artists in the late seventies and early eighties, followed by these projects with Serra and Holzer, prevented me from succumbing to the temptations of postmodernism even when it was at its peak popularity among architects.

JR – What made those collaborative projects different?

RG – Collaboration demands a conceptual exchange of ideas. Walter had it all in his head—how the piece should look, what the visitor's experience should be—and John and I helped him achieve that. Jenny reached out in 1994 to create a vaulted pavilion to contain a part of her *Lustmord* series. She wanted an enclosed space for the viewer to enter, where they would experience part of the work, and we worked closely together on its design. In the late 1990s I began working with Helmut Lang, a friend and fan of Jenny. He asked me to integrate her works into two of the stores we designed. Again, there was significant back and forth about how the installations of her work would interact with the architecture and influence the visitor's experience of the space. Another successful collaboration with Holzer was an iconic sign she did for our transformation of the Santa Fe Terminal Baggage Building for the Museum of Contemporary Art San Diego Downtown [2007]. It offered a vertical alternative to the historic neon sign on the ridge of the existing building.

JR – What about your collaboration with Serra?

RG – He was invited to participate in the competition for the Berlin Holocaust Memorial in 1994 and asked me to join him. He drove the design, but there was a lot of discussion over the architectural components of the project, the materials, the vertical circulation, and the visualization. He envisioned an elliptical tower, double walled, sunk thirty meters [ninety-eight feet] into the earth. The ramped entry into the ellipse led to an elevator and a double-spiraled stair between the two elliptical walls. The exposed section aboveground referenced a Martello tower, a type of coastal fortification, usually round or elliptical, built across the British Empire in the nineteenth century. Within the elliptical extrusion, a square tube with an open oculus extending to the top of the structure was the source of light. The experience would have combined the curved movement in his elliptical sculptures with the vertical perspective from his towers. Just before we submitted our design we learned that there was a four-meter [thirteen-foot] depth limitation that would be strictly enforced, and we were disqualified by the city engineers before it went to the jury. The height restriction was put in place because the water table in Berlin is fairly high. Building thirty meters down was an engineering challenge that could have been solved, but unfortunately it would have been very expensive. Richard did not want to compromise the design, and I supported that decision.

JR – I respect his decision, too, although, in a way, that's the difference between an artist and an architect: the former doesn't have to follow a brief, the latter does. How did you exchange ideas on these projects? Were you working on models together? Sharing drawings?

RG – We did a study model together that turned into a presentation model. I did some drawings, my office produced 3D visualizations, and Richard made sketches. He talks with his sketchbooks—he was constantly drawing whenever we discussed the design.

JR – So, in a way, drawing is your common ground with artists?

RG – It's also where the differences show up. He's drawing freehand with a black crayon, I'm using a straightedge with a 2H lead, and my associate is using a computer. That's not a criticism— Richard's drawings are very powerful and evocative. But, in a way, that's a metaphor for the distinction between our roles and responsibilities, between concept and execution.

JR – I appreciate your lack of ego in calling yourself an "expediter." I'm sure artists do, too, and that's one reason so many have wanted to work with you. But I can't help but wonder if you're selling yourself short. Listening to you describe your work with De Maria on *The New York Earth Room* and *The Broken Kilometer*, I'm struck by how carefully constructed, even artificial, the viewer's experience of these pieces is. Your architectural framework functions almost like a stage set or a diorama, which means that in both cases it has become an integral part of the artwork. I know these are extreme examples because the viewer can't walk around either space, but I'd still argue that they have something in common with most site-specific installations. This is a far cry from the autonomous artwork, the painting that can be moved from wall to wall or the sculpture that could sit on any given pedestal. In effect, the artist is leaning on the gallery architecture to coproduce the viewer's experience of their work. And yet so many artists—and critics, too—talk about gallery architecture as if it is, or at least should be, a neutral backdrop. Does that ever frustrate you?

RG – I don't consider the spaces to be neutral. Whether a found space or a created space, it's intended to interact with the art. It doesn't matter which comes first. In our studio, our primary goal is to create a diverse suite of spaces that accommodate different art typologies: paintings and drawings, sculpture, video, and installations. Good spaces need texture and scale and light, natural and artificial, to create a subtle context that relates to the visitor as much as to the art. There's a misconception that because I design so-called minimalist spaces, I'm trying to make the architecture disappear. After Dia Chelsea opened, Calvin Klein visited our studio to talk to me about designing a store. He noticed the toggle light switch on the wall and asked, "Why didn't you make that disappear?" I answered, "Because I'm not that kind of minimalist." As the constructivists said, "Not the new, just the necessary."

And that's the thing. I don't want every detail to be custom, and I don't want to try to erase the architecture—I'm not trying to make an abstract space. We know site-specific artists don't consider the frame to be neutral. There are always decisions that have to be made about what should come forward and what should recede. It's challenging to convert an industrial structure from the late nineteenth or early twentieth century into a twenty-first-century exhibition venue. From a mechanical or electrical perspective, these buildings are practically medieval. True, they were designed with plumbing, heating, electricity for equipment, and illumination from skylights and large glazing, but today's art spaces have much higher environmental standards. Our job is retrofitting all the infrastructure—sophisticated climate control, security systems, electronics, daylighting strategies—for a state-of-the-art museum into these buildings without completely cluttering them up. We don't abrogate the aesthetic responsibility to engineers, but we do bring them in early to work on the design of the technical components that are visible. We're trying to simultaneously update the space and preserve its original character, which means allowing its structure to provide scale and texture. That is an ideal frame for art—one that balances the relationship between the viewer, the art object, and the space they both inhabit.

JR – How has that decision-making process played out in specific projects?

RG – Dia Chelsea is a good example. It's four stories. The initial concept was for the ground floor to be a temporary exhibition space, and each of the other ten-thousand-square-foot floors would house a one-year installation of the work of a single artist. The inaugural set was going to be Joseph Beuys on two, Imi Knoebel on three, and Blinky Palermo on four. Their work established a subtle hierarchy for our intervention. The building has an ideal reinforced-concrete frame—high ceilings with generous spans supported by elegant square columns and deep girders. I wanted to make a slightly different play on each floor, to express more and more lightness as the visitor ascended. At level two, Beuys, the full structure was left visible to complement the materiality and weight of the felt and copper he works with; at three, Imi Knoebel asked for a long diagonal wall, so we kept the wall under the girders and beams while concealing the columns. He also asked us to design an array of five black cabinets, each containing ten thousand drawings in Solander boxes that could be taken out and examined on a tall, narrow steel table that we designed specifically for this work. At four, Palermo's small-scale abstract paintings were complemented by partitions that entirely covered the walls, girders, and most of the columns. We installed skylights, and the transformation of that floor was complete.

Richard Gluckman Architects, inaugural exhibition at the Andy Warhol
Museum, Pittsburgh, Pennsylvania, 1994

Richard Gluckman Architects, Dia Chelsea, New York, New York, 1987

JR – Do you feel like you need to know the artist you're designing for to make those kinds of decisions about how to treat the architecture?

RG – Not at all, although knowing the work makes it more intimate for me. Even at Dia Chelsea, I knew that the curatorial imperative of one artist per year per floor would eventually obviate the specific intent of that original conceit. But we knew who the Dia artists were. We take a similar approach when we design commercial galleries—the program influences our design thinking.

Gagosian on Twenty-Fourth Street, which we finished in 2000, is a good example—a single-story transfer warehouse with steel trusses one hundred feet long and nine feet deep. Incredibly beautiful and efficient. Natural light is important to exhibition spaces, but the structure is just as important because it provides scale and visual texture. The main gallery needed better clearance, so the trusses were raised ten feet and an insulated plastic clerestory window was installed on the south and west facades. In the middle galleries, a zoning restriction limited the height of the roof, so we cut the trusses in half laterally, which increased the ceiling height by four and a half feet. We added skylights and created a series of spaces with different proportions, going from large to small.

JR – Does that also mean the spaces are best suited to different kinds of art?

RG – To a degree, yes. At the opening, standing in the main gallery, someone said, "This isn't a very good space for paintings." I told them, "That's because it's not for paintings. It's for Richard Serra." I didn't design it just for him, but I knew Richard was a key part of Gagosian's program. The trusses were raised to accommodate his work, and the floor was reinforced to carry his work as well. Of course, the raised trusses and clerestory give the entire gallery light, lightness, and air. The top lighting and proportions of the interior galleries were primarily for paintings. In the end, all the galleries are used for both painting and sculpture. It's similar to Dia Chelsea: a series of differently proportioned, differently lit, and

Richard Serra, *Every Which Way*, 2015. Sixteen slabs of weatherproof steel.
Installed at Gagosian Gallery (West Twenty-Fourth Street), New York, New York,
May 7 through October 22, 2016

differently textured spaces, which is my formula for a good exhibition space.

JR – I'm glad you brought up this question of painting, because it reminds me that even though you had these incredible formative experiences with pioneers of minimalism, conceptual art, and land art, many of your museums have been for painters—the Warhol Museum in Pittsburgh, the Georgia O'Keeffe Museum in Santa Fe [1997], and the Museo Picasso Málaga [2005], to name just three. Have you felt any tension between designing for paintings and your early work for Dia, designing spaces for these other very different kinds of art?

RG – First of all, I like paintings. But you may be overstating the difference. Over the years I've learned a great deal about the relationship between art and architecture from my wife, Tiffany Bell, who is a curator and art historian, and from friends like the art critic Hal Foster. Tiffany and I took an especially influential early trip to northern Italy, which started in Varese at Count Giuseppe Panza's collection, which was a mirror of Dia's, installed in a stone barracks and his villa. We then visited Leonardo's *The Last Supper* [ca. 1498] in the Santa Maria delle Grazie in Milan, the Giottos in the Scrovegni Chapel in Padua [ca. 1305], and the Caravaggios in the Cerasi Chapel in the Basilica of Santa Maria del Popolo in Rome [1601]. All of these—including Panza's chapel-like spaces—were examples where the architecture frames the art, the art is created for that frame, and together the two create an environment that is focused on the physical presence and spatial experience of the viewer.

JR – It's true that the notion of the autonomous artwork that I raised earlier is essentially a modernist concept. When "site-specific" artworks came along in the sixties and seventies, they seemed radically new, but maybe in broad strokes they're not so different from a lot of historical models. Would you say that, at the end of the day, your task is to provide a spatial and material framework for the experience of art, and that's not so different whether it's a Flavin light installation or a Picasso painting?

RG – Yes, and Flavin's work at 393 West Broadway is analogous to those examples I just mentioned. But the other thing I want to emphasize is that museums continue to evolve. They're not just about architecture and art—there's a greater social dimension to them. We're not just framing art; we're framing a collective experience, comprising an ever-expanding range of art. I first became aware of this at Dia when Charlie Wright introduced poetry, dance, video, and other new art forms. When I began my career, I believed that the most important relationship in an exhibition space was that between the individual viewer and their object of desire—the work of art—and that my job was to facilitate that relationship. Particularly now, as artists are thinking more and more about cultural and social obligations, I've amended that original belief to acknowledge the importance of the relationship among the viewers. The institution isn't just providing an aesthetic experience; it's also offering—and facilitating—a cultural and social experience, one that has political ramifications. This is an important change, and we're still considering how our work can accommodate and expedite both contemplation and social engagement.

JACQUES

HERZOG

JULIAN ROSE – Today, we expect that architects of a certain standing will collaborate with artists. It's a way for them to demonstrate their success or affirm their cultural cachet. You and Pierre de Meuron are probably more responsible for this development than anyone else. Your own collaborations are legendary: one of the first projects you did after architecture school was a 1978 performance with Joseph Beuys for the Basel Carnival. But I would like to speak more historically—and theoretically—about how the relationship between the two fields pushed you toward collaboration in the first place. What did art offer in the seventies that architecture seemed to be missing?

JACQUES HERZOG – Pierre and I grew up in Basel, where institutions like the Kunsthalle and the Kunstmuseum showed important postwar artists before many other museums in Europe. We saw Donald Judd's sculptures at the Kunstmuseum in the early 1970s, when it was sometimes still difficult to see his work in America. In 1977 the museum purchased and exhibited Beuys's installation *Hearth I* [1968–1974]. It was very controversial, because he was not yet recognized as the great artist that he was, especially because he used materials that were not accepted in art, like copper wiring, grease, and felt. All of these things were captivating.

JR – Captivating because you hadn't seen anything like them before? Or because they suggested a fresh set of possibilities that you already saw yourself exploring in architecture?

JH – When I was young, I didn't think I would become an architect. Chemistry and biology and art interested me—and also Pierre—much more. When we eventually decided that we wanted to go into architecture, it was a naive decision. We thought it was a field that would allow us to combine these different interests.

JR – You were attracted to what you saw as architecture's interdisciplinary potential…

JH – Initially, yes. But we quickly became aware that architecture was filled with ideas that didn't really interest us. This was in the mid-1970s, when modernism was declining. We couldn't see ourselves continuing in the footsteps of masters like Le Corbusier or Mies van der Rohe. We felt that modernism as an ideology was discredited. Architecture didn't have a tradition anymore. At the same time, we were surrounded by the beginnings of postmodernism—deconstruction and historicism and all that stuff—and it felt limited, a narrow response to what had come before. So we turned to artists as models for new ways of thinking about architecture. This turn grew out of our fascination with art's freedom and openness.

JR – It's ironic that you found architecture to be so closed and art to be so open, because the major developments in both fields at that time were referred to in the same terms—as postmodernism. But in architecture this meant something very specific: a largely aesthetic rejection of modernism, either through the reintroduction of historical references or through the complex geometry of deconstruction. In art, there was never a monolithic postmodernism—it was the expanded field.

JH – Yes. And early on we recognized that open-ended approach as something that didn't exist in architecture at that time. The way artists work, especially those artists who work on concepts rather than refining a personal "style," was the way I thought—and still think—that architecture should be produced.

JR – You have mentioned, beyond this general sense of freedom, the influence of specific artists like Judd and Beuys. What drew you to their work, and how did you relate it to architecture?

JH – We were fascinated by how Beuys connected his work to natural history as well as to social and anthropological issues. We saw great potential in that approach, which was neglected by architecture at the end of the 1970s.

JR – I can see how a Beuysian conception of the natural world would offer an alternative to the stylistic debates between modernism and postmodernism, but how did it actually inform your approach to design?

JH – Architecture was primarily taught and practiced as either a technical or an aesthetic discipline, and, post-1968, as a social art, in which participation increasingly became a new topic. Beuys's work was a model for combining and integrating all these relevant forces into one complex reality. We did not like his sectarian side, but we were interested in the ways in which scientific and spiritual forces could materialize and become architecture. It was the moment of our early projects such as the Blue House [1980] and the Stone House [1988], when we were full of doubts about how to do even the most basic things, such as design a wall or a window or how to use color. Every one of our projects was radically different from the others. No traces of style or authorship were recognizable.

JR – At least with Beuys, then, artistic practice offered you less an aesthetic model than an attitude about authorship. But could the same be said of Judd? *Minimalism* is a term hotly contested between art and architecture, largely because many artists feel that architects reduced it to something purely aesthetic. If for Judd and other artists of his generation minimalism was about shifting the emphasis from object to experience, rethinking the way seeing is framed by the spatial envelope of the gallery and inflected by our movement through it, for architects in the 1980s and 1990s it became just a look or even a lifestyle—a branding slogan.

JH – Oh yes, I agree. Minimalism became an aesthetic school, especially in Switzerland and England, and then also in America and elsewhere. A number of architects became famous for their "minimalist" boxes. We felt responsible for that evolution, since we did radically minimalist work early on. Perhaps the Ricola Storage Building [1987] in Laufen [Switzerland] is the first example in architecture and the most Judd-like, in a sense. Also, we introduced the term *minimalism* to describe an approach to structure and materiality, which was different from what architects were doing at that time and was closer, in fact, to the concepts of artists such as Sol LeWitt, Robert Morris, and, of course, Judd. We proposed a new approach to materials: they should not be just functional but invisible elements of a wall or a floor. We wanted to give every architectural element a kind of individuality, a recognizable role within the whole. Bricks are great for that: a brick is still a brick, even when it becomes part of a wall; only mortar binds the wall together. In the exterior walls of the Stone House in Tavole, Italy, we even tried to get rid of mortar—each stone is piled up without mortar, holding its position through its own weight. When working on the Ricola Storage Building, we tried to give every element of the building its independence. The building itself is conceived and put together like a storage facility for architectural elements.

JR – You're referring not just to the fact that the building's program was the storage of goods but also to the construction of the facade, in which a shelving system is used to support the individual panels that make up the exterior wall of the building.

JH – We started from scratch, literally, like architectural analphabets who didn't know what a wall or a floor or a window was. We wanted to give materials more weight, to emphasize their specific and individual character. Look at the grayish-black basalt stones that are piled up in steel gabions to form the facade of the Dominus Winery [1998]. Depending on where you look or how close you stand, the wall seems either hermetic, like concrete, or transparent, like lace. The gap between the stones is as relevant as the stones themselves. When the sun shines, the gaps become lively actors, suggestive of thousands of photographic apertures.

JR – What about the projects in which you were dealing with images in addition to materials? In the Ricola Production and Storage Building you built in France near Mulhouse in 1993, a photograph of a plant was screen printed onto the facade's polycarbonate panels.

JH – That was related to our rejection of the way minimalism had been reduced to a style. Paradoxically, minimalism led us to

Herzog & de Meuron, Eberswalde Technical School Library,
Eberswalde, Germany, 1999

ornament, which seems to be its opposite. Since the time of Adolf
Loos, architects have rejected ornament as superfluous. We tried
to reveal its potential for contemporary architecture. In fact, we
discovered that ornament in past cultures was not just decorative,
but also an integrative element, one that could be used to produce
an understanding of architecture itself. We started to push ornament
as a method to test our own projects. Even if just applied on the
surface—like in early projects such as the Eberswalde Technical
School Library [1999] or the Ricola Production and Storage
Building—the prints and motifs would challenge the structural
and spatial concepts of those projects.

JR – It's an ingenious, if counterintuitive, move to apply the
serial, nonhierarchical strategies of minimalism to images on a
building's surface: you invented a minimalist approach to ornament.
This also suggests that translating ideas from art to architecture can
transform them in surprising ways. I wonder if direct collaborations
between artists and architects are equally productive, or if they

encourage more normative approaches. I'm thinking of the Laban Dance Centre in London, which you completed in 2003, for example, where you worked with Michael Craig-Martin on the facade's colors. On the one hand, this is admirably pragmatic. Architects are notoriously troubled by color, and Craig-Martin is a brilliant colorist. But is this simply offering the artist the building as canvas, and so reinforcing old disciplinary divisions between art and architecture, surface and space?

JH – We have tried out so many different forms of collaborations with artists. Why? Because the result should be interesting, new, and unexpected for both sides. The Laban is a spatially complex building with an ephemeral, translucent skin around it. We worked with Michael on the materiality and the colors both inside and outside that building. The color clouds that sometimes appear on the outside reflect the lively atmosphere inside. We could have done that ourselves, but it would have been worse! The use of color is not the business of an architect, even if quite a few have pretended to be experts in it. The exchange with Michael led to more provocative, more authentic, and more complex solutions. The result is the work of three indistinguishable authors.

At various times, we have also done these types of collaborations with Thomas Ruff, Andreas Gursky, Helmut Federle, Adrian Schiess, and a few others. The most radical collaborations were with Rémy Zaugg, with whom we collaborated from the 1980s until his early death in 2005, and Ai Weiwei, with whom we have been working since 2002. Rémy was more than just an artist friend. We traveled around Europe, talking and smoking and eating and drinking and designing many architectural projects and art projects in public spaces. It was always a very intense process. When we did the master plan for University of Burgundy [1990], we got together around a table at the very beginning of the project—in a very innocent way, almost as if we were children—and the work progressed through incredibly open-ended discussions. Our collaborations with Weiwei have a similar character and intensity to those we had with Rémy. We met him when he was still relatively unknown and when we all had more free time as well. We took trips together across China, and we began an ongoing conversation. Weiwei is critical of China but, at the same time, profoundly loves his country and knows an incredible amount about its history and cultural heritage. We've done and continue to do many projects together, large and small, some that materialized and some that didn't, but always intense and fun at the same time.

JR – This takes us back to your initial understanding of architecture as an inherently interdisciplinary field. It's true that, in a sense, architects are the last generalists and that an architect ideally should be able to interface with any number of specialists, whether an artist or a contractor or an engineer. But, at the same time, the production of buildings is now more technically complex than ever, and architects have an enormous amount of specialized expertise. Presumably, then, the collaboration can't continue indefinitely as a conversation among equals.

JH – We cannot do art and the artist cannot do architecture? That is a prejudice, and it is wrong. We have always tried to blur the boundaries between our roles to produce new ideas. Take, for example, the project we did with Weiwei at the Park Avenue Armory [*Hansel & Gretel*, 2017]. This was an art installation, a hybrid between a public sculpture and an opera. We were all involved, the three of us—Weiwei, Pierre, and I—and our teams, of course. It would be absurd to separate the contribution each one of us made to the final product. The truth is that nobody could have done it alone. It would have been different and less of a shared experience. I think it is also more complex than a work by one single person. The same is true for the Bird's Nest [National Stadium, Beijing, 2008]. Without Weiwei, that stadium would be different, and maybe it would not even exist. But, yes, you are also right when you say that the amount of specialized expertise has grown tremendously in the field of architecture. When Pierre and I work on a project, we cannot do it alone. We need the support of so many others inside and outside of our own company. *Collaboration* is the word for that.

Herzog & de Meuron, National Stadium, Beijing, China, 2008

We have practiced this way for many years. The art of collaboration is to find a denominator that is not a compromise—but the most powerful and daring concentrate.

JR – Besides technical expertise, politics is another potential point of difference between art and architecture. You described your initial turn to art as a way of escaping architectural ideologies. But, at the same time, much of the art you were looking at was profoundly ideological. The work of Beuys especially was driven by his political convictions, by a sense that he was operating outside of existing establishments and hierarchies. As an architect, is it possible to translate this critical position into your own practice, particularly as you become more successful and work for increasingly powerful clients?

JH – Architecture is like a quarry in which many strata of political and psychological conflicts have been deposited over centuries. But architects are rarely aware of that depth when working on a given project. Most are relatively apolitical and focus on the formal issues of their discipline. This has to do with the fact that they spend someone else's money: the client's. In that sense, an architect is a trustee for his client. This relationship is based on trust and respect. If you have a moral or political problem when working on a specific project—say, one in a nondemocratic country or one that forces you to design according to unacceptable guidelines— you should not accept the job or you should give it back. That is probably the most honest and credible critical position that you can have as an architect.

JR – Questions about power and criticality play out in very real terms in the architecture of art institutions, where artists and architects often seem to have competing desires. How do you create the kind of architecture you want while still granting artists the freedom to produce different kinds of work within the space, and visitors the flexibility to have different viewing experiences?

JH – We have never had a problem giving a building the specific quality that we want while also leaving enough flexibility and freedom for others to use it and play with it as they wish. It is a cliché to believe that a strong architectural position excludes or limits the freedom of artists in a museum. Frank Lloyd Wright's Solomon R. Guggenheim Museum was a nasty place for the artists of his time, but today it works very well, since artists have widened and expanded their repertoire. Ideally, a museum can offer a spatial topography of real difference: it should offer spaces that challenge contemporary artists to create new and unexpected work. At the same time, it should have galleries that work as a background for classical hanging.

JR – Difference is also important in the program of a museum, in terms of providing multiple kinds of space. But I wonder if there is a way in which difference itself becomes generic. Especially in museums for contemporary art, there's a checklist: "We need a big gallery for installations, and a small gallery for works on paper, and an auditorium for dance, and a black box for performance," and so on. How do you inject specificity into your design when there's such a standardized menu for museums?

JH – There is not just one ideal condition for a particular piece. It is interesting to install and experience the same work of art under different circumstances: you can hang a painting on a rough concrete wall, or a stone wall, or on wallpaper, under daylight or artificial light. You can put it in a large gallery or even in a stairwell. It's important to understand the hanging of art within the context of a whole building—how the proportions, materials, and surfaces of the galleries change as people move through space. Hanging is a very complex job, and I always admire those who can do it well—curators, but also artists. I was especially impressed by Rémy's installation of Alberto Giacometti sculptures—tiny little figures—in the Musée d'Art Moderne in Paris in 1991. The installation was an artwork in itself without being overwhelming or pretentious.

JR – How do you go about finding the right fit between a work and a space?

JH – It's not an answer that I can give abstractly. Give me two or three objects: a sculpture, a painting, and a drawing or a photograph; we could walk through a building—it doesn't even need to be a museum, nor do they even need to be art objects—and find ideal locations within a given space for each. It is an interesting experiment. We all do that all the time, often unconsciously, when we put a glass on the table, move a chair from one side of a room to the other, rearrange a curtain, et cetera.

JR – And you approach museum design in a similar way, with the collection in mind and in conversation with the curators?

JH – Yes, we try to be simple, forgetting what we believe is right or wrong. Of course we know how a white cube works, how a rough industrial space can be useful, how playful views of the landscape can be, and how visitors should be encouraged to enter the museum and stay for a while even if they are not immediately attracted by contemporary art. But every place is different, every collection is different; curators change and have new ideas.

JR – But what about institutions that don't have an established collection?

JH – The Pérez Art Museum Miami did not have an established collection when we started the project. But it had a plan—a curatorial plan that informed an architectural plan and vice versa. Based on intense conversations with the director, Terence Riley, and subsequently with other curators, we developed a concept based on anchor rooms, almost like centers of gravity, around which a narrative could be laid out using text, drawings, prints, photography, and all kinds of other materials. This concept—still active today—can be more easily completed with loans and newly purchased works than a conventional layout of rooms can. In other words, that institution's difficult beginnings at its new site led to a very specific architectural and curatorial solution that no other museum has. The concept is

Herzog & de Meuron, Pérez Art Museum Miami, Florida, 2013

also attractive because the anchor rooms offer opportunities to invite artists to create work in situ. We believe that the building, with its verdant topography inside and out, is equally inviting to visitors who spend time in these spaces and to artists who transform them.

JR – Art and architecture are increasingly evolving in tandem. **Your design for Tate Modern has been a primary site of this shift. Was it your intention, when creating spaces like the Turbine Hall or, more recently, the Tanks, to invite artists to explore new forms of production?**

JH – We are happy that these spaces have been so successful, because no architect can really predict if a space will work when finished. Getting back to your earlier question, it's not simply a matter of designing a large or raw or informal or flexible space. You can have all these things that sound interesting, and the museum can still be lousy. Nick Serota was a great director—he invented the program and collaborated almost as an architect with our team.

Artists were very happy to be involved, and later they brought life into that space in such varied and almost contradictory ways—like Doris Salcedo's piece [*Shibboleth I*, 2007] for the Turbine Hall, the crack in the floor, which I loved, or the Rachel Whiteread piece [*Embankment*, 2005–2006], which almost filled the space entirely. Bruce Nauman, Olafur Eliasson…each intervention was totally different from the rest. That is what makes the Turbine Hall a space that people want to go back to, and what makes artists willing contributors to its history.

JR – Is there is a darker side to the popularity of spaces like the Turbine Hall, though? Tate Modern has completely transformed London's South Bank. Cultural projects in general, and museums in particular, seem to be playing an ever-larger role in urban development, to the point that they have been almost entirely co-opted by developers. Your office is obviously involved in this: you recently proposed your first major project in Los Angeles, which was in the so-called arts district and included both art galleries and luxury housing. And here in New York, your studio has just transformed the Batcave, an old warehouse in Gowanus that was a famous artists' squat, into a high-end fabrication facility called Powerhouse Arts. The latter project has been bemoaned as the latest stage in the gentrification of Brooklyn. How do you retain a genuine or organic sense of culture and produce viable public space in the face of the forces driving this kind of development? This question seems particularly difficult today, because I don't think art practices still offer an alternative model. We began this conversation talking about art offering an appealing sense of freedom, a way of thinking outside of the systems in which architecture is entangled. But now art is, if anything, even more tied up with the market. I'm not sure architects can still look to art as a critical or conceptual model.

JH – A work of art can still be inspiring for anybody willing to look at it and spend time with it. But, yes, art has become more of a business model than a critical one. In a sense, the situation in art and architecture mirrors the rest of our society. Just as the middle

Herzog & de Meuron, Tate Modern and Tate Modern expansion, London, UK, 2000 and 2016

Doris Salcedo, *Shibboleth I*, 2007, installed in
Turbine Hall, Tate Modern, London, UK

class of citizens is shrinking, what you could call the middle class of artists and of galleries is shrinking and will eventually disappear. A few wealthy galleries control the market in America, Europe, and Asia. In architecture, developers control the real estate market; they are increasingly building our cities, and their logic strictly follows the profitability of the market. As an architect you can hate that. But you can also rethink your role as someone who not only designs but also influences a project on a programmatic level. More and more developers understand that iconic architecture is not enough—buildings need to be rooted in a city. They need to attract different social groups and offer different programs. Not every tower will have a public space like the Turbine Hall, but commercial buildings will need to have some kind of free and informal space. The alternative is empty, spooky towers, like those glass vitrines surrounding Tate Modern.

JR – It's impossible to imagine the Turbine Hall empty. In a sense, the stakes are higher for these so-called participatory spaces than for any other kind of museum architecture, because if you don't have public engagement, the space can't survive. Maybe in this brave new world the most important thing architects can do is refuse to design past a certain point, to avoid overdetermining their spaces and to allow for the unexpected, for adaptation and interpretation.

JH – Architecture is very archaic; you can see it, smell it, touch it, hear it—like nature. It has a sensual side, and it also encourages you to think. We see art, but also architecture, as tools of perception and reflection. Both disciplines can trigger a kind of creative, perhaps even erotic, energy in the viewer or user. That is an incredibly powerful energy, beyond any moralistic attitude or stylistic preference. I doubt that this will ever change, not even in a moment of transition toward greater commercialism.

STEVEN

HOLL

JULIAN ROSE – You arrived in New York in 1977 and immediately immersed yourself in the art scene. But the artists you connected with weren't necessarily the ones I would expect. At the time there were any number of artists who were engaging architecture directly, making large-scale installations or inhabitable structures—Mary Miss and Richard Serra come to mind—but you were drawn to people like Vito Acconci and Dennis Oppenheim, who are more associated with conceptual and performance art. What appealed to you about their work?

STEVEN HOLL – It was simple. I was interested in the ideas. In conceptual art, you have an idea that's driving the work. I felt like that kind of clarity was missing from architecture at the time.

JR – I'm also curious about how you discovered their work, given that they weren't exactly household names at the time. You had studied at the Architectural Association in London before coming to New York. The school was known for its radical pedagogy—did that include discussion of new developments in the visual arts?

SH – Not officially as part of the curriculum, but I met like-minded peers who were also looking to art for new ideas. Zaha Hadid was one of them. We became very close while I was in London, and when I moved back to San Francisco in the fall of 1976—I had been there working after I graduated with my bachelor of architecture from the University of Washington in 1971—she came and visited me so she could see Christo and Jeanne-Claude's *Running Fence*. We drove the length of the whole thing in my '59 Volkswagen. What an unbelievable project. It was up for only two weeks—it completely transformed the landscape and then disappeared.

JR – And it was certainly a very powerful exploration of space, if not quite architecture as such.

SH – That's true of a lot of the work I was interested in. It's exploring spatial experience, just not from the traditional perspective of an architect. Think about Vito's *Following Piece* [1969], where his meanderings through urban space are dictated by these chance encounters with strangers. That's a work about New York City.

JR – But, again, how did you know about a work like *Following Piece*?

SH – I was obsessed with art from the time I was an undergrad. I used to read everything I could get my hands on while I was living in San Francisco, and at some point I picked up Lucy Lippard's brilliant book, *Six Years: The Dematerialization of the Art Object from 1966 to 1972* [1973]. I still have my dog-eared copy; I read it over and over. It was the incredible story she told about the rise of conceptual art that made me want to move to New York. I knew I had to experience that atmosphere, that cultural density. I arrived on New Year's Eve in 1976. My brother Jim was finishing his master of fine arts at Columbia, and he arranged to meet me at the base of the Chrysler Building. He took me straight to a loft party with a bunch of artists, and that was it. I never left.

JR – I can certainly see the appeal of the incredible energy of New York's art scene at that time, but I have to admit I'm surprised that you were taken by Lippard's book in particular, because it was so polemical. The notion of "dematerialization" wasn't threatening to you? It could be seen as an attack not only on traditional art forms but also on architecture itself. After all, architects, even more than painters or sculptors, produce objects—that is, buildings.

SH – It was an attack on architecture! I never met Gordon Matta-Clark; he died the year after I moved to New York. But I got to know other members of the Anarchitecture group—like Jene Highstein, Laurie Anderson, and Richard Nonas—and they made that dimension of conceptual art explicit. And it makes sense, right? In some ways, architecture is the archetypal object. It's the status quo.

JR – It sounds like you were sympathetic to that attack.

SH – Absolutely. The time was right for it. Modernism was running out of gas. It had become what you might call a "late" style—there were still people trying to use the modernist language, but it was getting overcomplicated and pompous, almost baroque. On the other hand, I didn't like postmodernism at all—it seemed kitschy, reactionary, and commercial. But it felt like these were the only two options. During my first year in New York, there were two books everyone was talking about: *Five Architects* and *Learning from Las Vegas* [both 1972]. The first one was by Peter Eisenman, Michael Graves, Charles Gwathmey, John Hejduk, and Richard Meier. They were the late modernists. The second one was by Robert Venturi, Denise Scott Brown, and Steven Izenour. They were the postmodernists. We needed a fresh approach, and that was part of why I was looking at art.

JR – It seems like you were also looking back at the history of modern architecture itself. You started your own publication series, *Pamphlet Architecture*, in 1978, and I'm struck by the way in which you seem to have almost tried to skip a generation, presenting *Pamphlet Architecture* as a direct continuation of the early twentieth-century avant-garde. You cited Bruno Taut's legendary "crystal chain letters," an interdisciplinary utopian correspondence he initiated in 1919, as one of your inspirations, and one of the early editions of *Pamphlet Architecture* was authored by Alberto Sartoris, an influential Italian modernist who had been one of the founding members, with Le Corbusier and a host of other pioneering figures, of the Congrès Internationaux d'Architecture Moderne in 1928. You weren't so much arguing against late modernism or postmodernism—you were ignoring them and going straight back to the source.

SH – That was also something I had learned from conceptual art. I mean, that whole movement was based on Duchampian foundations. And I became very interested in how the art of the sixties and seventies was connected to Marcel Duchamp's legacy. The very first time I visited New York was in 1974. I was here to look at graduate schools, and there happened to be a Duchamp retrospective at the Museum of Modern Art. I'll never forget that show—I became obsessed with everything he thought and did to the extent that I made a pilgrimage to Philadelphia to see the secret room, *Étant donnés* [1946–1966]. I even started to read everything by Raymond Roussel, the French writer who influenced a lot of Duchamp's thinking. In fact, the first year I was in New York, I went to a Halloween party dressed up as a machine from Roussel's 1914 novel *Locus Solus*.

JR – You definitely were obsessed! I take your point, though, that, at the time, art seemed to have more historical continuity than architecture. After all, one of the terms initially applied to early performance art was "neo-Dadaist." So I can see that in art maybe there was a sense of ongoing experimentation, a way in which early twentieth-century ideas were being revisited and extended, in contrast to the reactionary tone of architectural postmodernism, which was more of an explicit rejection of early twentieth-century architecture. But how on earth did you convince Sartoris to get involved in *Pamphlet Architecture*?

SH – For the first few years, we were just flying by the seat of our pants: Who's going to do the next one? What should it be about? And at some point I was in Italy having lunch with Mario Botta and Paola Iacucci. We were talking about postmodernism. I think it must have been 1979, because Philip Johnson had just been on the cover of *Time* with a model of his design for the AT&T tower in New York—the one with the pediment borrowed from a Chippendale cabinet. It was this disgustingly postmodern moment, and we were talking about modern architects we admired. Sartoris came up, and Mario said, "You know, he's still alive. Let's go see him after lunch." So we did. He was in a kind of home, an assisted living place, but he was totally sharp. We spent the whole afternoon with him, and I explained what I was trying to do with *Pamphlet* and asked if he would do one. It came out as the tenth issue, *Metafisica Della Architettura*, which we published in 1984.

JR – His argument there was that modernism isn't so much a style as a mode of practice, one rooted in a long philosophical tradition. So it's not historically bounded; it doesn't make sense to proclaim its end or start adding prefixes like *post*.

SH – Sartoris felt that modernism still had something to give. And, you know, it was around this time that the philosopher Jürgen Habermas was writing about modernity as an "incomplete project." I still feel that way.

JR – But one thing that *had* ended by the eighties was the social democratic dream that modern architecture could bring about large-scale social change. Sartoris was part of that—he had worked on influential designs for low-cost housing in the twenties. But those housing schemes were never built, and the kind of state sponsorship those dreams would have required never materialized. You mentioned your frustration with the commercialism of post-modern architecture, but didn't you feel some commercial pressure as a young architect who had just opened your own office in New York, given that there wasn't much public architecture being built at the time?

SH – Not at all, because it was so cheap to live in the city then. It was a great time for creativity in New York. I had a loft for ten years, big enough for me to live and work in, and the rent never changed: $250 a month. That's like getting a decade-long fellowship. I was teaching a couple of days a week, and I could spend the rest of my time doing conceptual work. I wasn't in a hurry to start building. I was eager to find a theoretical framework for my practice.

JR – One of the frameworks you found was phenomenology, which you've written quite a bit about over the years. Most of the architects and architectural theorists who have been interested in that branch of philosophy—beginning with Christian Norberg-Schulz, who was one of the first architects to write about phenomenology, in the early 1970s—have engaged primarily with the ideas of Martin Heidegger. On the other hand, Maurice Merleau-Ponty was much more important for many of the artists who were exploring phenomenology around the same time, including people like Richard Serra, Robert Morris, and Bruce Nauman. You also cite Merleau-Ponty as the more important influence, and I've always been curious—is that a connection that came from your exchanges with artists?

SH – No, because I discovered phenomenology later, in 1984. But you could say my concerns were similar to theirs. I was after the experiential.

JR – So Merleau-Ponty's focus on perception and embodied experience spoke to you, as opposed to Heidegger's emphasis on being and essence. I think Heidegger can be a bad influence on architects, in a way, because his ideas become an excuse for what ends up being just a kind of symbolism or even mysticism: this or that material is supposed to capture the spirit of a place, and so on. But you don't seem to have succumbed to that.

SH – When you read Merleau-Ponty, unlike Edmund Husserl or Heidegger or anybody else, you feel like you're gaining an understanding of space, light, and architecture. In your mind you can actually find an architectural equivalent to what he's talking about. But, you know, I don't need the word *phenomenology* to explain my work. I like what Ludwig Wittgenstein said: "There is no such thing as phenomenology, but there are indeed phenomenological problems."

JR – What does that mean for you?

SH – Well, I'm interested in the actual problem of how our bodies interact with the world and how architecture shapes that interaction. That's a real, practical problem; it's best addressed through design, not through abstract theoretical concepts. And phenomenology is sort of a two-dollar word, so if you use it and some people don't know what it is, you might lose them.

JR – It's refreshing to hear that. Theory can become a crutch for architecture—and for art, too, for that matter—to the point that a given work is supposed to be meaningful because it's associated with a given philosophy or, worse, that you can't understand the work without understanding the philosophy first.

SH – Exactly. And let me say that architecture—unlike philosophy, or linguistic theory, or even art—has the potential to connect to everyone. That doesn't mean it can't have depth, too. Reading philosophy might be really generative for me, or someone like you might be interested in that aspect of my work, but I want my architecture to be able to speak for itself.

JR – Can you give a specific example of a project that was shaped by your engagement with phenomenology?

SH – Sure—the Kiasma museum, a building that completely changed my life. In 1992 I entered the competition for a museum of contemporary art in Helsinki. My design was based on the concept of the chiasm, "the intertwining," from Merleau-Ponty's last book, *The Visible and the Invisible*. So I called it the Chiasma Museum. When I won, they named the whole museum after my competition entry, but in Finnish they don't have the *ch* so they changed it to a *k*.

JR – But what was the specific relationship between the concept and the architecture? I know the museum's form comprises two interconnected volumes, but, to play devil's advocate, I could say that the chiasma is just a nice metaphor that helps you justify the shape you chose for the building.

SH – No, this is a really important distinction for me. A concept is not just a metaphor that justifies a formal strategy. A concept is experiential, and it drives the approach to the site and the internal logic of the building. The Kiasma museum is on a very important plot of land between the historic city center and newer development in Töölö, which includes Alvar Aalto's Finlandia Hall, so I was thinking about a kind of urban intertwining. But it's also about how you move through the building. One of the volumes is rectangular, and the other one curves in both plan and section. You enter an atrium formed by the space between them, and then the primary circulation system is a series of ramps, which curve up and out of sight. You *feel* the curves as the ramps draw you through the building, and the curves also create an incredible variety of spaces. There are twenty-five individual galleries, and each one is different in its shape, size, and quality of light.

JR – I'm interested in that diversity, given that Kiasma is a museum specifically for contemporary art. That's an almost impossibly varied category—"contemporary art" could mean a painting, or a video work, or a performance piece. Were you trying to create a variety of spaces for a variety of art?

SH – I spent a lot of time talking to artists while I was designing the museum. After I won the competition, James Turrell came to my studio, and we had long talks about light. The light in Helsinki is very northern—it's cool, and it's almost horizontal. So the curved walls and ceilings were about intensifying the light, bouncing it around. And then Vito was a friend. We were working on Storefront for Art and Architecture at that time, so he was spending a lot of time in the studio.

JR – I want to come back to that project, because I want to talk about your many collaborations with artists, but what did he say about museum design?

SH – He said, "Make the gallery as strange as you can, because my art needs something to react to." But then I invited Richard Nonas, whom I had admired since his Anarchitecture days, and he said, "Steven, my art exists between the floor and the wall. The wall has to be white, and it has to be perpendicular to the floor."

JR – How did you synthesize that contradictory feedback?

SH – Well, in the end, you have to go with your gut and the project has to have its own logic. That's where the spatial concept

Steven Holl Architects, Museum of Contemporary Art Kiasma,
Helsinki, Finland, 1998

of the chiasm comes in. It produces a range of galleries, so the building is sensitive to art without trying to serve one artist's vision.

JR – You weren't tempted to make flexible gallery spaces?

SH – Oh, no, not at all! That was part of the whole idea behind the project. I said: Look, before the twentieth century, the museum was a series of repetitive rooms. In the twentieth century, the museum became a large, flexible space with temporary walls. In the twenty-first century, the museum should evolve to have unique rooms that match the unique quality of artworks. And that was one of the reasons my proposal won, out of more than five hundred entries. The curators were bored to death with flexibility and movable walls. I used to call those flexible galleries "dumpster space" because you would go by the museum after a show closed and there would be huge dumpsters full of Sheetrock and metal studs. I would know, because I designed a few of them. I did the exhibition design for *In a Classical Vein*, a show of the permanent collection at the Whitney Museum in 1993. Marcel Breuer's museum is incredible— I love that building—but the show was up on the fourth floor and it's a big open space that you have to subdivide if you want to show art in it. So I was familiar with this problem.

JR – Of course, another version of the twenty-first-century museum is the architectural icon—Kiasma opened in 1998, about six months after Frank Gehry's Guggenheim Bilbao. But, like the large flexible space, the museum as a sculptural object is something you've avoided. Your addition to the Nelson-Atkins Museum of Art in Kansas City, the Bloch Building completed in 2007, could almost be read as an anti-icon, even an anti-object. You literally buried most of your building in the landscape. Was there a polemical aspect to your design?

SH – I never had the question of iconic or not in my mind. Again, you have to understand that my position is that the idea drives the design. That's what's important—whether someone sees the building that comes out of the idea and calls it iconic isn't

Steven Holl Architects, Bloch Building, Nelson-Atkins Museum of Art,
Kansas City, Missouri, 2007

important to me. And the idea there was to create an experience
that merged the building with the landscape.

JR – Where did your concept come from in this case?

SH – The rules of that competition were to add a new structure
to the north end of the existing museum, which is a neoclassical
stone building from 1933. There was going to be a new underground
parking garage there, and the logical thing would be to build the
new museum on top of it, right? All the other architects followed
that brief, but I decided to break the rules. The original building
wasn't the Parthenon, but it was well done. It was completely
symmetrical, and it had great detailing on all its facades—porticoes
with these grand columns. Why would you touch that? I didn't want
my building to smack up against one of those facades, so I came up
with the idea of complementary contrast. I would build downward
into the landscape in the park on the south side of the site, and my
design would feel weightless. The existing structure had very rigid
circulation—the plan is a series of enfilades, that's always the Beaux-
Arts solution to the museum—and I would create meandering
paths. Everything would be the opposite of the old building. I called
it the stone and the feather.

JR – I want to talk more about circulation because that's a crux of museum design. Architects often feel like the museum poses a problem of moving versus looking and they have to make a difficult choice about whether to combine the exhibition spaces with the circulation spaces or to separate them. The combination is generally more effective for handling crowds because it allows visitors to flow freely throughout the building, but it can also start to compromise visitors' experience of the art, because they're swept right by it. On the other hand, isolating the galleries and connecting them with a separate circulation system—say, a network of corridors or stairs— can create spaces for quiet contemplation but also all kinds of dead ends and pinch points that interfere with visitors' ability to navigate the museum.

SH – For me, museum circulation should be about choice. You should always have different options. So in the Nelson-Atkins, we connected the galleries directly, but we also created bypass points where you skip between them. And we studied the spaces very carefully to make sure that there were no dead-end galleries. You can always exit a different way than you entered. It has all these possible routes, and that's great, because a visitor can spend a whole day there and see every single thing, or they can just pop in and go to one or two of their favorite galleries. The curators like it, too, because they can close one gallery for installation without disrupting the whole sequence.

JR – It sounds simple when you describe it that way, but in three dimensions it's extraordinarily complex, given that you're connecting a long series of galleries on two levels and that the whole building is sloping downward to the south, in line with the topography of the site. It's almost impossible to understand how the space works from looking at the plans.

SH – That's because I didn't design it in plan! For a building like this, you have to work in perspective. It's not one building; it's a series of spatial experiences. It's all about how you're moving through space and how the elevation changes. It looks like a scramble in plan, but that's because the plan is just one flat cut through the space—it can't tell you about that three-dimensional trajectory. You've got to be there.

JR – As with Kiasma, light is a key component of your design for the Nelson-Atkins, and I'm particularly impressed with the granularity of your attention to the quality of the light in this building. When architects say things like "Light is one of the materials I work with," it's usually just a figure of speech. But you really did engage with the material qualities of light, right down to the color temperature. You designed a T-shaped vault that allows you to draw both north and south light into the galleries. You play with their differences—north light tends to be cooler and softer, south light is warmer and harsher—and blend them in different combinations.

SH – We called them the "fluttering T's" because we could vary the heights and the curves to get the effects we were looking for. And, by the way, you can't simulate this in a computer. The behavior of light is just too complex. So we built large models and looked at everything from the geometry of the vaults to the color of the walls to the precise orientation of the clerestories.

JR – The results are extraordinary. But I'm curious—did the museum staff resist it? In theory, everyone wants natural light in a museum, but then again curators and conservators will tell you that direct sunlight is the enemy of many artworks. By the time daylight gets into most museums it's been so thoroughly modulated and diffused that it's almost not fair to call it natural light anymore.

SH – We have blackout screens in all the galleries. They can be intermediate or pure blackout. So the curators can control the light as much as they want. But it's a lot easier to black out an existing window than to add a new one! I look at it like this: I designed an instrument for them to play. Like if you're playing the trumpet, you can have your mute if you want it.

Steven Holl Architects, Bloch Building, Nelson-Atkins Museum
of Art, Kansas City, Missouri, 2007

JR – What about the curved walls, which form the junctions of the *T*'s? Were those controversial?

SH – No, because we were very rigorous about it. We set a datum at twelve feet off the floor, and we said: Below this line the walls will be perfectly vertical; above this line, the geometry can be as expressive as we want.

JR – So you found a way to make both Acconci and Nonas happy with the same gallery.

SH – Absolutely. But it's also for the visitors. They can see paintings hanging on a vertical wall, and it's clean and simple and not distracting, but they also don't have to trudge through twenty identical white boxes in a row. And that's very important. You have to keep the spaces varied to keep people from getting fatigued.

JR – One of the fundamental challenges of the Nelson-Atkins was integrating your new building into the site of an existing institution, and you faced a much more extreme version of that in your most recent museum project, which is an expansion of the Museum of Fine Arts, Houston. It's an enormous complex—with your addition, it's now the second-largest art museum in the country, behind only the Metropolitan Museum of Art, and one of the largest in the world—and there was a whole collection of existing buildings to deal with. You had another neoclassical stone building, this one from the 1920s, but it already had a modernist addition by Mies van der Rohe (incidentally, his only museum building in America); plus, there was a more recent building by Rafael Moneo, completed in 2000, and a large sculpture garden by Isamu Noguchi. In a sense, you were even responding to yourself, because you had designed the new building for the Glassell School of Art, which is part of the MFAH and shares the site. How did you begin thinking about integrating a new building into this mix?

SH – In a sense, it was similar to the Nelson-Atkins project; I began by breaking the rules. In the original competition, which was held in 2011, the brief didn't say anything about the school.

We were just asked to build a new gallery building plus a seven-story parking garage, which would go behind the existing school. I told them instead of building that huge garage, they should build a new school and put the parking below that. They could double the size of the school and still end up with more open space on the campus. It was a big change, and it would mean more fundraising and a longer construction time, but in the end the board unanimously approved it. Of course, I also told them that if they built my design their sculpture garden would be larger than the one at the Dallas Museum of Art.

JR – There's nothing like a good civic rivalry to boost spending on culture! It's funny, though, I wouldn't have associated you with a program-based design approach, but this is the second museum project that you started with a radical rethinking of the brief. Would you argue that program is an important basis for museum design, albeit perhaps more at the urban scale, in terms of things like landscape and parking, than at the architectural scale, in terms of the organization of spaces within the building?

SH – It comes back to having a strong spatial concept. I wasn't really thinking about program, per se, but the concept—both for connecting the campus to the city and the building to the campus—was porosity. The building is notched in plan to create spaces for gardens that start to interpenetrate the building volume. And because we buried the parking, there's a huge amount of new green space. When you're standing in the lobby of the new building you can see gardens in four directions.

JR – There are also quite a few site-specific commissions from artists distributed throughout the building and around the site. Was working with these artists another thing that helped you bring a sense of unity to the museum campus?

SH – Absolutely. Especially because there are multiple paths into the building, and the artworks helped us draw visitors in and give an individual character to each entry. Cristina Iglesias has an

outdoor work, a kind of sculptural pool, near the main ground-level entrance, and Olafur Eliasson and Carlos Cruz-Diez designed light installations for the tunnels that link our building to the Glassell School and the other gallery buildings underground.

JR – It's not unusual for you to work with artists like this. In fact, you've made a consistent effort to incorporate artworks into your buildings that extend well beyond museums—I'm thinking of the Richard Artschwager piece in your Visual Arts Building at the University of Iowa and the Dan Graham pavilion installed on one of the terraces of your Simmons Hall dormitory at MIT. I'd like to talk more about your experiences working with artists, beginning with that early collaboration you mentioned with Acconci on the Storefront for Art and Architecture in New York, which you designed together in 1993. How did that project get started?

SH – Storefront needed to renovate the facade on its space on Kenmare Street, and somebody came up with the idea that it should be a collaboration between an artist and an architect. Vito and I were going to do the first one, but it was only supposed to be temporary. The facade was going to become the site for a series of collaborations, changing every two years. But Storefront didn't have enough money to continue the series, so ours ended up being permanent. They got a grant to pay for ours. It didn't cost very much, about forty thousand dollars, and Vito and I both worked on it for free, but Storefront was a small nonprofit and it couldn't do that every two years.

JR – What were the actual mechanics of the collaboration? Were you sending drawings back and forth? Building models together?

SH – Vito and I were both working with ideas. But he was trained as a poet, remember. So he would start with language. He would say something like, "OK, what if the wall turned inside out?" And I was working: drawing, making models, creating architectural versions of what Vito was saying. So we had this kind of conceptual back and forth. I thought his ideas were so strong. But, you know, it was very difficult. We worked on the damn thing for six months. I remember at one point Vito told me, "Working on this is like I'm coming in one side of a revolving door and you're going out the other side. Every time we pass, I try to make mine a little more like yours and you try to make yours a little more like mine, but we can never meet."

Steven Holl (left) and Vito Acconci (right) working on a model of the facade
for the Storefront for Art and Architecture, New York, New York, 1993

JR – A beautiful metaphor—just what you'd expect from a poet. And it's appropriately architectural and phenomenological, too. But if that's what the process was like, how did you ever get the project done?

SH – In the end, we simply ran out of time. It was going to open in a few weeks, and we just had to build something. We never even got a building permit. We did the work at night. I remember someone on the Storefront staff asked me, "What are you going to do if the building department comes?" And I said, "I'll tell them it's a piece of art! It's just temporary." The funny thing, too, is that we couldn't remove the existing facade until after ours was done, so we built ours on the outside, hanging over the sidewalk. So we never got a building permit, and it's a foot over the property line.

JR – Well, that uncertain status is appropriate, in a way, for a project that's not quite a building and not quite a sculpture. Are there any other collaborations with artists that have been particularly memorable for you?

SH – I'd have to say working with Walter De Maria at the Nelson-Atkins on his piece *One Sun/34 Moons*, which is integrated into the roof of our parking garage. As far as I know, it's his only realized collaboration with an architect, and it's a very meaningful project for me.

JR – Was it your idea to get him involved?

SH – Well, after we won the competition, Marc Wilson, the Nelson-Atkins director, told me he wanted a piece of art integrated into the design. And I said, OK, but if we're going to do this, let's really *integrate* it; we're not just going to put a big Henry Moore sculpture out front. And Marc got it; he was a courageous director and a great collaborator. So we talked about who would be right and came up with Walter. Walter came by the studio, and we decided to see if we could work together on something.

JR – How did the collaboration process unfold?

SH – He took my competition drawings, and he started rearranging things. He started to develop this idea of putting a platform in the reflecting pool that I had over the parking garage and moving the skylights around it. So the "sun" is this forty-by-thirty-three-foot bronze platform in the middle of the pool, and the thirty-four "moons" are the circular skylights that open into the garage below. And we talked endlessly about the light and how the platform would catch it and the water would reflect and refract it. In the end he decided to cover the platform with gold leaf, because it has a unique quality; it's amazing to see what it does with light. And when you enter from the parking garage you get to feel his piece before you even see it because of the quality of the light coming down into the structure. But what I remember more than anything is how slowly he worked and how committed he was to the process. He probably came here once a week for almost two years. And he must have changed the proportions of the piece—the edges of the pool, the dimensions of the platform—forty times. "What if we moved this one foot in that direction? What if we pulled back six inches over here?" He wouldn't even let me show the design to anyone for the whole first year. But I think Marc sensed that it was going to be an important work, and he didn't bother us about it.

JR – It's hard to imagine anyone waiting around for a year while an architect changes their mind forty times—artist and architects are often working under very different expectations. Do you think, then, that there's a freedom that working with an artist can bring to a project?

SH – At its best, yes. But, you know, I was complaining about the commercial side of architecture, and the art world has that side, too. We're in a very commodity-oriented time. Walter had so many invitations that he just turned down, either because he didn't believe in the project, or he didn't think he had time to do it well. He was the real thing—we need artists like that.

WALTER

HOOD

JULIAN ROSE – Even in the context of museum design practices, which tend to foster collaborations between architects and artists, yours stands out as fundamentally interdisciplinary. Not only do you have degrees in architecture and landscape architecture, but you also have a master of fine arts in studio art. You've designed both buildings and landscapes, and you've done everything from urban planning to public art.

But I want to start with your connection to music. Your first book, published in 1993, is called *Blues & Jazz Landscape Improvisations*. It strikes me as a fascinating break from a very long tradition of looking at landscape through the lens of painting. Going all the way back to the eighteenth century, there's the notion of the picturesque, which posits that a landscape can be composed like a painted image. Within modernism, too, this connection stayed strong; a seminal figure like Roberto Burle Marx was deeply influenced by the abstraction of people like Joan Miró and Fernand Léger—and, not coincidentally, he himself was first trained as a painter. When you turn to blues and jazz, you're referencing another cultural tradition, shifting from this formal approach toward a more temporal—even social—way of thinking about landscape.

WALTER HOOD – When I started teaching in landscape architecture at University of California, Berkeley, I knew that to get tenure I would have to have a research focus. At first, I thought I wanted to do cultural geography. This was in the early nineties, and I was looking at people like Richard Westmacott, who, in his book *African-American Gardens and Yards in the Rural South* [1992], was thinking about how landscapes are racialized places that are not only the manifestations of cultural histories but are also the creations of social and economic conditions. This was not just a different aesthetic but a different way of looking at landscape.

JR – But how did you shift from that analytical mode into practice?

WH – Through that work I found out I wasn't a cultural geographer—I was a designer. I remember I was halfway through the tenure process, I had gotten a National Endowment for the Arts grant to do fieldwork, and I just realized: This is not me. And around that time I ran across a quote from the anthropologist John Michael Vlach about the central importance of improvisation in the arts of the African diaspora, particularly during and after slavery. As he defined it, to improvise was "to reshape the old and the familiar into something contemporary and unique." And I just thought, Wow. That really resonated, because at that time I was taking a jazz appreciation class with the music historian Grover Sales, who had worked as a roadie for Miles Davis and had all these incredible stories about the West Coast jazz scene. There was a moment in the class where he was talking to us about improvisation, and he gave this one example where Charlie Parker went to LA and couldn't get his fix, so he sat in the studio with a half quart of vodka, and he played *Laura* over and over and over again. And every time he played the song, he played it differently. Grover told us this story, and then he played us five different takes of *Laura*, showing us how each time it was basically being reshaped into something new. I said to myself, "That's how I should be looking at landscapes."

JR – And that's when you started working on the book?

WH – That's when I realized that I had to begin with something very familiar. So the starting point for that book was a minipark in West Oakland that I knew well. It had been created by a Department of Housing and Urban Development initiative in the early seventies, and it was totally standard, completely generic— a small lawn, some trees, a few benches—and no one in the neighborhood was really using it. I basically decided to look at it through a series of individuals and then reshape the design by thinking about how each of them might inhabit the space.

JR – The book has a kind of iterative structure, and you present the reader with Park for a Dreamer, Park for a Musician, Park for a Single Mother, Park for an Anarchist, and so on.

WH – But they were all based on the exact same elements; each design just recombined them in a new way. And that was a very productive approach for me—it allowed me to bring culture into landscape while also, at the same time, critiquing the ways in which we usually make landscapes. That was really my connection to jazz. A lot of landscape architects might say something like, "My work is inspired by music. I listen to jazz while I design." That's not what I'm talking about at all. I was looking for more of a subtext to the music, a way it could actually show me how to work.

JR – So it's really a structural connection rather than an aesthetic one, and I can see how that would allow you to use an improvisational method across a range of different projects without limiting yourself to just one visual language. I'm wondering if improvisation has also informed your approach to history in landscape. Several of your early projects incorporate references to the history of the sites themselves—in Oakland's Lafayette Square Park [1999], for example, you created a domed grass hill that echoes the presence of a nineteenth-century observatory that once stood on the site. Is that also a case of making the familiar new? Someone might know how a neighborhood looks today, or even ten years ago, but you're helping them see connections to a longer and deeper history.

WH – To understand how I think about history, you have to understand that I was in landscape architecture school in the late eighties and early nineties, and postmodernism was huge. A lot of people were looking back at the history of landscape, but, just like in architecture, there was a fascination with all the traditional tropes of neoclassical design. What was disturbing to me about that was realizing that, in the US, it felt like there was no way to create a palimpsest other than by using this classical vocabulary. And not only does that mean turning your landscape into a colonial landscape, it's erasing a whole lot of history, too. So in Lafayette Square, I just thought, What if I could go back a hundred years without erasing anything? And then I just kept building up all the layers of history on the site as they happened. How would those forms manifest themselves, and what might those relationships be?

JR – It's worth emphasizing that in a lot of postmodern design, "history" remains pretty abstract. In the context of landscape this can become a kind of Jeffersonian fantasy of pastoral classicism. But in a project like Lafayette Square you're getting very specific about the material history of a particular place.

WH – Exactly. I did not want to begin layering history as pastiche, especially because in America that ends up being a kind of colonial regurgitation. The postmodern project was about going back to classical origins that literally did not include people who look like me. And that's where this historical specificity becomes incredibly important. Once I looked at the social and cultural history of Lafayette Square, I saw that in the late twenties and thirties, during the Depression, this was a place for out-of-work men. And they were diverse men. They were Portuguese, they were Black, and they shared a space. So in a way this place had always been for the marginalized, but that's not something a landscape architect is supposed to talk about, right? But by connecting to history, landscape can help us discover these lost narratives about ourselves.

JR – That's such a powerful role for landscape to play, but I wonder if it sometimes creates problems when you are working on a museum, because museums are often sites of decontextualization— or at least recontextualization—gathering objects from different time periods and from all over the world. Your first landscape design for a museum was for the de Young, which is sited in Golden Gate Park in San Francisco, and I know the brief included a large sculpture garden. Was there any tension between the need to create a new context for all those different works of art—or for that matter, for the building itself, which is quite sculptural—and your desire to engage the history of the site?

WH – Herzog & de Meuron started looking for a landscape architect after they won the competition to design the new museum building in 1999, and I think they were taken by the fact that I didn't have a large body of work. At the time I literally had just two built projects, Lafayette Square and another park. I think they liked that I didn't have a defined way of doing things, because their practice, as you know, is about the constant reinvention of typologies. And it was interesting timing for me because I had just gotten back from the American Academy in Rome, where a new approach to history was being fortified in my mind because I was hanging out with archaeologists. I mean, you go to Rome, and there are ruins under the streets—that's literally a palimpsest, right? And I was also talking to people and learning about the Roman presence in North Africa and the Arab presence in Portugal and Spain and thinking about all these networks and exchanges. So when I got back to the US, I knew I wanted to try to tell bigger stories.

JR – **How did that translate into this project?**

WH – When the architects brought us on board, they already had the basic parti for the building. It was a tripartite scheme, with the plan divided into three zones—the front being the most public, along the promenade, and the back being more private, opening onto the park. Their idea was that these three zones would be woven together by courtyards, so they really wanted the landscape to be integrated into the architecture. The problem was that it had to be a base-isolated structure for seismic reasons, so there essentially had to be a moat around the whole thing. But working closely with the engineers, we were able to make some of the landscape elements flow over that moat and give visitors the feeling that they could follow the landscape from the park right into the building.

JR – **It sounds like the landscape was a crucial part of the architectural concept.**

WH – It was, but I think in a way it was even more important for the client. It was very controversial to build a new structure in the

Hood Design Studio, de Young Museum, San Francisco, California, 2005

park—there were multiple lawsuits against the museum, and in a way our design became the client's response to that. Whenever they presented the project to the public, they always showed the landscape first. Because our design helped people understand that, yes, this is a world-famous park, but it's also a highly constructed, dynamic landscape, and it's always been changing. Golden Gate Park was actually carved out of a giant sand dune, and then throughout the park's history many of the plants were brought in from other places. The fern grove came from Australia; the palm trees came from different countries around the world. When you bring in these plant species, you have to bring in dirt; they need topsoil to live and thrive, so there's a whole material transformation that took place. It made no sense to talk about preserving the "original" landscape or using only native plants. Instead, we started thinking about the terrain itself as a kind of museum, where the plants were part of this larger cultural landscape.

JR – So you were weaving the museum into the site in two senses—there's a literal porosity between landscape and building, but you also connected the new project to a long history that stretches back to the beginnings of the park itself.

WH – Yes, but the project wasn't all about continuity. At a certain point the museum approached us and said, "We have two donors. One wants to create a children's garden and one wants to do a sculpture garden." And those two initiatives were really outside of the architecture. In a way, it was like we had three clients, and you can tell when you go there. There's one piece that feels like it's part of the architecture, and then there are these other pieces that feel like they're being informed by something a little different. It was an important lesson for me to realize that the project was big enough to allow each space to be its own thing—it was the first time I had designed a landscape where I didn't feel like everything had to be congruent.

JR – Would you say that this kind of noncongruence has become a theme in your museum projects? I'm thinking about the traditional role of outdoor space in the neoclassical museum typology; landscape typically takes the form of the courtyard and the plaza, and it's primarily about reinforcing the monumentality of the architecture. You worked on a major renovation of the Cooper Hewitt, Smithsonian Design Museum [2015], which is in the Carnegie Mansion, a Georgian revival building from 1902. The original landscape design was just what you would expect— a very formal garden. And your intervention was extraordinary— you introduced a series of much wilder elements inspired by Central Park, which is just across the street. There are chunks of New York's bedrock, Manhattan schist, which Frederick Law Olmsted famously incorporated into his design for the park, and you created echoes between plantings in the park and the museum garden. I don't quite want to call your design oppositional, but you certainly play with contrast and difference, and you open the building to a new range of experiences and associations.

Hood Design Studio, Cooper Hewitt, Smithsonian Design Museum,
Arthur Ross Terrace and Garden, New York, New York, 2015

**Would you say you were aiming for a kind of dialectic between
the landscape and the architecture?**

WH – Again, it depends on the context, right? The Cooper
Hewitt is on a very confined urban site. If I had tried to make a
landscape by looking only inward at that site, it probably would
have been pretty predictable. Landscape, to me, has always been this
inward and outward thing. And you said it at the beginning of this
conversation—it's about time, and it's about experience. You see
through landscape, and that continually shapes and reshapes your
understanding of a place. Cooper Hewitt is a classic example. Go
through Engineer's Gate, the entrance to the park that's right across
the street, walk up to the top of the hill there, and look back at
Cooper Hewitt. In the summertime, you see nothing. Just the green
of the park. In the wintertime, you can see all the way into the
museum gardens, and they become part of your landscape. That's
why I wanted to bring plants from the park into the site. When
things are blooming over there, why can't they be blooming over
here, too? There's this conversation unfolding, and to me that's

a much more interesting way of thinking about landscape than just as a two-dimensional composition. It's giving people a connection to the time and the place. Somebody might be visiting the museum and stop for a moment and say, "Oh, wow, it's springtime." That sounds mundane but it could be revelatory.

JR – It's not mundane at all. As museum architecture has moved away from the white cube, away from the idea that galleries should provide spaces of autonomy, there's been a real struggle to reestablish a connection to place, to introduce a level of temporal and locational specificity into the museum experience. It's almost funny, though, to think about how limited an architect's means are in this regard compared to what you can do with landscape. I'm thinking of a project like Louis Kahn's Kimbell Art Museum in Fort Worth, Texas. People rave about its natural light, and justifiably so, because Kahn designed the skylights so that the galleries register subtle changes in the sunlight depending on the weather or the season. But that seems like a very small thing compared to what you can do with blooming trees!

Talking about this profound connective power of landscape makes me think of your renovation of the Oakland Museum of California, which opened in 2021, because your work with the grounds transformed the institution. The irony is that landscape was always intended to be an important component of the design. It's a classic brutalist building by Kevin Roche and John Dinkeloo— a kind of cascade of concrete boxes—which prominently features a series of expansive terraces and roof gardens, all designed by the well-known modernist landscape architect Dan Kiley. If you go back and read what those three said about the project when it opened in 1969, it's clear that they fully intended it to function as a kind of public park within the city. What went wrong, do you think?

WH – That's a good question—why do some brutalist structures work and others don't? My studio is working on a renovation of the Barbican, by Chamberlin, Powell and Bon, in London right now, and we were just talking about this the other day. Look at Brazil, where you have all these huge brutalist buildings that aren't so different from what Roche and his team did in Oakland. But the Oakland Museum was hated by the community, and it was neglected and not maintained, and it basically atrophied as an institution. And in Brazil those structures are loved, and they're used, and they take on a completely different complexity. Why is that? I think a lot of it has to do with the nature of public space in America. The museum is a building of its time. It actually was supposed to open in 1968. What else is going on in the city then? Huey P. Newton, one of the founders of the Black Panthers, is on trial at the Alameda County Courthouse right across the street. There's so much civil unrest that they have to delay the opening by a year. And they change the design, adding a massive concrete wall on the north side of the site, facing the courthouse.

So what I'm getting at is that so many of these public spaces from the postwar era emerged at a time of terrible contradiction in America. There's an optimism that we want to live together, that we should create new civic spaces in our cities—this is the era of "urban renewal." But actually, we absolutely don't want to live together. Integration literally has to be legislated. The Oakland Museum can't function as a new town square because certain groups of people are just fleeing the city. And the groups that are left in the city are probably not going to museums.

JR – We've been talking about connecting a museum to its site as a kind of design choice, but this project is a powerful reminder that an institution's context is going to affect it no matter what— which is all the more reason that architects and landscape architects should consider it. How did you start rethinking the relationship between the city and the museum, particularly given all the changes that Oakland has gone through over the past fifty years?

WH – By thinking about how people use the space. Before my studio joined the project, the museum had started having Friday night events on the lawn outside of the wall, along the street. And it became a big deal. Every single Friday a lot of people would show up. When we looked at how well those events were working, we had this epiphany: Why don't we just open this whole thing up?

JR – That's fascinating—the event series showed you that people would come socialize outside of the wall, so you were able to isolate the wall as a problem.

WH – Exactly. And so expanding that programmatic use became the driving force for the renovation. But it was also interesting to look at who was coming to these events, and where they were coming from. And the people showing up were from the suburbs. These are the people who left the city. That's also part of the story of what the city has become today. You can live in an affluent suburb like Walnut Creek, drive into the museum on a Friday night, bring the kids. That's your experience of the city. I taught a class at the museum one semester, and I remember interviewing some of the people at one of the events. I'd ask where they were from, they'd say, "We're from the suburbs, but we *love* coming here. It's very urban!" And again, that actually makes sense if you look at the history of Oakland since the museum opened in 1969. Those tensions and those relationships are still playing out today.

JR – So how did you approach connecting the institution to the local community?

WH – The other important piece of the story is that the museum had a new director, Lori Fogarty, and she convinced the city to let go. Since it opened, the Oakland Museum had been a public, city-run institution. And because of problems with bureaucracy and funding, museums run by cities don't have great track records.

JR – Unfortunately not, at least in the US. It is a bit of a painful irony that she had to free the museum from the city to better serve its community.

WH – But it was a crucial step. Once she was able to get her own board of trustees, she could start a meaningful campaign for change. She asked us to do a master plan for opening the museum up, and

Hood Design Studio, Oakland Museum of California,
Oakland, California, landscape redesign, 2021

one of the first things I did was take the board for a walk. I wanted
them to look at the museum in the context of the city, so we went
for a three-hour walk, from the museum to downtown and back.
And none of them had done that. Because, again, these are people
who might work in the city or visit certain places in the city, but
they don't traverse the city, they don't walk through the city, they
don't inhabit the city that way. And it was so interesting to see them
starting to understand these connections. We looked at the museum's relationships with other gardens—there are lots of gardens all
around it, from rooftop gardens to horticultural gardens. And we
built this huge model so that we could think about the project at
that scale.

   And then one of the most important steps was what I called
"breaking the box"—we worked with the architects and engineers on
the team to figure out where we could create new openings into the
building. That was crucial, because you can't address everything
through programming. At a certain point you also have to change

the space. Before we got involved, the museum had moved its entrance from one side to the other. But that didn't really work. Either way, you basically have this huge structure that takes up two city blocks and you're saying there's one way to get in and out. I told them, "You have to be a multi-interest, multi-entrance place." So now we have three entrances, and that supports the programming. On one side, you can still go straight into the museum. But you can also enter the site from the lake side, which brings you right into the lawn. That's where concerts and other events can happen. From the other side, there's a ramp that takes you up to the café. And you can do either of those things without even going to the museum—which of course you could have done before, too, but no one did, because no one knew the gardens were free.

JR – I love the idea of using a garden to break the box. This kind of dialectical, even transformative, relationship between landscape and architecture also seems to be part of your most recent museum project, the International African American Museum in Charleston [2023]. It's hard to imagine a more charged site for this institution: it sits on the exact location of Gadsden's Wharf, which was the arrival point for almost half of all enslaved Africans brought to the United States. The scholar Henry Louis Gates Jr. has called it "ground zero" for the Black experience in America. The building, designed by Harry Cobb [of Pei Cobb Freed & Partners], feels almost deferential. It's a simple concrete box, floating above the site on a series of columns, so the architecture seems to be both stepping back from the ground and sheltering it. Was that a deliberate strategy you developed together to create an open field for the landscape design?

WH – Well, first of all, I can't take any credit for the site of the museum. That all has to go to Harry. The building was originally going to be down the road and across the street, directly across from the aquarium. That site had been chosen by Joseph P. Riley Jr., who was the mayor of Charleston for many years, and he's the one who brought in Harry to design the building. But then in the meantime excavations uncovered the physical remains of Gadsden's Wharf, and

Harry had the idea of moving the museum. The city had owned that land at one point and then sold it—I think someone was going to build a restaurant on it—so they had to buy it back.

JR – That's such a powerful example of the importance of preserving all the layers of history on a site—of undoing selective erasure—which you already talked about with your earliest projects like Lafayette Park. You go to Plymouth Rock, where the *Mayflower* landed, and there's a monument shaped like a little Greek temple looking out over the harbor. Yet this other landing site, this other point of origin, literally has to be exhumed.

WH – And it's not like it was a lost history. I mean, people knew Gadsden's Wharf existed. But the site had to be uncovered because in America this is not the history we celebrate. So that was Harry's idea, to build on the actual site of the wharf. And then he brought me into the project. I had never even met him prior to that. But he had done his homework—he knew all about the studio and the kind of work we do—and he just basically said, "Walter, this museum is all about the landscape—that's the project. I don't want to create a building that's highly rhetorical about the ground below." I had never worked with an architect as generous as Harry, and I probably never will again.

JR – It's interesting that he described his building as non-rhetorical, because it does seem like the architecture is trying hard not to make a statement. It defers meaning to the artifacts and exhibits inside and to the landscape outside. I'm not sure if this was a deliberate response to that nonrhetorical strategy on your part, but you chose to multiply meanings in the landscape. You're bringing in language, with an inscription that has the words of Maya Angelou; there's a figurative element, with a tidal pool that washes back and forth over a field of bodies sculpted in silhouette; there's an ethnobotanical dimension to the design, where you're combining native plants with plants that were imported from Africa; and there are spatial interventions, where you're carving into the landscape

Hood Design Studio, International African American Museum,
Charleston, South Carolina, 2023

to create places of gathering. How did you think about weaving together all these different ways of engaging with the site?

WH – That's a very difficult question to answer. But I think at the root of it was my struggle with the ways history is dealt with at other cultural sites and institutions across the US. I was looking around, and most of them deal with history in a very abstract, very pedagogical way. How can I put it? They're very traditional in a certain sense of wanting to be respectful and inclusive and, basically, to please everyone. But for me, if there's any space where we *don't* need to please everyone, it's a museum like this. And the other thing was that I knew I didn't want history to be abstract. Yes, the Pilgrims came to the US, but slavery also shaped the nation, right? Both things are true, and I wanted people to engage with that. And, I have to say, in the studio we find that, even now, people don't want most of the projects we present in this way. Because it's work to engage with them. They want the project that says, "OK, so this happened, and we were complacent about it, but now we acknowledged it. We raised $1 million for a piece of public art and now we're done."

JR – But given the importance of this site, and the momentum behind the project, you saw an opportunity to do things differently?

WH – I just thought, OK, we're not going to do something that everyone else has already done. This is ground zero. We need to do something very particular. Early in the process I organized a three-day workshop with about twenty-five people—scholars, historians, local residents, politicians, architects, and city workers. We toured a plantation. We toured the Gullah/Geechee communities in the Lowcountry.

We went out to Sullivan's Island to look at the place where enslaved Africans were basically interned in these "pest houses," where they were checked for disease, and I had an important realization there. Toni Morrison did a project called the Bench by the Road. The idea came from an interview where she basically said, "There's no place for me to sit and think about my ancestors." So the idea of the project was to place benches at important sites for the

African diaspora all over the world. The first one was sited on Sullivan's Island and was just a simple standard park bench with a little plaque on it. And here we are, surrounded by all this history—there are buildings and exhibits all over the island—and that bench was the one thing everyone was taking pictures of. That hit me really, really hard.

And I just decided—I'm going to come up with the most audacious ways to talk about the experience that this museum site represents. I'm not going to let that experience be abstracted. And that became part of the workshop. We came up with more than thirty different ideas, and, the whole time, we were having these amazing conversations. That's how these approaches emerged—the figurative sculptures of the bodies, the different plants that showed how the ecology of the place had also been shaped by this transfer of people and culture, and so on. So there was never a moment of saying, OK, this is the scheme. The design kept evolving, and that gets back to improvisation—taking these elements and reshaping them into something completely new.

LIU

YICHUN

JULIAN ROSE – I would like to begin by asking what role, if any, the visual arts played in your education. You studied architecture at Tongji University in Shanghai, where the pedagogy has been deeply influenced by twentieth-century European and American modernism, in part because the first director of the Department of Architecture, Huang Zuoshen, studied under Walter Gropius at Harvard in the late 1930s and early 1940s. At the Bauhaus, Gropius famously called for "unity" between architecture and the visual arts, and similar ideas were advocated by other influential modernists— Le Corbusier's "synthesis of the arts" is another well-known example. Did your teachers emphasize interdisciplinary collaboration as an important part of the legacy of modernism?*

LIU YICHUN – European modernism was still very influential when I was studying at Tongji in the 1990s, because the director at the time, Feng Jizhong, had graduated from the Vienna University of Technology in the 1940s. He brought back a system of architectural education based on modernist concepts of spatial composition. The curriculum at most other architecture schools in China was based on the Beaux-Arts model, and these were very different. But I learned about modernism primarily in terms of architecture's relationship to industrialization and new technologies; we were not looking at modernism as a model for thinking about how architecture connects to visual art. The lessons of modernism were about how architecture could be used to improve people's lives.

JR – That focus makes sense, given the incredibly rapid urbanization China was experiencing in the late twentieth century. How did this emphasis on modernism affect the way you were taught about architectural history? Several of your early works draw from traditional Chinese architecture, and in Europe and America that kind of engagement with vernacular building was closely associated with postmodernism, because it was part of a reaction against the

---

*The author would like to thank Zhang Wenyi for her invaluable assistance in translating this conversation.

modernist obsession with reinventing architecture from the ground up. It's interesting to think that for you the two influences—modern architecture and vernacular architecture—might have coincided.

LY – I did learn some Chinese architectural history at Tongji University, but the way history was taught was not really connected to design. During the period I was a student, postmodernism was very popular around the world, and it was also influential in China. But this approach simply used the symbols of traditional Chinese architecture. So, for example, a new building would have a modern form, but a huge traditional roof on top. I was very critical of that kind of combination, and so were many people in the field. This made me a little bit reluctant to turn to traditional architecture. I thought maybe my architecture should be entirely modern.

Later, in 2001, I established my studio, Atelier Deshaus, with two collaborators, Chen Yifeng and Zhuang Shen. At that time, we asked a fundamental question: How do we define ourselves as a Chinese architecture practice? We thought a lot about how to combine what we had learned about modern architecture with something that was specific to our situation. In the end we came back to history, but this was our own independent research after we had established our practice. And we did not choose to use the symbols of traditional Chinese architecture or borrow its forms. Rather, we wanted to introduce into our own work the kinds of spatial experiences we found in traditional buildings.

JR – That's the thinking behind projects like the Xiayu Kindergarten, completed in 2005, where you organized the classroom buildings in a kind of loose cluster that recalls the way the pavilions might be arranged in a classical Chinese garden, even though the materials and the geometry of the buildings are themselves quite contemporary?

LY – Exactly. That project is in one of the "new town" developments built in the suburbs of Shanghai, so there was no existing urban fabric to respond to. Instead we looked to architectural

Atelier Deshaus, Xiayu Kindergarten, Shanghai, China, 2005

history, and our design was based in part on a careful study of the Master of the Nets Garden in Suzhou. But thinking about history provided a method of design rather than an architectural style or a visual language.

JR – I have another question about how historical precedents might have shaped your approach to design. I think one reason that many modern Western architects, from people like Gropius and Le Corbusier onward, have been so interested in connecting art and architecture is that there is a powerful mythology, dating back at least to the fifteenth century, of the genius who is a master of both fields. This is the idea of "Renaissance man," embodied by someone like Michelangelo, who sculpts the *David*, paints the Sistine Chapel ceiling, and also designs St. Peter's. There's a deep sense, in other words, that art and architecture have historically been closely connected—perhaps even that this is their natural state—and that if they're not connected today, this fragmented state suggests some sort of failure of contemporary practitioners to live up to the example provided by the great figures of the past. Is there a historical tradition of connecting the architecture and the visual arts in China?

LY – There are some similarities between the histories of Chinese and Western architecture in this regard, because in both the practice of building was closely related to other aspects of culture, as you were saying about architecture and visual art. But the difference is that in the context of ancient China, there was no such thing as the profession of architecture—the architect, in a modern sense, did not exist. Rather we had the literati [shidafu], who were kind of hybrid figures of scholars and government officials in the imperial court. You could call the literati "interdisciplinary," because they would make paintings, practice calligraphy, and write poems and literature. And they would imagine ideal environments, like gardens or buildings, in these works, but then they would engage a craftsman to build that environment for them. So in a way it is in the art form of the poem or the painting that the architecture is created by the literati, but then it is constructed by other people.

JR – That's fascinating because there is an analogous separation of the architect from the craftsman in the Western tradition. In fact, a key part of the emergence of the modern figure of the architect in the Renaissance was the idea that they were an intellectual, someone who imagines buildings and makes drawings but who does not build with their hands. At the same time, the architect was still a specialist in making buildings and was expected to have mastered very specific techniques of architectural drawing, which were the technologies used to communicate their ideas to the craftsmen who would build their designs.

You're describing a looser relationship between the idea of a space and its realization. Has that cultural archetype of the literati influenced how you think about your own practice? In a way, it sounds like it may have been appealing to you that the literati were not creating detailed plans for specific buildings, because you were not looking at history for formal models.

LY – I am interested in the literati's relationship to space and the way they thought about creating a specific kind of spatial experience. If you look back at how the Chinese garden developed, it was a kind of refuge. The literati would spend many, many years studying, and then they would take the civil service exams, and if they passed they would progress through different positions in the bureaucracy of the imperial government. It was a very rigorous, demanding career, and they would need to have a place to take comfort in nature and have time to think. The form of the garden emerged from these needs. It was both a place to escape everyday life and a place to find inspiration for their other art forms—calligraphy, painting, and poetry. And the space in a garden would be composed very carefully, arranged according to specific rhythms and sequences. So, for example, if you enter a very small space at first, then you might immediately go into a large, open space. And because there are many pavilions in gardens, they can teach us a lot about the relationship between inside and outside. There are many devices that frame the landscape and create special points of view. Walking through a garden gives you a much greater range of different spatial experiences than walking through a normal building, and I am interested in introducing these experiences into the buildings I design, whether a kindergarten or an art museum.

But the literati are also important because they provide a body of knowledge, a philosophy about architecture and space, that is distinct from both the theories of modern architecture that I learned about at university and from the Western philosophies that were important to some postmodern architects, like deconstruction. In my recent designs, I have been inspired by the concept of yin jie ti yi, which is described in one of the most famous manuals of garden design, *The Craft of Gardens*, written in 1631 by Ji Cheng during the late Ming dynasty, when garden building was at its peak. It is very difficult to translate into English, but it means something like "adapt to the circumstances." It is made from four characters—yin, jie, ti, and yi—and each one carries a specific meaning. *Yin* means "because" or "due to." It suggests that the design of the garden should be based on the existing conditions of the site, taking into consideration its topography, climate, and other local factors. *Jie* means "borrow" or "utilize." It implies that the designer should make use of the existing landscape or scenery surrounding the site, such as distant mountains, nearby rivers, or other natural features. *Ti* means "form" or "structure." It emphasizes the importance of the physical form and layout of the garden, including its arrangement of pavilions, terraces, ponds, rockeries, and other architectural and landscape elements. *Yi* means "suitable" or "appropriate." It suggests that the design should be in harmony with the local environment, culture, and aesthetics and should be adapted to the tastes and needs of the users of the garden. Overall, this word encapsulates the idea that a well-designed Chinese garden should always be adapted to its site and should take advantage of the full potential offered by local conditions.

JR – It sounds like *The Craft of Gardens* has provided you with a conceptual framework for thinking very deeply about the relationship between architecture and its context, but I'm struck by the fact that in garden design context is understood primarily in terms of nature, while many of your projects are sited in cities. How do you apply these ideas to an urban environment, for example at the Long Museum West Bund in Shanghai, where the existing scenery included not just the Huangpu River but also enormous pieces of defunct industrial infrastructure?

LY – I think the two situations are actually very similar. As we enter a period of urban renovation along the waterfront, these existing industrial ruins are another kind of nature. In other words, they are part of the natural condition we are faced with, so they are also a part of the foundation of our design.

JR – I'd like to speak in more detail about how your design for the Long Museum responded to its context. The site was originally a wharf where coal was transferred from barges to railcars, and a massive loading bridge with coal hoppers—over one hundred meters

Atelier Deshaus, Long Museum West Bund, Shanghai, China, 2014

long, ten meters wide, and eight meters tall [328 by 33 by 26 feet]—
had survived from the 1950s. But by the time you started working on
the museum, in 2011, there was also an underground parking garage,
constructed as part of an urban redevelopment scheme that had since
been abandoned. You were dealing with a true palimpsest, in other
words, which must have been quite challenging. How was that site
selected for the location of the museum?

    LY – It's a situation that might only occur in China. The city
government had been planning to redevelop this part of the old
industrial waterfront for some time. They commissioned another
architect to design a visitor center for tourists on the site, which was
supposed to be completed for the Expo Shanghai 2010. The below-
ground parking structure was finished in time, but the aboveground
piece was not, and so the project was stopped in a half-finished state.
About a year later, the government approached us to see if we could
create a new design, still for a visitor center, that used the existing
garage as a foundation. We accepted, but then a month after we
started the design, the government began to reconsider who was
going to administer the building and to think more about the

audience they wanted to draw into the site. They realized that maybe it was better to make the building an art museum instead. This decision was part of a broader plan to transform this former industrial area, which at the time was called the Xuhui Riverfront, into an arts district.

JR – So the idea was to use the art museum as an engine to drive urban development?

LY – Exactly. The idea was modeled on the South Bank of London, where a series of industrial facilities were converted into art facilities. So the government paid for the construction of our building, imagined as part of a series of art museums that would help to transform the district. In fact, we also designed the West Bund Art Center, which is housed in a converted aircraft factory, about two kilometers [about one and a quarter miles] south of the Long Museum. Afterward, the riverfront was rebranded as the West Bund.

JR – I know that the Long Museum is a private museum that exhibits the holdings of two major Chinese collectors, Liu Yiqian and Wang Wei, so I'm surprised to hear that the government paid for its construction.

LY – Again, this is a situation that could perhaps only occur in China. The government financed the construction, but then the museum was sold to Liu and Wang. The pair already had another Long Museum in Pudong, which opened in 2012—it displays their collection of Chinese art, which includes Chinese antiquities and works by contemporary Chinese artists—so initially they were thinking about putting their collection of international contemporary art in our building. But then they found that the public had a great interest in their Chinese collection, so they decided that the new museum in the West Bund would exhibit both.

JR – Did you know about this combination of ancient and contemporary art during the design process? The main galleries are on the ground floor, formed by interlocking concrete volumes that you described as umbrella vaults because their curved surfaces are cantilevered out from a central structural core. They are extraordinary spaces—luminous and fluid—but I imagine that their scale and abundant natural light would make them challenging places to display historical artifacts.

LY – The decision about the collection came while we were still working on the design, so we introduced different gallery typologies to distribute the different kinds of art. The Chinese antiquities are in underground galleries that we created from the original parking structure. Here, the light is controlled to protect the paintings, and there are glass vitrines for ceramics and other fragile objects. There are also some galleries underground for modern art from 1900 to 1949; these spaces are standard white cubes. The aboveground galleries are for contemporary art, and we wanted to make these spaces large and open so they could accommodate new forms of art in the future. At one point, Liu thought that some of the ancient Chinese art should be moved aboveground because it generates so much public interest, but we persuaded him that these precious artworks should be kept in the underground galleries, because they are rather small in scale and so suit that environment better.

JR – Several artists have done site-specific installations in the museum. For example, when Olafur Eliasson had a survey there in 2016, he created several new pieces especially for the museum, and he spoke about how he wanted his work to respond to your architecture. Was part of the original concept for the Long Museum the idea that "contemporary" art would mean not just the art of the recent past, but artworks created for the museum in the present? And did you imagine your space as a kind of invitation, or even provocation, to artists?

LY – It's true that it is a provocative space for artists. At first, Liu and Wang imagined that the museum would be just for displaying what they had collected through the years. And they thought that the space might be too difficult. The aboveground galleries are raw concrete, and one of their curators even suggested painting them white, just like traditional galleries, to make them more accommodating to the art. But then after the building was completed, it began to attract the attention of curators and artists around the world because the space is so unique, and they became interested in doing exhibitions there. Also, many Chinese artists have come to see a solo show at the Long Museum as an important milestone in their career, because they know it will receive attention, not just here but abroad. So the museum has become a center of communication, in a way. It has become a window between contemporary Chinese art and the global art world.

JR – It's an impressive example of the power of museum architecture. I know Liu and Wang have also invested significant resources in the museum's operations and programming, but it's hard to imagine that the Long Museum would have become such a focal point without your building. And while we've been talking primarily about its spatial qualities, the building's tectonics are also remarkable—or really, to be more precise, I should say that those spatial qualities are produced by extremely sophisticated tectonics. You mentioned the raw concrete surfaces of the umbrella vaults, which are certainly one of the most striking features of the contemporary galleries. It's impressive that you were able to cast concrete with enough precision to create finished gallery walls. But it's even more impressive that all the building's mechanical systems are cast into the central shafts of these vaults—they're hidden in the frame of the umbrella, so to speak, and that is a huge part of why the structure feels so light and the spaces feel so open.

I think in many places in the world, and certainly in America, an architect would be hesitant to design a cast-in-place structure that included things like ductwork because the construction tolerances with concrete are simply not tight enough. A more typical approach would be to use concrete for the primary structure only, then place the mechanical systems outside of it and clad everything with a veneer of some other material. But in that situation the walls are much thicker, the surface you see isn't the actual structure of the building, and the space has a very different feeling.

What gave you the confidence to try this? Had you worked extensively with concrete before, or did you have an especially close relationship with the contractor?

LY – I think we were too young to be afraid. It was one of our first big projects, and we designed it in what we felt intuitively would be the ideal way and said, We'll just see how it goes. Of course, we did tests and mock-ups, and we knew that if the casts failed we could try breaking the structure into smaller units, or if the surfaces of the walls were not good we could have finished them with another material or painted them white, as the curators had suggested. I don't know if I would be brave enough to do it today, now that I have much more experience in construction.

JR – Well, sometimes it's helpful to be young and inexperienced! In several of your lectures you've mentioned that, while you were working on this project, you studied Louis Kahn's Kimbell Art Museum, which also uses a system of concrete vaults. But what strikes me about the comparison is that, in Kahn's project, the gallery space provides the basic organizational principle of the building— the plan is a series of rectangles, and the vaults are evenly spaced and arranged in neat rows according to that logic. In your building, it seems like you abandoned the idea of the gallery as a spatial unit, and instead you focused more on designing the structure itself. By varying the spacing between the vaults and allowing them to intersect in different ways, you created an enormous variety of spatial conditions, all of which work for exhibiting art without necessarily being legible as traditional galleries or even discrete rooms. Would you say that, for you, museum design starts with structure rather than space?

LY – The time that I was working on the design of the Long Museum was a period of very intense thought for me, and it was a turning point in how I think about the role of structure in architecture. In most of the new buildings that were appearing in China at the time, the structure was wrapped up in a facade, so the only time you would see the real structure was while it was under construction. And I felt that somehow this was backward because the structure is the most fundamental element of architecture. In a museum, of course, to some extent you have to organize the space according to function. But in my experience visiting museums around the world, I found that it is a problem when the gallery space is repetitive. It's very tiring if you have to go from room to room to room and there is only one way of moving through the building. So for the Long Museum I thought about compressing the idea of a room into a wall. We always say a room or a gallery is where we place artworks, but, actually, most of the artworks are on the walls. That means that the walls are the basic requirement. And so I imagined an entire museum that would feel like it was made of walls, not rooms—where the walls are both the space and the structure. In fact, we used the umbrella vaults so that the wall could become the roof and cover the space, too. And the walls are independent from each other on the plan so you can move freely between them. That's how they're different from the vaults of the Kimbell, because in that case the distribution of the vaults is decided by the organization of the plan. We worked more three-dimensionally, adjusting the vaults so that sometimes they are parallel, sometimes they are perpendicular, and sometimes they have different heights. In that way, we created many different kinds of space within the building.

JR – Given the importance of structure in this building and the technical challenges I mentioned earlier, I imagine that the role of the engineer was particularly important. Did you begin collaborating with an engineer early in the process, as you were designing the vaults?

LY – Actually, the funny thing is that, for the Long Museum, we did the design first. And then, as we were thinking about how to realize the umbrella vaults, I interviewed many engineers. Most of them did not want to get involved in the project, because they saw it would be really difficult. The engineer we worked with is Zhang

Atelier Deshaus, Long Museum West Bund, Shanghai, China, 2014

Zhun. At the time, he was just starting out in his own practice, and prior to meeting him I had sought out one of his professors, because I thought I needed someone very senior. But the senior engineer was too busy, so he suggested I speak to Zhang, who became very excited about the project. Our collaboration was so productive that after the Long Museum I suggested to Zhang Zhun that he move his structural engineering practice to the same building as our architecture studio. Now he is right downstairs, so we are physically working together. In all our projects now, we work closely with him from the beginning. And I think that was a little bit of a pioneering move, because it has become much more common in China for architects to involve engineers early in their design process.

JR – So the Long Museum initiated a whole new approach for you. I'm also interested in the other collaborative dimension of your practice, which is your work with artists. In a sense, these collaborations seem to complement each other—you work with engineers on the structure of your buildings, and it seems that you often work with artists on their surfaces. I'm thinking of a project like the Blossom Pavilion, from 2015, where the artist Zhan Wang designed the surfaces of the structural supports based on his well-known stainless-steel sculptures of scholar's rocks, or the main building of the Artron Art Center, completed in 2014, where you worked with Ding Yi. Ding is known primarily as an abstract painter, and you worked with him to create a series of colorful ceramic tiles that were used for the building's facade. You mentioned earlier that you feel a lot of contemporary architecture puts too much emphasis on surface at the expense of structure. Is one solution of this problem to work with artists on a building's facade? Do you think that some artists are specialists in surfaces in the same way engineers are specialists in structure?

LY – Well, the facade is a standard part of architecture, and we are accustomed to thinking about how a building's envelope is related to its program and its interior space, so it's not necessary to work with an artist on every project. But sometimes the facade

Atelier Deshaus and Ding Yi, Artron Art Center, Shanghai, China, 2014

Atelier Deshaus and Zhan Wang, Blossom Pavilion, Shanghai, China, 2015

becomes an independent layer, or it even becomes the theme of the building, and I would question that. If we find that a specific project needs a facade to be somehow special, I prefer to collaborate with an artist on it. Then they can use the building surface as the canvas for their own creation, and it adds to the complexity of the architecture. I learned this approach in part by looking at the work of Herzog & de Meuron in Europe. I noticed that they often collaborate with artists on the surface specifically.

JR – You mean, for example, the Eberswalde Technical School Library, built in 1999, where the artist Thomas Ruff selected photographs to be screen printed onto the concrete facade of the building?

LY – Exactly. Looking at projects like that, I noticed that when artists do the surface of a building, they often have a more sensitive touch, and the way they deal with different materials and textures and colors is very different from how architects deal with them. For example, when I collaborated with Zhan Wang for the Blossom Pavilion, I was thinking of the steel plates primarily as structure, but he had the idea of treating them in a more subtle way. So I find these collaborations to be very inspiring because they can expand my own thinking about different elements of architecture.

JR – In the Blossom Pavilion, the surface of the steel is hammered by hand, just as in Zhan's sculptures. Today, architects are usually under tremendous pressure to control construction time and labor costs to produce a building in the most efficient way possible, so they are rarely able to introduce handmade or even hand-finished elements into their projects. Do you also work with artists because it allows you to reintroduce a level of craft that would otherwise be missing from architecture?

LY – Yes. I would prefer to work with craftsmen, because there is a powerful emotional connection created by the traces of their hands on the building materials. And, of course, historically that was how buildings were made—for example, traditional Chinese wood construction. But this is rare, given how buildings are made today, so working with artists is one way to bring more of this emotional connection back into architecture.

JR – You mentioned that the Long Museum was part of a major urban development plan in Shanghai. Since it opened, you have gone on to build many more art museums all over China, and many Chinese cities have continued to grow at a rapid pace. Part of this growth is a shift from the industrial city to the postindustrial city, where financial centers and cultural institutions are replacing factories and infrastructure. A similar shift has taken place in many Western capitals—for example, on the South Bank of London, as you pointed out, where a defunct power station became Tate Modern in 2000. How do you envision the role of the art museum in the future of Chinese cities? Will it be similar to what we have seen in the West?

LY – There are a huge number of art museums emerging in China, and this is certainly a symbol of the transition from the industrial era to the postindustrial era. This is surely the same in China as it is in the West, and China is trying to learn from Western experiences. But, at the same time, the situation might be a little bit different in China, because we don't have so many public institutions in our cities. And museums are, first of all, public architecture. Even if they are privately owned, like the Long Museum, they are designed for the public and their purpose is to deliver culture to the public. In that sense, they are similar to libraries in that they play a role in improving the quality of life for people in the city. So museums are not just for tourism and urban development, and we need to think about how their function expands beyond these things and even how it expands beyond exhibiting art. If museums are welcoming public spaces, they can have a very important influence on the public life of the city, and I think in that sense they might be even more important in China than in the West.

JR – That's certainly an admirable goal for the museum. But a concern that is commonly raised in the West is that, as cultural institutions become more and more intertwined with urban development, architects themselves start losing control of these projects. As the economic stakes of constructing a new museum get higher and higher, the investors behind the project are less and less inclined to take risks. So they are unlikely to allow an architect to experiment, and the role of the architect shrinks because more and more strategic planning and decision-making is being taken over by the financial team. China's economic system is obviously different, and it also seems that in the last decade or so the government has made a concerted effort to promote Chinese architects. In the early twenty-first century, rapidly growing Chinese cities were famously the playground of European and American architects—nearly all the major buildings constructed for the 2008 Beijing Olympics were designed by Western "starchitects," for example—but recently more and more major projects in China are going to Chinese designers.

Do these conditions give architects more power than they have in the West?

LY – The last decade has been a good time for Chinese architects. And this is partly because they have, besides their professional knowledge in architectural design, a lot of expertise in planning and organizing. Our cities have grown so fast that we have gained a huge amount of experience. For the same reason, it has actually been a difficult period for government planners because they have been faced with such a vast amount of development. So when we are working with developers or with local governments, we can give suggestions in the early stages of a project and beyond our design proposal; we can also contribute our expertise in how to operate a new institution. For example, if we do an art museum, we can think about questions like, Who will run the museum? What will the collection be? What will the exhibitions be like? These are questions that a developer or a government planner might not have the experience to answer, so they rely on the expertise of the architect. This is not unique to me. I see many other architects working in similar ways. I'm not sure if this will continue in the coming years, but because Chinese architects have so much experience in the recent transformation of the urban environment, their voices are highly respected.

RENZO

PIANO

JULIAN ROSE — You are by far the most prolific museum designer in the world today. In retrospect, this affinity is somewhat surprising, because there was nothing about your education or early career that suggested a particularly close connection to visual art. Other architects who have become well-known for museum design have gone to art school or spent formative years working alongside artists as part of the same cultural scene; you went to the Politecnico in Milan, Italy's largest architecture and engineering school, and your earliest projects were experiments with new building technologies like modular construction systems. How did you progress from such a technical background to such expertise in museum design?

RENZO PIANO — Looking back, I had a very different start than many architects. I was born into a family of builders: my grandfather was a builder, my father was a builder, my uncles were builders, my older brother was a builder. So I grew up in a kind of culture of construction. But I didn't know much about art, or at least the things you would probably describe as art. For me, "art" meant the art of making things, of putting things together.

JR — How was that understanding of art expressed in your work?

RP — My father made very simple buildings, which were also very massive, because concrete was his material. So, as you do when you're eighteen or nineteen years old, I set out in exactly the opposite direction. I became fascinated by lightweight structures and by the idea that my architecture could fight against the force of gravity. I wanted to make buildings from the least amount of material possible. Stripping away the excess from architecture, refining it to its essential elements, became an art form for me.

JR — These interests seem particularly unusual for the time. You graduated from architecture school in the mid-1960s, when the field was dominated by arguments about style. There was widespread acknowledgment that modernism was no longer sustainable as the ascendant international style but little agreement about what should come next. So-called late-modern approaches like brutalism were pitted against the first stirrings of postmodernism. There were also emerging design collectives—like Archigram in the UK and Archizoom and Superstudio in Italy—that were questioning the importance of building itself by creating provocative paper architecture. Did your grounding in construction allow you to avoid getting caught up in these aesthetic debates?

RP – It was a good beginning because I started from scratch. For me, architecture was not theoretical, not academic, not cerebral. It was about reality, about making shelter for human beings. Architecture is fundamental—after clothing, it's the primary thing we use to protect our bodies. This is quite a simple understanding of architecture—a bit too simple, probably—but it saved me from falling into the trap of a kind of academic practice, of worrying about belonging to this or that style.

JR – Is that approach still at the core of your practice?

RP – Well, eventually I grew up and started to understand that architecture is not that easy. It is those essential elements—shelter, structure—but it is also about community, about ethics, about utopia. And it's about beauty, poetics, and desire, too. Architecture is about many things that don't belong to the world of practicality.

JR – You mention utopia, and I wonder if that is the concept that began to bridge the technical and the cultural in your work. In 1971, you and Richard Rogers won the competition for the Pompidou Centre with a design that completely reimagined both the form and the function of the museum: an unprecedented combination of programs housed in an overtly high-tech exoskeleton. Was it your sense that embracing a new approach to building technology would also open new possibilities for social interaction and new roles for the cultural institution?

RP – I have an office in Paris now, and every time I pass by the Pompidou I am amazed. I understand why we did it, but I still don't understand how we were allowed to do it. It's completely mad—it is a sacrilegious object in the middle of the city.

Piano & Rogers, Pompidou Centre, Paris, France, 1977

JR – Because of how it looks or what it does? Or both?

RP – That building emerged from a special moment in the history of the modern world—a moment of rupture. The competition was only a few years after May '68. We had the sense that our job was to break the museum—to say clearly and loudly that culture should be open and accessible instead of closed off and intimidating, that the museum should be a place for culture with a lowercase *c*, not a capital *C*.

JR – How did that mission fit with your own understanding of culture, and of institutions, up to that point?

RP – Back then, I did not spend much time in museums. Neither did Richard. That was not our world. We were in love with music, especially the experimental music of people like Pierre Boulez and John Cage. We loved cinema. We loved the art and literature that we saw coming out of America because it had a sense of freedom. But we didn't love museums, for the simple reason that we thought they were places only for the few. Museums were sacred spaces, places of ceremony and ritual.

JR – In fact, some two decades earlier, when Theodor Adorno made his famous comparison between museums and tombs— essentially arguing that the museum was where culture went to die—he used another Paris institution, the Louvre, as one of his examples. It sounds like you were trying to bring the museum back to life.

RP – One idea that Richard and I picked up was from André Malraux, who was France's minister of cultural affairs under Charles de Gaulle. He had talked, well before, about decentralizing culture, and he had the idea of doing this in part through what he called the maison de la culture. Every city, even a small one, would get a building where people could gather and interact and experience different forms of culture—look at art, listen to music, read books, and so on. In a way, the Pompidou Centre was a kind of maison de la culture on a much bigger scale. But the size was not about grandeur, of course. It was about bringing all of these things together— a huge public library, as well as places for art, music, and cinema.

JR – But then you had to invent a new architecture for this new institution and persuade the world to accept it. How did you do that?

RP – The competition jury was so important. It was an amazing group of architects—including Philip Johnson, Jean Prouvé, and Oscar Niemeyer—who were willing to select the most radical solution. And it was also planets and stars crossing at the right moment, the involvement of Monsieur Pompidou and of his wife, who was very engaged with art.

JR – How did you imagine your building communicating with the public? The Pompidou is often cited as one of the first built examples of so-called high-tech architecture, but it also has a pop, almost playful side. In some ways, the building's relationship to technology seems symbolic—the color coding of the ventilation and plumbing on the exterior, the escalator snaking up the facade. You mentioned Malraux's maison de la culture, but now I'm thinking of his *Museum Without Walls*. That book was about coming to terms with what happens when works of art circulate primarily as photographs, and of course that happens to buildings as well. In some ways, Malraux presaged the rise of an image-based culture that has also absorbed architecture—buildings circulate as images, and increasingly seem *designed* as images, too. Did the Pompidou, intentionally or not, recast the museum itself as an image?

RP – That building is innocent. It's not a celebration of high technology. If it was a machine, it was one like the Yellow Submarine. It was in the spirit of those times—a bit of May '68, a bit of the Beatles, a bit of Archigram. To us, a machine seemed less intimidating than a marble building. It's also not an image. You can call it what you like—a machine or a ship or a factory or a refinery—but most of all the Pompidou is a small town. And the escalator is like its main street. The building is about society and community and openness and accessibility. That is the real point.

JR – And has that emphasis on community carried over into your other museum projects?

RP – The Pompidou was really the beginning. When I make a museum, I'm making a place of shared values, a place for people to meet. The first museums were only about art; today they are also social centers.

JR – Much of the current discussion about museum architecture focuses on what happens inside. But it sounds like, for you, museum design is also an urban question.

RP – I have built twenty-nine museums in my career, and my studio has four more under construction now. Every one of those buildings is about making culture accessible to the community. This is not culture in the sense of an establishment; it is culture as a source of wonder, surprise, exploration, material for collective engagement.

Sometimes people ask me, "Aren't you tired of making museums?" No, because each of those thirty-three buildings tells a different story. They are all connected by one idea about how museums can operate, but they all belong to different places, and each is woven into a unique civic life. Some of the places we build are challenging. We are working on the Istanbul Modern, which is right on the Bosporus. We are building the Beirut History Museum. These are not the easiest locations to work in, but the museums can become points within the cities that make them better places to live.

JR – Would you argue that cities like these are in fact the ones that need museums most?

RP – Cities need so many public buildings. They need schools. They need universities. They need libraries. They need hospitals. They need courthouses. But, yes, I think among those things they also need museums—on one condition: the museum must be open and accessible and provide a place for people to meet. That's the essential thing.

JR – Of course, the problem is that, inevitably, a museum's civic role depends in part on so many things that are outside of the architect's control, from institutional policy to government regulation. What spatial or material moves can you, as the architect, make to influence the way a building connects to its community?

RP – The building's relationship to the ground is key. That's why the plaza outside the Pompidou slopes down to meet the building. That's why the building for the Whitney Museum of American Art flies, lifting up to let the street inside and to embrace the High Line. That is my philosophy not just for museums but for all public buildings. We recently finished a new courthouse in Paris. It's a building for ten thousand people, and of course it has to be secure, but, even there, the ground floor is very accessible. Any building is always in dialogue with its surroundings. But museums are essentially about that dialogue.

This is part of an evolution. The first museums in Europe, in the seventeenth century, were what in Italian we call quadreriae, picture galleries deep inside of palaces, and their purpose was essentially to preserve the artworks and keep them safe. At that time, culture was something that needed to be protected from the world outside. But museums today are not for protecting their contents— they are built to bring culture out into the world.

Renzo Piano Building Workshop, Whitney Museum of American Art, New York, New York, 2015

JR – The idea that the museum is a place of refuge extended well into the modern era. As you said, your building for the Whitney brings the street into the museum. One of the things that interests me about that project, which was completed in 2015, is that it almost completely inverts the concept of Marcel Breuer's Whitney, which was finished in 1966. In some ways, that's not so long ago—it was only five years before you designed the Pompidou—but Breuer had a completely different attitude toward the relationship between the museum and the street. He spoke explicitly about the need to create a retreat from city life. And whether you love it or hate it, the building's entry—some people call it a moat—is very clearly an architectural gesture of separation between building and street. Were you consciously trying to turn the old Whitney building inside out in your design?

RP – You are touching on an important point. I have always loved that building, especially the strength of its materials—the stone, the concrete. Part of the idea of a museum is that it is built for duration, and Breuer's design is a beautiful embodiment of that. But just because you love something doesn't mean you have to copy it.

I was actually asked to do a proposal for expanding the museum on that site, but they were not going to be able to demolish the brownstones next door; it wasn't feasible. The director Adam Weinberg and the board decided to postpone the project, and eventually we found the new site downtown.

JR – And was the downtown site more compatible with your philosophy of museum design?

RP – Once you start working on a new building, you don't just apply your principles. You forget the principles and find something specific in the site that the design can respond to. Sometimes that is the local history, or another building to expand, as in my projects for the Art Institute of Chicago [2009] and the Morgan Library [2006] and the Kimbell Art Museum [2013]. But even an empty site will have something. When I was designing the new Osaka Airport [1994], we were building on an artificial island out in the middle of the bay, and even there, with only the water, there was something that I could work with. It's the spirit of the place, what the Romans used to call the genius loci.

I will never forget the day I visited the Whitney's new site. The High Line was there, and the water, and the traffic on the highway, and the sun, and the busy streets. These things are the essence of the building. There was already a double relationship, with the city on one side and the water and the traffic on the other. Then I thought about the logic of the street, and that maybe the building could rise up and the street could come inside in such a way that you wouldn't even understand the distinction between inside and outside, so that the city and the museum could merge. And stairs and terraces on the outside of the building would allow you to play, because by walking up or down from one level to another you can see the city in different ways.

JR – I can see how important the stairs and the terraces and the openness to the street are for the Whitney's engagement with the city, but I wonder if there is a point when these kinds of design moves start to conflict with the galleries themselves. It strikes me that many of your early museum designs, starting with the Menil Collection in Houston, which opened in 1986, were one-story buildings on relatively open sites. That building, in particular, has been celebrated for its masterful use of natural light in the galleries— for essentially creating the perfect conditions in which to view art. Is there ever a conflict between connecting a museum to the city outside and creating ideal viewing conditions within?

RP – Honestly, when I can, I prefer to make a horizontal museum, for the very simple reason that it allows all the galleries to have natural light. That's why the Menil is one floor, the extension to the Kimbell is one floor, the Fondation Beyeler [1997] is one floor, and the Nasher Sculpture Center [2003] is one floor (with a basement). But there are situations when you just can't do that, when you're working in parts of the city that are obviously too dense.

Renzo Piano Building Workshop, Fondation Beyeler, Riehen, Switzerland, 1997

Renzo Piano Building Workshop, Menil Collection, Houston, Texas, 1987

Again, it's about responding to site. Texas thirty years ago was a place with very little history. There was not much to respond to in that sense. But I was always interested in natural light, from my very first buildings, and the magic moment came when I was talking to Dominique de Menil. She told me, "I want a building that is big inside but small outside." And then I thought, This must be about light! To make a building feel big inside even if it's not monumental, you have to fill it with light. Dominique said she wanted to feel the day going by; she wanted to feel the clouds passing over. I began to understand that natural light is magical because it's not stable. Today a museum can have technically perfect lighting with halogen bulbs or LEDs, but it's flat, it's plain. It doesn't change.

JR – So working with natural light can be one way to connect a building to its site. But the topic of light in museums also brings up an interesting paradox. I think one reason many people think sunlight is ideal for viewing art is because it seems not just natural but neutral. Even describing it as "natural" makes it sound like it has nothing to do with anything man-made—as if it had no connection to architecture at all. But of course you can't just leave a painting out in the sun and call that natural lighting! In fact, the architectural elements that are required to mediate natural light are often extremely sophisticated and complex. The roof of the Menil is a perfect example. The Texas sun doesn't simply pour into the building—you designed curved ferro-cement "leaves," held in place by a steel superstructure, which filter and diffuse that light. This is an ingenious architectural solution, and it's also highly visible from the galleries below. Do you ever find that the materiality and tectonics of your gallery architecture conflict with the vision of artists or curators who simply want museum architecture to disappear?

RP – You are right that there are some people who believe that attention to architecture takes attention away from the art. I don't agree. A white box kills art.

JR – But the white box was invented because curators and artists and viewers complained that architecture was a distraction. Isn't it possible for architecture to be overly assertive?

RP – When it's good, architecture is like an iceberg—you only see a piece of it. But to make that visible piece you need hundreds of people: builders, fabricators, engineers, draftsmen. It's important to make that labor, that craft, visible. I think, unfortunately, that sense has been lost in architecture. People make entire buildings that don't show any trace of their construction. Of course, today we don't make buildings entirely by hand, but you should still be able to see traces of how the building is made, how it comes together piece by piece.

JR – And by revealing only the tip of the iceberg, you're able to show that process without distracting from the building's contents?

RP – Yes, but I don't see a conflict between the architecture of a museum and the experience of viewing art. I don't want to sound moralistic, but, as an architect, when you design a museum, your job is to make a house for art. This is a noble job. When you design a concert hall, you start with sound. You think about noise, vibrations, clarity, how sound will travel through the space, how it will reflect off different materials. In this way, music inspires the design. No one would say that because you are working in the service of music, your freedom as an architect is limited. So, when you make a building for art, it's stupid to believe that you have to do white boxes because that is the only way to show art. And it's just as stupid to believe that you should do a piece of monumental sculpture that overwhelms everything inside of it. You have to accept that you're working for art. That is why thinking about light is so important. That is why working on the perspectives people will have within the space, how people will move through the space, and the sense of conviviality among the visitors is important. I don't see any of these as limitations.

JR – Do you think artists understand your architecture in the same way?

RP – I have many friends who are artists, writers, or musicians. I like talking to them because we all have so much in common. Every discipline has its own language, but the problems of creating are the same. Everyone is connected by the same need for clarity and structure, and the same sense of exploration. Take cinema and architecture, for example—or music. They're all about sequence, about time. It's just that, in architecture, you move through the building. In music or cinema, you remain still, and the sequence unfolds around you.

JR – So you're actually giving two distinct reasons that the museum shouldn't be a site of conflict between art and architecture. First, you're arguing that setting up the right conditions for viewing art is in itself an architectural problem. And it's true that by focusing on the design of lighting systems, of street connections, and so on, you seem to express your own architectural language in a way that doesn't oppose the requirements of exhibiting or viewing art. But your second, more fundamental point is that art and architecture are on separate but parallel tracks, exploring many of the same issues but through different means. Instead of assuming that the work of artists and architects is competing for the same territory, perhaps we should be thinking about how each can extend the other?

RP – That's why when you talk about building, you can't talk just about shapes or styles. It's also how you do it. You don't begin with some conceptual inspiration and then start thinking about nuts and bolts—you think about the two things together. And this is true for everybody. Maurizio Pollini, the great pianist, is a close friend of mine. Every time we talk, we talk about Steinways. You can't disconnect the music from the force of fingers on a keyboard. That is the power of technique: it is the link between idea and execution. Art needs that kind of depth, and so does architecture. That need will always connect them.

DENISE

SCOTT BROWN

JULIAN ROSE — Before we discuss your museum buildings, I'd like to talk about your connections to visual art. The idea of architects learning from artists is nothing new, but it's typically been a matter of architects taking art as an aesthetic model, and this has tended to limit architects' interest to the kinds of art that are easiest to translate into architectural form—for example, abstract painting or sculpture. You, on the other hand, were one of the first architects to take pop art seriously. This was a revolutionary shift from form to content; you recognized that art and architecture could be connected not just by aesthetics but also by a broader set of cultural strategies, and this has opened a whole range of new possibilities for both fields. How did you first become interested in pop? Was it during your time in London as a student in the 1950s, when you encountered the groundbreaking work of the Independent Group?

DENISE SCOTT BROWN – No, no, much earlier. It started with my birth in Africa, or rather with my grandparents' move there, and the two generations of rich cultural influences that I absorbed in my first twenty years of life there.

JR – Well, let's start at the very beginning, then, and we can come back to your student years. When did your family settle in Africa?

DSB – In the 1890s, three of my grandparents left Latvia, and one (my father's father) Lithuania, for Africa. They settled in the Rhodesias, two British colonies, now the nations of Zimbabwe and Zambia. Willie Hepker, my mother's father, bought a one-thousand-acre farm fifteen miles from the town of Bulawayo. Beckie, my mother's mother, was sent as a mail-order bride to marry Willie. Years before, her father had set out for South Africa to prepare a new home for his poverty-stricken family. But yellow fever quickly killed him, and relatives assumed responsibility for the children. So Beckie emigrated at eighteen, a soignée young woman with social grace and domestic skills, whose mettle would soon be tested. Willie, meeting her boat at Cape Town in 1903, fell in love with the poised and beautiful person descending the gangway. Beckie and Willie spent their early life farming, and raising and homeschooling four children.

My pop origins lie in this place, but so does everything else, and isolating it is like parting curds and whey. The fifteen miles of lion country between Bulawayo and their farm meant that visitors were rare, and Beckie was a homemaker and mainstay. She even served as family doctor. And she taught herself Jewish cooking in Rhodesia, much as I, as a foreign student at Penn, studied African housing, or Bob [Venturi], at the American Academy in Rome, read up on the American shingle style. She cultivated, cooked, and made almost everything my family had, including clothing. And, in the "pop" line, she covered paraffin cans with frilled floral chintz fabric to make an elegant bedroom dressing table. What a grand make-do artist!

JR – So there was an ethos of adaptation and reuse in your family that influenced how you later thought about art and architecture?

DSB – Yes, but even more influential was the incredible range of cultures that were mixing and colliding in the South Africa of my youth. Beckie herself, for example, brought a mixture of Jewish, Baltic, and European cultures with her, but she also consciously acculturated to the British way of life. So, whereas she would serve wine to guests as a Latvian, as an English colonial lady she served tea from a silver Georgian teapot made in the late nineteenth century (we still have it) with milk. To give you another example, our piano was one of our prize possessions. It represented the centrality of music in our lives, but it was also a link to Jewish and Eastern European culture that remained important wherever we went. I remember someone saying, "Every Jewish household should have a piano in it." So whether it was Africa, Israel, or anywhere else my relatives settled, there was always a piano to be used by the women of the family. The one in my grandparents' house came by train to the railhead in Bulawayo, then made its final lap to their farm in a wagon drawn by oxen along a riverbed. Shortly thereafter, a storm blew the roof off their house, leaving this prized possession open to the rain.

JR – It sounds like your family has a fascinating background, but I'm interested in hearing more about how this range of influences affected your own development.

DSB – Well, it made me into a thoroughly cross-cultural individual. I was raised in an environment of jarring combinations, contradictory feelings, and many languages. My grandmother knew German, Lettish (her name for Latvian), Russian, English, and French. And in line with upper-class practice in Russia and Courland, where she grew up, she demanded that the English governess she hired for her children also speak French. Both she and my mother also spoke Northern Ndebele, a Bantu language related to Zulu—I, too, speak a few words. When I was young, my mother raised me with French and English nursery rhymes paralleling each other. Plus, my childhood was full of melodious Afrikaans folk songs, mixed with a few Yiddish and German ones from my grandmother, later to be joined by Zionist and Hebrew songs and, when I entered primary school, a slew of Anglican hymns.

Similar cultural mixing was going on all around me. My most vivid impressions derived from local African craftspeople who adapted Western commercial and industrial artifacts lying around them—empty Coca-Cola bottles, for example, that they covered in traditional beadwork.

JR – Pop art is usually discussed in terms of tension between high and low culture. But your example suggests another opposition: between the global and the local, Indigenous craft meets the commodity object. Would you say that is part of what pop means to you?

DSB – Again, my version of pop comes from all these different cultures and legacies. And you might think my discovery of pop was about moving away from modernism, but it's not quite that simple because all these influences came alongside another one that may surprise you: very mainstream modernism.

JR – That does surprise me. What do you mean?

DSB – You see, my mother studied architecture in South Africa, and she was part of this little group of disciples of Le Corbusier. She never got her degree, but one of her classmates, Norman Hanson, became a successful architect, and he designed a house for my parents. My family moved there when I was four, in 1935. It was probably the second international style house in Johannesburg. And even at a very young age, I could tell how different it was. In a traditional house, the door handles are about three feet high, which means you can reach them as a three-year-old. But I had to wait until I was five, because in our house the doors had steel lever handles up at four-foot-something. And although I had no attic to play in, I had an enormous flat roof to explore.

JR – I have to admit I've never thought about Le Corbusier's obsession with flat roofs from a child's point of view, but it sounds wonderful. Modernism wasn't an abstract idea for you, then; it was something concrete and personal, something that you lived with. Can you explain how this early connection to modernism influenced your subsequent architectural education?

DSB – It certainly did impact my architectural education, but there were stepping-stones between the two. My mother, my sister Ruth, and I shared an interest in art in all forms—music, dance, and especially painting. I would spend hours paging through my mother's coffee-table books, mainly of impressionists and post-impressionists. My mother took us to exhibitions, too, and I noticed that many European refugee artists who painted African subjects were producing picturesque scenes that looked just like the European impressionists. But there was a Dutch Jewish refugee, Roza van Gelderen, who held classes for children that I joined. She was a social realist, and she said, "You will not be artists if you don't paint what's around you." That was a very important lesson.

JR – And then you went on to study architecture at the University of Witwatersrand in Johannesburg?

DSB – Yes, the same university where my mother had studied in the 1920s.

JR – Was it unusual for a woman to be enrolled in architecture at the time?

DSB – In retrospect, yes. But to me, because my mother had done it, it wasn't unusual. I grew up thinking architecture was women's work. When I entered the first year, there were only five women in my class. And I remember looking around the studio and thinking, What are all these men doing here?

JR – It's extraordinary that you had such an example to follow! When you moved to London in 1952 to continue your studies at the Architectural Association [AA], what new influences did you encounter there?

DSB – None at the beginning. England, as the head of the British Empire, had already deeply affected me as a South African. The BBC had been our chief source of news during the war, which we, too, were fighting, and our school textbooks and most other books sold in South Africa were published in England. But at the AA, I began to look more deeply into the history of architecture. I took the course John Summerson offered on classicism twice, because I was learning so much from it, and I met the great historian Nikolaus Pevsner through him. I was particularly fascinated by mannerism, which Pevsner had written about. After I graduated from the AA in 1955, I traveled in Europe with Robert Scott Brown, my first husband, carrying a copy of Pevsner's *An Outline of European Architecture* [1943] and a long list prepared for us by my friend Robin Middleton, who was doing his dissertation under Pevsner, of every mannerist building and painting we would pass between England and Rome.

JR – I imagine you were learning not only about history, though, given the radical developments in London's art and architecture scenes at the time. I know you met Peter and Alison Smithson, the trailblazing advocates of new brutalist architecture who were key members of the Independent Group. Did you encounter other members of that group as well?

DSB – Absolutely. The Smithsons' housing studies of London were very important to me. And from the Independent Group I also got to know Reyner Banham very well—he invited me to call him Peter, as his close friends did—and Eduardo Paolozzi, who had been doing his collages since the late 1940s, so that was very early pop art.

JR – Given that you've used exhibitions so effectively to present your own research—I'm thinking particularly of *Signs of Life: Symbols in the American City*, which you organized at the Smithsonian in 1976—I'm curious to know if you saw the Smithsons' famous exhibitions, *Parallel of Life and Art* at the Institute of Contemporary Arts in London in 1953 and *This Is Tomorrow* at the Whitechapel Gallery in 1956?

DSB – Yes, I saw both, and they helped me see how new perspectives on urbanism were needed to rebuild Europe after the Second World War. But you have missed an important group also connected to new brutalism, which was Team 10, made up of young members of CIAM [Congrès Internationaux d'Architecture Moderne] who were in revolt. They were very young and idealistic like us. At this time, almost everyone in architecture faced its problems via urbanism, and many wanted to study in the United States, where urbanism was considered to have been given more thought than in Europe. So Robert and I planned to go to the United States. Peter Smithson, while not employed by the AA, was frequently in the studio and took a liking to Robert. He recommended that if we were to study in America we should go to Penn [University of Pennsylvania], because Lou Kahn was there.

JR – But you studied both architecture and planning at Penn, correct?

DSB – Yes, I got full master's degrees in both architecture and planning. Robert and I felt it was crucial to study planning because we thought we were going to go back to South Africa to participate in building a more just nation. Lou was not teaching planning, but he could see why I was going to study it if I was going back to South Africa. But Robert was killed in a car accident in 1959, and that changed everything. All my advisers encouraged me to finish my degrees, so I did, and the next semester I stayed at Penn and began teaching. I got the students thinking about the way urban patterns were formed by social, economic, and physical forces. And my required readings were also generously laden with works by the Smithsons and Team 10, neither of which were known by the student body or the faculty. There were many social movements beginning then, and everyone fought and learned and fought and learned. Herbert Gans was teaching at Penn during that time, and he was so important for giving me a proper view of sociology. My connection to that field continued with people like William L. C. Wheaton, who founded the Institute for Urban Studies at Penn and later was head of the College of Environmental Design at Berkeley. He said to us one day, "Why do architects design public spaces that people don't use? Why don't you go to Las Vegas and try to understand why people like it there?" So our entry into pop was also based on social questions, not only love of art.

JR – You conducted your research in Las Vegas with Robert Venturi. Did you meet him while teaching at Penn?

DSB – Yes. At one of our faculty meetings, the topic of demolishing Frank Furness's Fine Arts Library building came up. There was a lot of argument back and forth, but I made a very passionate case to save the building, and eventually the whole architecture school faculty voted against demolition. Bob came up to me afterward and said, "I absolutely agreed with what you said about the Furness building. My name is Robert Venturi." So the first thing I said to him was, "Well why didn't you say something then?"

And that became sort of a joke between us, because Bob never used to speak. He was very, very shy early in his career, although eventually he got so keen on what he was doing that he stopped being shy.

JR – Obviously you shared an interest in historic preservation from the start; was pop art also a common interest? There is some discussion of pop in both your and Venturi's writings from the 1960s, and it comes up in *Learning from Las Vegas,* which you wrote together with Steven Izenour and published in 1972.

DSB – Bob and I used to play a game called "I Can Like Something Uglier than You Can Like." That was part of how we started to think about learning from things like storefronts and signs and Main Street. Looking at pop art was part of that. It was about taking popular culture and the everyday American landscape as seriously as Herbert Gans did.

JR – Can I hear more about your encounters with American pop art? I see how your friendship with the Smithsons would have led you directly to the British pop of the fifties, but in the early sixties American pop art was far from mainstream—it's not like you could just stroll into the Philadelphia Museum of Art and see a pop show. I know that one of the first group exhibitions of pop art in America—including Jasper Johns, Roy Lichtenstein, and Claes Oldenburg, among others—was at the Young Men's and Young Women's Hebrew Association in downtown Philadelphia in 1962. Did you see it?

DSB – Yes, although I'm surprised you know about that show because I think not that many people remember it. But I had been going to the Venice Biennale since the 1950s and first saw American pop art in an Italian government exhibition of emerging pop artists from various countries.

JR – There wasn't a single formative encounter, in other words.

DSB – My really formative encounters were with African folk pop. The Smithsons' interests in English and American pop and in mannerism caused me to take my first photographs of billboards, in Natal, on a visit home to South Africa in 1957. Long before I got to America I was already interested in the everyday, and in Philadelphia I had been photographing vernacular architecture and advertising and things like that since I arrived. I had a small single-lens reflex camera that I learned to use while traveling in Europe in the 1950s. Photography had become part of my way of seeing the world.

JR – Speaking of photography, how did you discover Ed Ruscha? You illustrated your 1969 article "On Pop Art, Permissiveness, and Planning" with images from three of his now-legendary books— *Thirtyfour Parking Lots* [1967], *Twentysix Gasoline Stations* [1963], and *Some Los Angeles Apartments* [1965]. Your text appeared in the *Journal of the American Institute of Planners*, and I've always been fascinated by the collision between this buttoned-up, academic publication and Ruscha's avant-garde work. Particularly given that he was still relatively unknown, using his work in that context seems, for lack of more scholarly terminology, very cool.

DSB – Well, I started teaching at UCLA in 1965, and there was a nice bookstore on my way to the university from Santa Monica where I lived. I used to stop there, and I found those little books of his. And by the way, they're worth a fortune now! I'm glad I kept them.

JR – It's a good thing you did! So you looked him up after coming across his books?

DSB – When Bob Venturi and I taught the Learning from Las Vegas studio at Yale in 1968, we and our students stopped in Los Angeles before going on to Las Vegas. And I called Ruscha and said I'd like to bring my students to meet him.

JR – Was it a productive visit?

DSB – He was very friendly and nice, but quite young and didn't really know what to say to them. I think he liked playing the dumb

Robert Venturi, Denise Scott Brown, and Steven Izenour, *Signs of Life: Symbols in the American City*, Renwick Gallery, Smithsonian Institution, Washington, DC, 1976

artist. Eventually they solved it with a large quantity of beer. They all drank beer, and I left.

JR – Another well-known artist that you had an early collaboration with is Stephen Shore, who took the photos for your 1976 Smithsonian exhibition. Shore was undeniably precocious—he was taking photos in Andy Warhol's factory at age sixteen. But, when you worked with him, he still hadn't exhibited widely, and he hadn't yet published any of his famous books. How did you find him?

DSB – By the time we were working on that exhibition, I had gotten so involved in our architectural projects that I couldn't do photography. Steven Izenour, who had been our teaching assistant for the Yale studio and coauthored *Learning from Las Vegas* with us, was very interested in photography, and he started looking for people to work on the exhibition. He's the one who found Shore, and he also found John Bader, who does paintings that look very photographic. We had both of them traveling around the country, paid for by the Smithsonian—or really paid for by us because the Smithsonian money ran out very soon.

JR – Were you interested in the work of people like Shore or Bader—or Ruscha—as pop art in itself, or did you see it primarily as a form of documentation? In other words, were you more interested in the images or the things they depicted?

DSB – Well, I certainly saw it was art, but it was also very much in a long documentary tradition. I love the American photographers of the Depression era—people like Dorothea Lange and Walker Evans—and I saw the new work we were exhibiting in *Signs of Life* as connected to that.

JR – The year that your Smithsonian exhibition opened, 1976, was also the year you completed your first museum building: a major addition to the Allen Memorial Art Museum at Oberlin, a 1917 neo-Renaissance design by Cass Gilbert. There's a good case to be made that your project was the first-ever postmodern museum, in that you incorporated historical references that connected your addition to the existing structure. To my knowledge, it was years before any other architect tried something similar.

DSB – But I think you may be misunderstanding, because the piece we added on was a modernist box, more or less. It was a great big, long shed.

JR – Well, I'm thinking specifically of the oversize column you placed at the back corner—the "ironic ionic," as it's been dubbed. But I take your point that the design is not explicitly historicist. I suppose what I'm really getting at is that your design seems to make a concerted effort to harmonize with the classical style of the existing building. Your stone facade incorporates decorative patterns that reference the original building in terms of color and texture, for example. That marks a clear shift from the approach taken by someone like, say, Gordon Bunshaft in his 1962 addition to the Albright-Knox Art Gallery. He slapped down a sleek box of black glass next to a 1905 Greek revival building clad in white stone— the contrast could hardly be more extreme, and that was often the modernist approach to dealing with historical structures.

DSB – There is a great big Greek column clad in wood, which you see at the back of the new gallery we added. It's outside, but you see it through a window—very bold. That was the gallery where they put their contemporary art, which included some pop paintings and sculpture, so the column was sort of in conversation with those works. I was not so involved in that aspect of the design.

I was very much involved in trying to work out how we wanted to get these two structures clashing but also relating; we wanted to get a pattern on the one that was like, but also not like, the other. You see, the program was quite complicated. As well as the new gallery, they needed a fine arts library, a conservation lab, and studio space. So it was quite a feat to get this new building, which was by necessity quite large, to fit together with the old. We had this big problem with the roof, because it was going to be terribly, terribly

Venturi, Scott Brown and Associates, Allen Memorial
Art Museum expansion, Oberlin, Ohio, 1977

complex to interrupt the sloped terra-cotta roof of the existing
building. I'm proudest of the contribution I made when I saw
that we could take the roof of our new gallery and lift it up above
the eaves of the existing building, but still keep our height lower
than the crown of the old roof. So the two structures are kind of
interlocked, and it's quite wonderful.

Venturi, Scott Brown and Associates, Allen Memorial Art
Museum expansion, Oberlin, Ohio, 1977

JR – The curator of modern art at the Allen Museum, Ellen
Johnson, was a well-known art historian who became something
of a legend for her early support of many pop artists who would
become internationally famous. Did you meet her while working
on the project?

DSB – Well, yes—our contemporary art gallery is named in
her honor! But she had also commissioned an important work from
Claes Oldenburg, *Giant Three-Way Plug* [1970], and they decided
to put it on the pathway to our building. It's a nice place for it.

JR – Your next major museum was the Sainsbury Wing of the
National Gallery in London. That project presented a problem
similar to the one you faced in Oberlin—combining a new building
with a historical structure—but with much higher stakes: it's one of
the most visited museums in Europe, located in the heart of London.
How did you get involved?

DSB – Well, there was a whole competition for an expansion
of the National Gallery in 1982, and the winning entry was in a
high-tech style that was quite a sharp contrast to William Wilkins's
neoclassical building from 1838. Prince Charles, as he was then, had
what the English call a wobbly, which means a temper tantrum. He
looked at that steel-and-glass thing and said, "What is proposed is
like a monstrous carbuncle on the face of a much loved and elegant
friend." And then the whole world fell apart. There was a huge

uproar and endless discussion about what should be done—should the design go ahead, should a new one be chosen, and so on. Someone wrote an article comparing how different architects would tackle it, saying so-and-so would do this, so-and-so would do that, but of course they didn't mention us. I remember reading it and thinking, Hold on—I studied under Summerson, I know a lot about classicism and mannerism, we've already designed a museum, and we've done several museum exhibitions: the Smithsonian show and also *200 Years of American Sculpture*, which we did in 1976 for Tom Armstrong when he was director of the Whitney.

JR – Which was another project that involved some complex historical juxtapositions. You had artists like David Smith and Donald Judd alongside everything from Hopi artifacts to New England weather vanes.

DSB – Exactly. And so I began to think, They just don't know what we can do. I was getting crosser and crosser, and eventually one of my former students asked, "Why don't you call Jacob Rothschild?" At that time he was the chair of the National Gallery's board of trustees. So I did. I was visiting my parents, who had moved to Switzerland, and I was thinking about stopping in London on my way home. Rothschild told me that he wouldn't be there but that the director and the assistant keeper would be, and that I should talk to them. I did, and it was a great success. They told me that they happened to have a team in New York interviewing architects and asked if Bob and I would come up from Philadelphia to be interviewed. We did that, and then eventually they held a second competition, an invited one, and we produced something they liked very much.

JR – In addition to your experience with museums and exhibitions, you had a deep connection to London from your time as a student. Did that influence your approach to the National Gallery?

DSB – Of course! When I got to England, I had to be in school all week. I used to go to museums on Sundays, and they were terribly crowded; I would be trying to look at paintings while I was being swept along in a phalanx fifteen people abreast. So when we were working on our design, we educated the board. They didn't know what it was like to see the museum on a busy weekend, and I don't know if they understood the importance of urban outreach.

JR – It sounds like you saw the museum in part as an urban design problem. Did your experience in planning influence that perspective?

DSB – Certainly. It's a public building, so the question is how to shape it so that the public can flow through it. We thought of it as a kind of transportation problem. In the fall of 1967, Bob and I had taught a studio at Yale together that analyzed the New York City subway. And that was inspired partly by what we had seen at the Expo in Montreal that spring. I wrote an analysis of the Expo for the *Journal of the American Institute of Planners* ["Planning the Expo," July 1967], and I talked about how most of the shows were designed so that you couldn't see them at all, because the pavilions simply weren't planned to deal with such masses of people. We learned quite a few things from looking at crowds, and that's how we came up with the circulation system for our design. We called it a people freeway going through the building.

JR – The Sainsbury Wing was designed to house the National Gallery's early Renaissance paintings, including very famous works like Piero della Francesca's *The Baptism of Christ*, from 1437–1445. That's a far cry from Oldenburg and the other contemporary artists you were designing space for at Oberlin. Do you see the National Gallery as connected to this pop trail we've been tracing through your work? Is it a pop building?

DSB – Yes, and it is many other things as well. It's a pop building in the sense that it considers the populace—it's a building that takes usage, connectivity, and necessity into account, as any great museum should. We wanted people to use the building in many different ways—to spend a whole day there or to down a quick

Venturi, Scott Brown and Associates, Sainsbury Wing,
National Gallery, London, UK, 1991.

lunch, then view their favorite painting. We wanted Trafalgar Square
to assert its new identity in relation to the museum and what they
offered each other. And, in the galleries, we wanted the sky outside
and its changes to register, and Lord Nelson and his column to
be visible from within and without. And I love the way our building's motherly arms welcome the crowds in Trafalgar Square.
Recently, there was a protest against Trump and the whole square
was full, with people pressed right up against the museum.

JR – What about the historical references incorporated into
your design?

DSB – Well, in many ways the design reflected our personal
experience with the history of architecture. We learned lessons in
lighting from the Dulwich Picture Gallery by Sir John Soane. And
we were thinking about Palladianism, both in Italy, its country of
origin, and in Europe, America, and parts of the British Empire.
We were especially influenced by Italian palazzos we had visited that

Venturi, Scott Brown and Associates, Sainsbury Wing,
National Gallery, London, UK, 1991

had been converted to galleries, where intriguing parts of the city peeked out between window curtains. This amalgam of national styles was influenced as well by my two months of living and photographing in Venice when I was there for a CIAM conference in 1956. From the young Italian architects I met there, I learned about the great palazzos, which had formal entrances reached by gondola on the Grand Canal and working entrances served by sandoli, smaller boats for the delivery of services. I saw, too, how the Venetian floods caused the piano nobile to be well above the water, and I studied the stairs that connected the ground floor, where merchandise was often stored, with the living areas above.

In the Sainsbury Wing, Bob and I tried to imitate the skill with which the relationships of scale and circulation were handled in these buildings. We also studied the joining of the spectacular front facades to more workmanlike buildings behind. The broad stair that connects the Trafalgar Square entrance to the elevated walkway linking the Sainsbury Wing to the Wilkins Building—which we called, in another Venetian reference, the Bridge of Sighs—was the trickiest part. It stumped us until Bob had the idea of borrowing a baroque device that Edwin Lutyens had used for a bank in the City of London, giving the stairway a diagonal shape in plan that produces a trompe l'oeil deception as you climb it. Unfortunately, the board has recently supported changes that scratch away at our design, and since the Sainsbury Wing is one of my best-known works, I feel this is a sad end to my career. I'm still fighting hard to save it.

JR – But surely your legacy goes far beyond your buildings: You've produced an incredible range of writing and thinking about architecture. And many scholars and critics are continuing to explore your pioneering role in the field. Looking back over the press coverage of the National Gallery opening in 1991, I was shocked to see the building almost universally described as designed exclusively by Robert Venturi, despite the fact that your name is right there in the name of the firm hired to create it: Venturi, Scott Brown and Associates! I can't see anyone describing the National Gallery in this way today. Certainly, our understanding of your work has shifted, and indeed the whole field of architecture has shifted, thanks in part to you.

DSB – My legacy is showing now. The architectural historian Frida Grahn recently put together a beautiful book called *Denise Scott Brown in Other Eyes: Portraits of an Architect*, a collection of twenty-two perspectives on my works. It covered my architecture, planning, and education projects and was published in 2022 to mark the fiftieth anniversary of *Learning from Las Vegas*. I'm happy that so many people want to continue the conversation.

KAZUYO

SEJIMA

JULIAN ROSE – A conversation about museums is also, inevitably, a conversation about the relationship between art and architecture more generally, so I'd like to begin by asking you about your first encounters with visual art. Was art part of your curriculum as an architecture student? Were there artists whom you admired as a young architect or who influenced the development of your practice?

KAZUYO SEJIMA – Not at all. In Japan, architecture and engineering are closely linked and are normally taught in the same schools, but art is separate. Only a few art schools have architecture departments, and they're very small. That is gradually changing, but here architecture is still more associated with industry than with art.

JR – I'm surprised to hear that, because the materiality of your work reflects what could be called, for lack of a better term, an artistic sensibility. Your use of glass, especially, involves extremely subtle and sophisticated plays on the relationship between physical movement and visual perception. And, presumably for that reason, critics have linked your buildings to the work of artists such as Donald Judd and Dan Graham. But of course their work, in turn, could be said to address fundamentally architectural problems, so there is no reason you would have necessarily arrived at your current practice through visual art. It sounds as though your first training with materials like glass, aluminum, and steel was practical, even scientific.

KS – Yes, purely technical. I didn't have much experience with art until I started designing museums.

JR – At what point in your career did you begin doing that?

KS – The 21st Century Museum of Contemporary Art in Kanazawa was the first big museum that Ryue Nishizawa, my partner in SANAA, and I did. It opened in 2004, and the competition was a few years earlier. But before that there were some smaller projects for exhibition spaces, like the N-Museum in

Wakayama [1997]. There, the client asked for just one very small gallery to show the work of painters from the area. Traditional Japanese paintings are very sensitive to sunlight, so the main function of the gallery was to protect the works.

JR – Many museums want to bring as much natural light as possible into their galleries, but in this case you had to keep it out.

KS – The main gallery became a concrete box. It was very generic. But if the same concrete volume had become the facade it would have been unfriendly, so we surrounded the box with a glass corridor that is large enough that it becomes a public space in itself, to be used by the local people.

JR – Inventive interchanges between circulation space and gallery space are a hallmark of your museum designs. Often architects try to either hybridize them—as in the familiar enfilade of most neoclassical museum buildings—or separate them completely, which usually results in vast galleries with stairs and corridors pushed to the perimeter, as in the Pompidou Centre or other open-plan museums. In Wakayama, it sounds like your approach to this relationship evolved from the exhibition requirements of that specific collection.

Kanazawa is a museum explicitly dedicated to contemporary art, which is more amorphous. What did you know about the collection, and how did that knowledge inform your approach to the design?

KS – Yuko Hasegawa, the museum's chief curator and founding director, was deeply involved from the beginning. We learned a lot about contemporary art while working with her. But we also learned that our principal role was to understand the relation between the building and the art and to think about that relation in terms of the visitor's experience. For example, when you walk through a museum, sometimes you want to go back to see one piece again. It's a little bit boring to simply retrace your steps, so we considered connecting the gallery spaces in many different ways. It was an interesting challenge. Of course, if the design gets too complicated, that is also problematic.

JR – So you saw your role less as responding directly to the art than as framing its relationship to the viewer and, in the process, finding a balance between simplicity and complexity.

KS – Yes. In that way, a museum building should be like a city. It's boring to immediately understand everything. But it should not be impossible to understand, either. Every time you go back, you should get to know it a little better.

JR – That's a particularly good analogy in the case of Kanazawa, because there is not just a variety of pathways through the building but also a mix of private and public spaces, including amenities for the community. Were some of your conversations with the curator also about how to make it feel more accessible?

KS – The 21st Century Museum is a public institution. As is typical for a building like this in Japan, the program was defined by the local government. At the time of the competition, more than twenty years ago, contemporary art was still not very popular in Japan. There were many citizens who might protest spending money on that. So the government decided to make two buildings on the site, one a museum and one a kind of community center. We proposed to combine the two, and we won the competition.

JR – That's beautiful, but it also sounds almost paradoxical. How did you mix those elements within one building?

KS – It's not like a gallery is always quiet and a public space is always busy. It's strange to create such a sharp distinction. And also, for us, the museum's focus on contemporary art meant that it should somehow be connected to contemporary society. So we tried to mix the gallery and the circulation, increasing the proportion of circulation space until the two were almost equal. At that point, it was not really circulation space anymore, but an area that could be used in different ways. Architecturally, our solution was to make a circular glass building, with public programs—a lecture hall, a library, a workshop—all around the facade. The perimeter is transparent, so it feels open, and there are four entrances to invite people into the

SANAA, 21st Century Museum of Contemporary Art, Kanazawa, Japan, 2004

building from all different directions. You don't have to pay the admission fee until you get into the center of the circle, which is the museum zone.

JR – And the galleries themselves are pavilions, essentially small freestanding buildings within the outer glass circle. Were these structures simply a response to the necessity to create wall space? There is a long history of attempts to exhibit artworks in transparent buildings, and they've usually been unsuccessful. In Mies van der Rohe's Neue Nationalgalerie in Berlin, the iconic transparent volume is really just an entry pavilion, with more traditional gallery space on the ground level below. Lina Bo Bardi famously invented glass easels to show paintings in her Museu de Arte de São Paulo, but they have rarely been used. In Kanazawa, were these gallery pavilions your way of reconciling the desire for transparency with the needs of the museum?

KS – It was also a way of introducing diversity into the exhibition space. The galleries have different shapes and different proportions—even different heights, ranging from thirteen feet to thirty-nine feet. And because all the galleries are independent, it makes the entire building more flexible. The curators can redefine the "museum zone" for every exhibition, changing which space is free and which space you pay admission to enter. They can also change how you enter the exhibition and how you move through it.

JR – That's fascinating, because it seems like you've invented a new approach to flexibility. Architects and curators are always talking about how important it is to have flexible spaces in a museum, but that is usually defined at the scale of the individual gallery—say, with movable partitions. You're providing flexibility across the building as a whole.

KS – We defined the plan, but artists and curators can develop it further. There is an opportunity for the architecture to be created through use.

JR – I want to return to the question of transparency. You mentioned the need to balance simplicity and complexity in planning your buildings' circulation, and I wonder if there is a similar balance that you have to achieve in phenomenological terms. You don't just use glass to create transparency—often you layer it or curve it to produce reflections and other visual effects that make the experience of moving through your buildings very complex. Is there a point where this begins to compete with the art?

KS – In the case of Kanazawa, there were some limits. We couldn't achieve what we originally proposed, which was to have windows in the gallery pavilions themselves, to make visual connections among them. The curator asked us to make them opaque: no windows, only skylights. Some of the other programs—the conference room, the lecture hall—are in glass enclosures. In the Glass Pavilion we did for the Toledo Museum of Art in Ohio [2006], we had more freedom, because the space is mainly for exhibiting glass works. So that meant we could think of the museum itself as part of the exhibition.

SANAA, Glass Pavilion, Toledo Museum of Art, Toledo, Ohio, 2006

JR – That building is similar to Kanazawa, in that a cluster of galleries is contained within an outer glass skin. But in Toledo the interior rooms themselves are also made of glass. Did that design similarly begin with a desire to mix gallery and circulation space?

KS – In Toledo, we started by trying to avoid circulation entirely. We began with a grid of gallery spaces. Then we looked at how we could open the points of intersection so that different spaces would be directly connected, making one big gallery. All the spaces are made by manipulating this grid.

We also tried to make all the interior walls out of glass, so from inside one gallery you can see into others and also outside to the city beyond. But we couldn't connect everything. We needed buffer zones. The curators wanted to include fabrication facilities so visitors could learn about the process of glassmaking. This process requires a lot of heat, so it needs a buffer zone around it. And then the gallery needs to be an even more stable environment than the buffer zone, to protect the objects.

JR – So you're layering space not just visually or programmatically but also environmentally to create different climate zones within the building.

KS – And the interesting thing is that the many transparent layers begin to affect the light in different ways, so as you move through the building the glass changes its character, becoming more and more reflective, to the point that you cannot see through it at all. After many layers, even the transparent becomes opaque.

JR – So you can build up opaque boundaries through these strata of glass. It's almost like you're creating a horizon, or multiple horizons, within the building—in a sense, you're actually shaping and separating spaces through effects that at first seem purely visual.

KS – Right, and the different spaces are still related. Each space is always influenced by the space around it.

JR – In both Kanazawa and Toledo, then, thinking about how the visitor moves through the space was a key starting point. Was that also the case with the New Museum of Contemporary Art in New York [2007], which you must have been designing at around the same time? That's a multistory building on an urban site, so movement—at least in the horizontal direction—is very limited.

KS – Yes, the site of the New Museum is very small. The only way to go was up. That means we needed to think about both horizontal and vertical circulation. But at the time we were working on the design, the neighboring buildings were still very low. From the beginning we knew that our building would need to be very high, so we tried to articulate separate volumes and then stack them and shift them as they moved up. This allowed the building to retain a similar scale to its neighbors. The shifting also means that boxes can open on the top or the sides to bring in light or to create terraces.

JR – Did the curators resist any of this?

KS – At first, the curators asked for closed boxes. But we proposed that if the boxes opened, they could start to communicate. Our idea was not only to bring light in but also to allow an exchange between inside and outside. We wanted visitors to enjoy the views, the site, the city all around, and we also wanted to show the public on the street that something is happening inside the museum.

JR – When it came to setting the galleries' dimensions and proportions, did you have specific works in mind? You must have been facing a similar problem to the one presented by Kanazawa— this museum's mission is to exhibit the new, which is by definition unknown.

KS – Again, we tried to create a variety of spaces within the museum and, more importantly, many ways you can move through it. Sometimes people can use a stairway along the perimeter, and sometimes they can use the central one. Sometimes the space in front of the elevator is for circulation, and sometimes it becomes

SANAA, New Museum of Contemporary Art, New York, New York, 2007

incorporated into the gallery. We also tried to think about how it would be possible to divide the space and still have good proportions, whether it's making one gallery into two or one into seven. So it's very diverse. But in the end we realized that the curators will still view the space in ways that we did not anticipate—and that's really interesting.

JR – In all the projects we've discussed so far, you seem to maintain a certain distance from the art that will be exhibited in the spaces you designed; you treat it almost as an abstraction. You created containers for art that curators could use in many different ways, and then you focused your own efforts on exploring how visitors can move through and between these spaces.

I'd like to ask about your work for Benesse Holdings on the island of Inujima, Japan, where you have been involved with something called the Art House Project. It seems to involve more direct collaboration with artists. How did that begin?

KS – There are many islands in that region, which is in the Seto Inland Sea. The island of Naoshima was the starting point for Benesse, where they built the Chichu Art Museum [2004] and the Benesse House Museum [1992] with Tadao Ando. We designed a ferry terminal there in 2006. And then Benesse asked me to think about Inujima, which was challenging because it's a remote, tiny island. In the early twentieth century, there was a copper refinery operating on the island, and the population was around three thousand, but now only about thirty people live there. Our client's idea was to revitalize the remaining village by introducing art projects. Yuko Hasegawa, whom we had worked with on the Kanazawa museum, was the project's artistic director. There were many empty houses in the village, and we began by thinking about which ones we could transform into galleries. The idea was not to have any permanent works or exhibitions but only a series of temporary installations.

JR – How was that different from designing a museum?

KS – Even in a normal museum—Kanazawa, for example—
the exhibitions need to be changed from time to time. But the
curators do not want to show that transformation in progress,
so as architects we must think of how to hide it, to create behind-
the-scenes space that allows these processes to be invisible. In the
beginning, at Inujima, we believed that we would have to disguise
the transformations, perhaps by altering the pathways people would
take around the houses we were changing into galleries. But in a
village it's impossible to hide anything. And eventually we realized
that it's nice to show the transformations: the process of converting
a house into a gallery or changing an installation should be exposed.
And the people in the village, or the visitors who come to see the
project, can enjoy this.

JR – Then the construction becomes part of the work?

KS – And also part of the community. The first thing we did
was transform four houses into galleries, and a crew of artists and
workers stayed for a month or so to install the inaugural exhibitions.
It took maybe ten people to do this, and so for a time the population
of the village increased from thirty to forty. But after the opening
party and a period of intense activity, they disappeared, and the
village was suddenly quiet and sad. So we wanted to make the
process more continuous, with people living in the village and
artists working and the transformations ongoing.

JR – So the project has become integrated into the daily life of
the village. Did that affect your choice of materials and construction
techniques? The first galleries were all transformations of traditional
houses, correct?

KS – Yes. But even the wooden houses I tried to make transparent, so that visitors can enjoy the art in relation to the existing
context. Again, in the beginning Yuko insisted that the galleries
should have walls, but eventually she agreed that transparency could
work, because this is a very special situation. And the artists can

create their installations specifically for these spaces—they know there are no walls.

JR – You also did a transparent pavilion on the island?

KS – Yes, it's two walls of Plexiglas, and art is installed between them. We started with the houses, but some of them were in such poor condition that they couldn't be transformed, so I decided to build this pavilion, to create something new. But I realized that the important thing with any construction on this island, new or old, is that it must be made with small pieces. There is no large-scale construction equipment on the island, so even modern materials like Plexiglas or aluminum still need to be brought to the island in small pieces that can be connected by hand. So there will be some continuity, even if the materials are different, between the new and the old, because the construction technique is similar.

JR – It's interesting that you began by talking about the Kanazawa museum building as functioning like a city, because now you're describing a literal transformation of a village into a museum.

KS – In our early work, we were very interested in the program of the building, in understanding the social aspects of what happens inside. But now I think the program itself is not as important as connecting the building to the environment, to its surroundings.

JR – Is that a lesson that came specifically from museum design?

KS – I think so. Of course, we are interested in different building types, but we have had many opportunities to think about museums. And a museum is best when it is part of public life.

ANNABELLE

SELLDORF

JULIAN ROSE – You grew up in Cologne, a city with a legendary art scene, and you've spoken about its influence on your work. But you left after high school to study architecture in the United States. How did you come into contact with Cologne's radical art at such a young age?

ANNABELLE SELLDORF – It goes back to my parents, who were very much part of that scene. They were friends with artists such as Hann Trier and Joseph Fassbender, who had started the Donnerstag-Gesellschaft [Thursday Group] after the Second World War to promote modern art in Germany—Joseph Beuys and many other important figures were involved. My childhood in the late 1960s and early 1970s coincided with a very dynamic period in the city, and I grew up looking at art and being around artists. There were these artists' associations that would bring together painters and photographers and writers and musicians for exhibitions and events. These people were my parents' friends, so naturally we would go. We would go to museums and galleries, too. Galerie der Spiegel [the Mirror Gallery] was right in the heart of the city, and it was a sort of outpost for artists like Victor Vasarely, who was famous then as one of the founders of op art. A friend of mine worked for Heiner Friedrich's gallery, so I would go there, and I would be this fourteen-year-old kid hanging out in a Dan Flavin light installation or something.

JR – That's amazing.

AS – But it wasn't amazing for me then—it was simply what we did. I wouldn't even say that art was a particular interest of mine. It was just part of life. And then, of course, when I became a teenager, going to openings was cool: standing on the street outside the gallery and drinking beer, which is what one does in Cologne.

JR – Right, I can see how that would appeal to a teenager! What did your parents do that brought them into contact with so many artists?

AS – My father was an architect, but he was not academically trained. I believe this exists in America as well, but in Germany you can become licensed on the basis of having practiced for a certain period rather than having a degree from an architecture school. And he was a practitioner in the true sense of the word—he did all the drawings for every one of his projects himself. My mother had gone to art school, and she became an interior designer. She worked with my father, advising on some of his projects, and she also had some of her own clients.

JR – Was it unusual for them, as an architect and an interior designer, to be so close to practicing artists? In other words, were there a lot of connections between architecture and design and the visual arts in Cologne at that time?

AS – I think my father was a bit unusual in the sense that he was definitely *not* in the architecture scene. He hadn't gone to university to study architecture, and as a result those were not the people he was in dialogue with.

JR – That suggests that the art scene was more informal and fluid, and probably more welcoming, which certainly fits the free-wheeling ethos of Fluxus and other movements that were developing in Germany at the time. Looking back, how do you feel that this time spent in museums and galleries informed your own approach once you started to design exhibition spaces for art?

AS – It didn't register with me consciously at the time, but there was a building in Cologne designed by Rudolf Schwarz for the Wallraf-Richartz-Museum—it still exists, but now it's the Museum of Applied Arts [Museum für Angewandte Kunst]—that I think did everything a good museum building should do. It was built in 1957, and it's an unassuming modernist building. The entrance is very modest, and you pass through a low-ceilinged reception area into an open communal space. On one side, there's a glass wall with doors leading out into a courtyard garden, and on the other side there is a large staircase leading to the exhibition spaces, which, on the top floor, have north-facing skylights. The rooms are very well proportioned. There are places to rest and windows that orient you. The circulation allows you to make a loop, so you never have to retrace your steps. It's all very simple, but it's really deep in my memory.

JR – What was its most important lesson for you?

AS – That it was possible for a building to give you a sense of freedom and a sense of orientation at the same time. You're never lost, but you also never feel coerced to follow a particular path. In that way, the visitors are central to the design, and I think that's one of the fundamental values that architecture can bring to a museum.

JR – What did you think of the art inside? Today the Wallraf-Richartz is known primarily for its medieval and Renaissance collections, but you would have been visiting before the Museum Ludwig had moved into a separate building in the 1980s, so I imagine you saw modern and contemporary art there, too.

AS – Yes, the Ludwig collection was focused on contemporary American art, and it's one of the greatest collections of pop art in the world. There was a big Jasper Johns flag hanging in the stairwell. The galleries were full of Rauschenberg, Warhol, Lichtenstein—you name it. That art was formative for me in almost a textbook kind of way. There was this fantasy of America present in those works that was so different from the older European art in the rest of the museum. I think the Ludwig collection eventually prompted a new building because it overshadowed the historical collection—which is, by the way, also fantastic, but it can't compete directly with the scale and color and graphic quality of pop.

JR – The combination of those two collections within one building does sound almost like an allegory—the New World versus the Old. Was that fantastical vision of America part of why you wanted to go to architecture school in New York?

AS – Well, it wasn't so linear. My path to architecture was a little bit circuitous. In Germany, when you finish high school, you usually go straight on to university, and by that time you are already supposed to have chosen your profession. There's no such thing as a liberal arts degree. But after high school I was very uncertain, mostly because I didn't particularly want to do what my father did.

JR – Why not? You had seen how his work connected him to such a vibrant community.

AS – It wasn't the artistic community I was uncertain about, it was the job of architecture itself. It seemed unglamorous—like an awful lot of work for which you received very little gratitude. Through my father, I had seen what it was like to be at the mercy of your clients, and I didn't like that at all. I did apply to architecture school, with mixed feelings, but I didn't get in because my grade point average wasn't high enough. I was actually relieved, and I decided to take a year off—what you'd call a gap year today—and travel and try some internships. I had relatives in Peru who invited me to come visit them, and my godfather lived in New York, so I had this idea to travel to South America via New York. My parents told me, "You can do it if you can pay for it." So I got a job and worked for a few months until I could buy my ticket to New York.

JR – What were your first impressions of the city?

AS – I was overwhelmed. This was the late seventies, and New York felt like this unbelievably vibrant place. I don't want to get overly nostalgic, but I think the city made me feel that I could exist there with a new sense of freedom. Germany is a very interesting place, but it's also very small. Everybody knows everybody. There was a sense of anonymity that I really loved about New York.

JR – Did you seek out art during that first visit? Did you go to museums and galleries?

AS – Systematically! I saw absolutely everything—every museum, every gallery. And then once I lived in New York, the routine of going to openings and exhibitions—that sense that there was always something interesting to see—became very natural.

JR – Right. I can imagine that there were many similarities between what you had experienced in Cologne in the late sixties and early seventies and the art world in New York in the late seventies and early eighties. Both were very dynamic environments where a lot was changing in a relatively short time.

AS – There were direct connections, too. My first job in New York, during the summer before I started at Pratt, was for Stelle Gluckman. At some point somebody at Heiner Friedrich's gallery in Cologne had said, "Oh, you want to do an internship in an architecture office? These two guys in New York are doing a lot of work for us, and I can connect you with them." Fred Stelle and Richard Gluckman were working on all the spaces for the Dia Art Foundation, which Heiner had founded with Philippa de Menil and Helen Winkler. The funny thing is, I didn't even speak English well enough to write a proper application. A friend of mine had to help me, and he said, "You just have to say that you know everything, because that's what they do in America." So I represented myself as really great at architecture. It would be hilarious to see that letter now!

JR – It must have worked, though, because they offered you a job.

AS – But they very quickly realized I knew absolutely nothing. I hadn't been to architecture school, and I had pretty well avoided learning what my father really did. I think they were a little bit disappointed, but, nevertheless, they were very welcoming. They found things for me to do: "OK, you can help measure the site. Can you please go get lunch?" And I began to learn. I remember somebody showing me how to sharpen a pencil. In those days, when you were making a drawing, you'd have your scale, and each time that you'd draw a wall of a certain thickness, you were supposed to measure it. I thought that was ridiculous. It seemed like such a waste of time. Each time, you measure *again*? So I would always cheat and say to myself, I know what five inches is, I'll just eyeball it. And I would make these terrible drawings. But really slowly, little by little—and by the way, I'm still this slow now—I started to grasp why the drawings had to be measured, why it mattered to do things with accuracy. People always say, "Oh, of course it makes sense that Gluckman was your teacher," because we've both designed a lot of spaces for art. But he wasn't really teaching me so much as just being very patient and supportive and even jovial. That office was a good place for me, and I kept working through school and for a few months after graduating.

JR – It's interesting that you had that grounded, practical experience as a counterpoint to your architectural education, because Pratt—like most schools in the US at the time—was very theoretical. Before we talked, I was looking through some issues of the *Pratt Journal of Architecture* from the eighties, and there's a lot of heavy-duty stuff: reprints of Heidegger texts, essays on architecture and deconstruction. Do you think working for Stelle Gluckman helped you escape that?

AS – I think my time in that office taught me that it's always the human connections that fuel architecture. At the end of the day, it's people who build buildings and it's people who use buildings. So yes, in a way, I suppose the lesson there was that architecture is not just an intellectual exercise.

JR – I want to get back to the art you encountered in New York, because it strikes me that you arrived in the middle of a paradigm shift in the art world. In the 1960s and 1970s many of the most radical artists in America were making work that engaged space in some way—minimalism, postminimalism, installation art, even performance art—which meant that their practice often had a direct connection to architecture. In 1978 the art historian Rosalind Krauss famously argued that the entire "expanded field" of contemporary sculpture could be understood by mapping its relationship to either landscape, on the one hand, or architecture, on the other.

But the 1980s were marked by the resurgence of the image. The art world was dominated by painting and photography—this was the era of the so-called Pictures generation. So you get to New York and you're not walking into a gallery and seeing an architectural-scale construction by Donald Judd, you're seeing film stills by Cindy Sherman. In some ways that kind of work seems less appealing to an architect, or at least less provocative or engaging.

AS – Well, the truth is, I didn't connect art and architecture in that way, and I still don't. I think that the two are separate things driven by different motives. Having said that, I wouldn't be passionate about art if it wasn't something that inspires me. You mentioned Cindy Sherman, and those early film stills are hugely inspiring to me because they're making such a powerful statement about how women's identities—their places, their roles, their senses of self—are constructed in our society. But it doesn't mean that I put those film stills into my architecture. I carry my experience of that work, that inspiration, with me. It's part of what makes me the person that I am, and then as that person I go make something else. I think all the arts are probably like that. There might be a painter whose inspiration is music or a dancer inspired by architecture. But I think if you try to borrow your aesthetic from another art form, that's a bad thing; it's so simplistic.

JR – It does sound almost silly when you put it that way, but I think a lot of modernism was about trying to translate aesthetics from art into architecture. You have someone like Le Corbusier making paintings inspired by Picasso and Léger and then trying to turn those into buildings, or you have the Bauhaus teaching that the same basic principles of composition can be applied to painting and architecture and graphic design.

AS – I don't agree. I think that Le Corbusier, for example, was both an architect and an artist. His paintings, I believe, are about processing certain ideas at a human scale—they're very related to the body. And I'm not sure they are the principal inspiration for his architecture. If you look at his early works at La Chaux-de-Fonds, they very clearly grow out of the Swiss vernacular. And when you look at his sketchbooks from Italy, you can see how deeply he was influenced by classical buildings there. So there's a sense in which the trajectory of his work unfolds very much within an architectural tradition—into which he introduced great innovation. Are the paintings related to the buildings? Of course, but I'm not sure you can make such a linear connection.

JR – I think it's generous to call Le Corbusier an artist, because his paintings were fairly derivative, but I take your point that he used painting as a form of research to explore ideas beyond architecture. You're helping me see that I may be reading these connections too much through the writing of art and architectural historians, who often lean on this idea of translation as a means of explaining the evolution of modernism. In the catalog of his pioneering 1936 show *Cubism and Abstract Art* at the Museum of Modern Art, Alfred H. Barr Jr. famously argued that one of the reasons Mondrian's painting was important was that it had inspired architects like Mies van der Rohe. And in his *Space, Time and Architecture* [1941], Sigfried Giedion basically credited cubism for inspiring all modern architecture. Perhaps that's more of a reflection of how difficult it is to understand complex relationships between different fields of cultural production—stylistic influence is always a handy crutch for historians. That said, later generations of architects did return to modern art in a more literal way. I'm thinking of, say, John Hejduk's Diamond Houses [1962–1967], which were explicitly based on the diamond canvases of Mondrian. But maybe by that time there was an element of irony or pastiche.

AS – What you're alluding to is an intellectual exercise. That question of the formal relationship between art and architecture can become very academic.

JR – It's certainly true that, whether they're made by a historian or an architect, references to the visual arts can serve in a way that's analogous to the theoretical references I mentioned earlier. The discipline of architecture has long struggled to define itself as more than the mere practice of building, and both art and philosophy can offer a form of cultural and intellectual legitimization.

AS – It's not an either-or situation—architecture can very well be an intellectual pursuit. But I think it creates problems when architects focus too much on that.

JR – What do you mean?

AS – Let me give you an example. I'm currently working on a renovation of the National Gallery in London. Someone suggested I should read Harry Cobb's book [*Words & Works 1948–2018: Scenes from a Life in Architecture*] because it has a long discussion of his entry into the design competition for the addition of the Sainsbury Wing to the National Gallery, which was won by Robert Venturi and Denise Scott Brown in 1986. In the book, he publishes part of his original project description, and then there's the transcript of a recorded conversation that took place at the Century Club in New York sometime after the competition, where John Hejduk, Peter Eisenman, Charles Gwathmey, and a few others got together with Harry to talk about his submission. This is less than forty years ago, but it truly feels like another era. There were no questions like, "Who are the visitors?" "How do people look at art?" "How do we get people into museums in the first place?" It's all about "rotational geometries" and "the expression of the building's autonomy," this or that axis as the basis for the composition. The conversation is entirely formalist. It's clear that the problem wasn't "How do you make a good museum?" It was "How should the language of contemporary architecture relate to the language of classicism?" I was absolutely flabbergasted by that.

JR – It's almost impossible to imagine a conversation like that taking place today.

AS – And there was not a single female voice anywhere within miles. That absence stood out to me as so significant. I can't tell you how frequently I get asked, "What is it like to be a female architect?" I've never been preoccupied with that question. But reading this conversation made me look back on the work environment I was in at that time and the architects I admired.

In 1986 I had finished architecture school, and I was thinking about starting my own practice. These people were my heroes then, and I still admire them all a great deal. But it was also such a limited vision of architecture—of what it is, who it's for, and who can make it.

JR – It certainly bears emphasizing that formally driven approaches to architecture are often based on the pretense of universal validity, while in fact they're underpinned by exclusionary assumptions. I'm interested to hear more about how you approached your own National Gallery project, though, thirty-some years later.

AS – It's not that I don't care about how my buildings look; obviously I do. But I think there's a hierarchy in architecture, and I think people should be at the top. This is what I was saying about the Wallraf-Richartz—the museum should center the visitor.

JR – Would you describe yourself as a kind of functionalist then?

AS – No. The problem with function is that in the end it is totally subjective. It becomes an excuse, because you can always claim that you made this or that formal move to improve this or that aspect of the building's function. It's the experiential aspect of architecture that, for me, becomes the guiding principle. At the National Gallery, my team was tasked with refurbishing the Sainsbury Wing to be a welcoming space for the twenty-first century, one that receives more than five million visitors per year. So we began by asking, "Who goes to the museum? What can we do to make them feel more welcome?" And then we asked, "Who *doesn't* go to the museum? What can we do to make them feel welcome, too?" Institutions like the National Gallery have achieved many amazing things over the centuries, but one of their achievements has also been to draw a very clear class distinction between those who go to museums and those who don't.

JR – How does that desire to be welcoming translate into architectural terms?

Selldorf Architects, rendering of National Gallery renovation,
London, UK, anticipated completion 2024

AS – I think the most brilliant thing Venturi Scott Brown did
in their design for the Sainsbury Wing was to create an entrance on
the ground level. To enter the 1838 William Wilkins building, you
had to climb up a monumental flight of stairs, and that's the case
at almost any neoclassical museum around the world. Venturi Scott
Brown did a neoclassical facade, but then they cut a big hole into
the bottom so you can just step off the street into the museum.
I think that's a beautiful idea, and I want to reinforce that. When
the Sainsbury Wing opened in 1991, it wasn't intended to be the
main entrance to the whole museum. Now it is, and there are all
kinds of new protocols that didn't exist then. Visitors didn't have to
pass through a security checkpoint in 1991. The entry has become a
bottleneck—there are lines to get into the museum stretching across
Trafalgar Square. So our proposal is to create a newly configured
entry sequence in which you enter through a compressed zone and
then feel the space expanding on either side; you're drawn into a
new, wide-open space with daylight streaming in from both the east

and the west. What we're doing is relatively discreet—we're not touching the galleries at all—but it will make the ground floor a dynamic receptacle for crowds of visitors, and it's vital to keep the heart of that building pumping.

JR – Unlike Cobb, then, you didn't see your problem as primarily a formal one.

AS – We did not, and one of the difficulties we encountered in the project was that we heard from preservationists who wanted us to keep more of Venturi Scott Brown's neoclassical fabric. But I don't think you can just pick and choose like that. We're not intervening on the level of the formal language; the architectural moves we made are based on the spatial and experiential logic we've created. And we have to keep that coherent. You can't treat the design like it's just a bag of tricks and say, "This stays; that goes."

JR – Your National Gallery project is somewhat unusual in that you're working on spaces that are primarily for visitors: the entrance, the lobby, the circulation areas. Does your approach change when you're designing spaces for both visitors and works of art?

AS – I'm really proud of the Museum of Contemporary Art San Diego, because it's as close as I've come to building a new museum. We built a new building with forty thousand square feet of exhibition space, and it happens to be attached to an existing museum. It was the most difficult context you can imagine: the museum had acquired a new parcel on the south edge of its land. The site is on a steep hill right along the coast, literally across the road from the beach, so there are very strict height restrictions for new construction. As we studied the problem, it became evident that we would have to combine a two-story space at the bottom of the hill with a single story closer to the top, and the path through the museum would be long and somewhat involved because you have to traverse this topography somehow. That made it crucial to help the visitor feel oriented. We were very deliberate in the rhythm of the galleries and the circulation spaces, and we placed windows so that you have

Selldorf Architects, Museum of Contemporary Art San Diego expansion,
San Diego, California, 2022

specific long views out to the ocean and also back to the city, so that you understand the direction in which you're moving. The views create places to pause and rest, and, when you have a sense of where you are, you're less susceptible to museum fatigue.

JR – It sounds like you took an almost narrative approach to the design.

AS – I'm reading a memoir by the writer Amy Tan [*Where the Past Begins*, 2017], and she talks about having to be able to visualize the whole arc of the story as she works. I thought that was interesting because, in a sense, it's how I do things. Somebody else might start with structure or with materials, but that's not my process. Once in a while, when we have a new project, someone in the office will say something like, "Here's a great material we could use for the facade." And I have to tell them, "I don't want to think about the material yet!" I want to design the museum from the inside out. I want to know, What is the sequence of volumes that I will experience as I move through the space? What is my path through the building? I think you have to be able to walk around the building in your mind's eye—which, by the way, is why I design so much in plan. Of course, you then have to translate it into three dimensions and solve the elevation and the section and all of those things. But in plan, I can walk around a space and see it. Imagining yourself within a space is the only way to capture the experience you're after—the only way to make sure it's inhabitable.

JR – I'm intrigued by the fact that you're talking about "inhabiting" the museum, which is a space more typically discussed in terms of "visiting" or "viewing." There's a powerful polemic implicit in that term about who—or what—the museum is really for. Do you ever find yourself in conflict with curators or museum directors who want to focus more on the art?

AS – I believe that a museum has to be made for the visitor in the first place. Otherwise it could be just a storage container for art. Obviously, there are all kinds of art—from old masters to contemporary—which may need different considerations or even have contrary requirements. And, particularly with contemporary art, you have to accept that you cannot predict the future. Nevertheless, I don't want to be distracted by that too much. I would rather think of space in terms of circulation and proportion and light—and I'm also thinking about flexibility. For a while, paintings were becoming bigger and bigger and bigger. Then we had installations. Now there are all kinds of new media art. And, of course, artists are going to keep challenging the museum— that's part of their job.

Around fifteen years ago the Swiss artist Christoph Büchel got into a major conflict with MASS MOCA [Massachusetts Museum of Contemporary Art]. The museum had invited him to take over their biggest gallery—one of those huge, old factory floors—with an enormous installation [*Training Ground for Democracy*, 2007]. They basically said, "You can do anything you want." And it just became more and more elaborate—I remember he wanted both an airplane and a house to be part of the installation. It was like the museum staff had made a commitment to the artist and the artist was rubbing their faces in it. At some point it just became impossible to finish, both in terms of cost and logistics, so the museum went ahead and showed the incomplete work without the artist's permission. It was a huge controversy. And who was right? Nobody was really "right." But I found it very instructive to watch this whole process unfold.

When we build a museum, there is so much we can't predict. Where is art going next? We can't determine that. But we can make a commitment to demonstrating that we want people involved in the experience. And I think it's the mutual responsibility of curators, directors, and architects to keep that in mind.

JR – I can see why you were not so interested in the aesthetic affinities of art and architecture when I brought them up earlier; if you don't feel your architecture necessarily has to engage or reflect art on a formal level, that probably frees you up to think more flexibly about what it means to experience the artwork and about how that particular experience relates to the overall experience of inhabiting the museum, as you put it. But since we're talking so much about the public, I have to ask: How do you bridge the gap between the intensely personal experience at the heart of your design process—imagining yourself moving through the space, and so on—and the huge and incredibly diverse audiences that these institutions serve? You mentioned that your building in London will get more than five million visitors per year, and I'm sure that number will only continue to grow, thanks in no small part to your renovation.

AS – Well, another crucial part of the design process is that we speak very specifically with the people at each institution about their goals for public engagement. And I'm not just talking about the usual numbers and statistics. In London, for example, we worked with a group that studies public engagement in a hands-on way: they put together questionnaires, and they fan out into the neighborhood. Sometimes they were out in Trafalgar Square at midnight asking people questions. And they invited people—from London, from other places in the UK, students, tourists—into the museum for discussions and really built a rapport and got them to speak frankly. And, believe me, you hear things that you might not want to hear.

JR – I'm sure you do! But do you feel that the issues that people raise are things you can actually address architecturally, or do they have to do more with, say, institutional policy?

AS – Well, one thing that almost everyone agreed on was that the most important part of entering a museum is how you are treated when encountering another person. They want to have a positive human interaction. Often, they don't want to buy their ticket from a machine; if they came to see a particular artwork or a specific show, they want to be able to ask someone how to get there. And that was fascinating because I don't believe it lets architecture off the hook. Quite the opposite—now my job is to create an architecture that enables that human interaction.

JR – It's interesting to think about the precedents for using a questionnaire as part of your design process. Today it might sound a little corporate, like market research, but there is a long history of the avant-garde using similar tools to engage the public. The constructivists circulated questionnaires about the role of art and museums in Soviet society, for example, and Cedric Price used surveys to help himself think about the programming of his utopian Fun Palace. And, of course, artists have used public surveys to directly critique the museum—as in Hans Haacke's famous MOMA *Poll* [1970], where he asked visitors what they thought about Nelson Rockefeller, who was then New York's governor and serving on the museum's board of trustees and who vocally supported the Vietnam War. At the same time, I doubt this kind of public engagement and demographic research was something that many museums were doing fifty years ago, or even ten years ago. Do you think it will become an increasingly important aspect of museum design in the future?

AS – I think that progressive institutions are learning more and more about—and from—their audience, and I think that the more information architects have, the more responsive we can be. We're working on an expansion of the Art Gallery of Ontario right now, and it's incredible what they know and how they think about their public. They've worked hard to study how people look at art and what they respond to, and as a result they've achieved a highly diverse visitor profile that reflects the diversity of Toronto itself as a very international city. They really do put people first, and that's inspiring for my work as an architect.

Increasingly we're finding this with many of the museums we work with. You might expect the Frick to be conservative, right? But, working with them on the expansion, I've realized that the museum wants to do all kinds of things to engage with the full variety of their visitors and also to attract more people who don't traditionally find their way into an art museum. We're now provid-ing them a new reception hall and a large education center to

Selldorf Architects, rendering of Dani Reiss Modern and Contemporary Gallery, Art Gallery of Ontario, Toronto, anticipated completion 2027

Selldorf Architects, rendering of Frick Collection renovation and expansion, New York, New York, anticipated completion 2024

draw visitors in. These are spaces where people can come together and have a new experience of this venerable institution. "The public" isn't an abstract concept for us, and, when we think about the museum's engagement with the public, it's not on the level of a symbol or a monument. This is not the old Enlightenment idea of the architect saying, "I will build a temple of art for the city." We have a much more detailed understanding of who these buildings are for, and we're able to engage that audience in a much more specific way. When I work on a project like this, I often feel like I'm not really redesigning a museum; I'm redesigning its connection to the public.

JR – How would you say that this new understanding of—and engagement with—the public has changed your role as an architect?

AS – It doesn't mean design by committee. An architect's job is still to interpret and translate all this information into a piece of meaningful architecture. Ultimately the work of the architect is still about creating volume and space using the tools available, and careful considerations of context, proportions, structure, light, circulation, and material are still among the most important tools that architects have. The work should not be about style or form, nor should it be self-referential. Architecture must find authentic expression in serving the people who bring it to life—and that is a tall order.

SHOHEI

SHIGEMATSU

JULIAN ROSE – You graduated from Kyushu University in 1996, and at that time there was a very dynamic architecture scene in Japan, led by people like Toyo Ito, for whom you had interned as a student. But you left to pursue graduate studies at the Berlage Institute in Amsterdam. What drew you to the Netherlands?

SHOHEI SHIGEMATSU – Well, the thing about Japanese architectural education is that it's very technical. It's more like what in the US or Europe would be the program for an engineering degree. And I think there's a frustration about the technical nature of the education, in a way, because you can see how abstract and poetic the work of people like Ito and most other successful Japanese architects is. But I didn't feel drawn in either direction—toward the technical or the poetic—and I found myself looking for a more conceptual approach to architecture. At that time, Dutch architects had developed a very sophisticated approach to communicating architectural ideas through diagrams and models. It wasn't just Rem Koolhaas and OMA [Office for Metropolitan Architecture] but the whole generation that came after as well. This was the Superdutch moment, and offices like NL Architects, MVRDV, and UNStudio were winning major international competitions and their work was being published all over the world. It was a fascinating time. And I think that was the reason that I decided to go to Holland.

JR – In architecture, "conceptual" can be another way of saying "theoretical," which usually refers to practices that are trying to ground themselves in philosophy or critical theory. But it sounds like you mean something different. You're talking about an intellectually rigorous approach to design, grounded in research and analysis.

SS – Exactly. I knew I wasn't interested in that kind of theoretical approach to architecture because in my first years at university deconstruction was still very popular. Everyone was reading Gilles Deleuze and Félix Guattari's *A Thousand Plateaus* [1980] and not really understanding a single word of it. I had doubts that I needed to read Deleuze to be an architect. So the Dutch approach seemed more straightforward and essential, and also more fun. But I have to say that most of my architectural education really happened after the Berlage, at OMA, where I started working in 1998.

JR – What do you mean by that?

SS – OMA liberated me. Before, I always thought that you had to be such a great designer to be an architect. But what Rem was doing was somehow more journalistic—he would really get into the depth of program and context and then conceive an architecture that was truthful to the given conditions of the project. That premise showed me that I don't have to be a creative genius, I just have to be true to the context, and then a unique response will come from my careful observations. That was a very tangible lesson.

JR – I can see how that would have been a refreshing contrast to so much of what was happening in architecture at the turn of the twenty-first century. That period was defined by the ascendance of the "starchitect." After the Guggenheim Bilbao opened in 1997, Frank Gehry probably became the most famous example, but there were many other architects in both the US and Europe—I'm thinking of people like Zaha Hadid or Daniel Libeskind—who were becoming globally famous for their sculptural buildings. There's always a risk of oversimplifying in hindsight, but I think it's fair to say that there were a lot of high-profile buildings that looked unlike any architecture that had come before, and so, in a way, the whole field became obsessed with form-making.

SS – That's true, but I think that Bilbao had a profound effect at OMA, too. Before then, Rem had an almost stoic commitment to the box. There was complexity in his architecture, but it was all internal complexity. Somehow Bilbao turned that into the more complicated geometry of projects like the Seattle Public Library [2004], the Casa da Música in Porto [2005], and CCTV Headquarters in Beijing [2012]. All those projects are still based on programmatic research, but they share a new language, an acceptance that maybe looking deeply into the complexity of the building's program will produce a complex form. And that's crucial because it's still the OMA approach, which you can learn and then apply in your own way. I think that's why Rem has influenced generations of younger architects. When I look at Gehry's work, I admire it, but it's not something that I can learn from because it's so personal.

JR – Let's talk about this OMA approach. In the twenty-five years since you joined the practice, you've become known as the museum expert. But it strikes me that the museum has resisted the kind of programmatic reinvention for which OMA is famous. You just mentioned three classic projects, and each starts with a known building type: the library, the concert hall, and the office tower. Then there's a rigorous programmatic analysis that basically asks, What does this typology mean in the twenty-first century? And then a kind of radical reshuffling of functions follows, which is deeply grounded in logical analysis—I really like your use of the term *journalistic* to describe the approach—but it results in a revolutionary new architectural form. In both the Seattle Library and the Casa da Música, the box has morphed into a striking, prismatic volume, and in CCTV the traditional office tower has been twisted into a loop!

In OMA's proposal to expand the Whitney Museum, from 2001, which I know was one of the first projects you led, there was a similarly radical proposal to overhaul the typical museum program by splitting the Whitney's spaces equally into zones for "exhibition" and "experience," with the latter mixing art into spaces for circulation, entertainment, and consumption. This new combination of functions resulted in a similarly striking new form. But that project remained unbuilt. Is the museum somehow a more conservative institution than, say, a library? Does it have a more static program and a more entrenched architectural typology?

SS – I think at that time Rem, and everyone at OMA, had a profound belief that typologies could evolve quite fast. It was almost like: because it was the turn of the millennium, every typology was supposed to undergo a quantum leap.

Shohei Shigematsu/OMA, model of proposed Whitney Museum
of American Art expansion, New York, New York, 2001

JR – That was very explicit in the rhetoric around the design for the Seattle Public Library. There was a lot of discussion about what books meant in the age of digital media and what the future of the public library could be.

SS – Exactly. But with the museum, I think we misunderstood the speed. Now that it's been more than twenty years since we made that proposal, some of the provocations we made there are starting to happen. In my design for the expansion of the New Museum of Contemporary Art in New York, we had the idea of putting monitors inside the elevators to activate the circulation space with art, and the curators really liked it. But it has taken time. I also think part of the problem with a project like the Whitney was that the architect was trying to impose radical change on the client from the outside. Even today, if we try to tell the client, "A museum is x, and so you have to do y," it doesn't work. So for me the question is not just if a design is ahead of its time or not, it's also whether the architects are telling the specialists what to do.

JR – You're raising the question of expertise, which is complicated. On the one hand, I appreciate that you don't want to be the megalomaniac architect who assumes that their creative genius can be applied to solve any problem in any field. But on the other hand, specialists within any given field can be notoriously myopic, and I think that one of the most valuable things that architects can provide is an outsider's point of view. In *Delirious New York* [1978], Rem proposed a "paranoid-critical method," of design, but to continue your analogy, we could describe the architect as a kind of investigative journalist, someone who is willing to dig into a project and then reveal truths that some people might not want to acknowledge.

OMA's entry into the 1997 competition for the Museum of Modern Art [MOMA] expansion, which I know was just before you joined the office, stands out in my mind as a great example. Among other things, the project suggested reimagining the museum as "MOMA Inc." At the time there was a lot of pearl-clutching: "How dare you insinuate that this bastion of the avant-garde has any taint of corporate commercialism?" But looking back, it seems like OMA was just willing to be honest about what the museum was becoming before anyone else was. It's hard to see MOMA and other major museums as anything *other* than corporations today. And this isn't even a particularly controversial viewpoint—in 2014 the New Museum opened an incubator called New Inc.

SS – I agree, but I think the way OMA communicated at that time was a little bit too imposing. After the Kunsthal in Rotterdam, which was finished in 1992, OMA didn't win a museum competition until my proposal for expanding the MNBAQ [Musée national des beaux-arts du Québec] in 2010. In my proposals, I'm trying to capture the needs of each museum, and that might mean accepting some level of conservatism from the institution. In Québec the design is not really imposing the kind of experience that visitors are supposed to have. We are trying to give the curators a space that they can play with.

JR – Do you ever feel like the design suffers from this approach? To be polemical, I could say that deferring to the curators can become a cop-out for the architect. Especially with spaces for contemporary art, it's easy to say, "Well, I don't know what art will look like in ten years, so I just made a big empty box, and the curators will keep adapting it."

SS – I don't think generic architecture is good for the museum. But the impulse to be generic doesn't always come just from the program. At OMA there was a time right around when I moved to the US, in 2006, that was a little bit of a post-Bilbao moment, where everyone felt that museum architecture should be generic rather than expressive or iconic. When I was working on the design for Québec, I was still sort of caught up in that. So the addition is a simple stack of boxes, although the stair that punches through one facade resists that simplicity. Of course it's been well received and well used, but after it was finished, in 2016, I kept thinking that maybe the architecture was a little bit too generic. A museum should be a memorable space—if you look at the history of the typology, these were always very special buildings.

JR – How did that thinking inform your design for the Buffalo AKG Art Museum expansion, which you started the same year the MNBAQ building was finished?

SS – The AKG was interesting because we were dealing with two very established museum typologies—there's the original 1905 building by Edward B. Green, a typical neoclassical "temple of the arts," plus an expansion from 1962, a modernist box designed by Gordon Bunshaft. I always joke that there are only two kinds of museums in the world: the museum in the park and the museum in the city. But ironically the AKG was sort of neither. It's located at the north edge of Delaware Park, which was designed by Frederick Law Olmsted. But the two buildings had not really engaged the park, and, in fact, they had created a kind of urban wall. Both are very solid and hermetic—Green's building is a stone temple, and Bunshaft's is black glass—and because they are side by side, they block circulation between the city and the park, closing off views and access. So our concept was to use the park as a domain for art. We wanted to create a much more transparent building that would

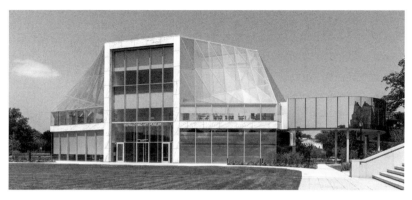

Shohei Shigematsu/OMA, rendering of Jeffrey E. Gundlach Building, Buffalo AKG Art Museum, Buffalo, New York, 2023

be situated in a way that created more of a campus feeling for the whole museum. That transparency was very important, because it's not just a literal quality, it expresses the fact that the museum is committed to open engagement with the community. And, for the same reason, I wanted our design to feel nondirectional. It doesn't have a front or a back like a Beaux-Arts temple. It connects to its surroundings on all sides, a 360-degree building.

JR – And that's where your geometry comes from? The building has a distinctive crystalline form, very different from the boxes in Québec.

SS – Actually, it's more of a hybrid than you might think. The galleries are still boxes because that was the most efficient way to provide the space that was called for in the brief. But we arranged the smaller galleries on the ground floor to create a plus sign, and then we stacked two larger, flexible galleries on top, plus there is a double-height gallery that connects the plus sign below to the boxes above. In plan, this organization creates open corners that the museum can fill with different programs. Three-dimensionally, there's a kind of ledge between the plus sign and the boxes that becomes a promenade. So we've created the flexible and efficient gallery space that was called for in the brief, but when we wrapped everything in a transparent glass veil, we also created these new spaces—at the four corners of the ground floor and on the promenade—that the client never asked for. And in these interstitial areas the museum can start really thinking about programmatic diversity, like new media galleries, performance spaces, or venues for public events and education.

JR – I'm fascinated by the idea that you provided spaces that the museum wasn't asking for. This gets right back to the question of architects telling specialists what to do. In your experience, how conscious are, say, curators or museum directors of the need for these kinds of additional or alternative spaces? Do you feel that part of your job is to design a kind of Trojan horse museum, where, yes, you're conscientiously following the brief, but you're also sneaking other things in?

SS – Definitely. I think the strength of our approach is that we can suggest other programmatic needs coming from our observations. But it's not imposed. It's presented more as found space, which comes out of the concept and the three-dimensional diagram. And I think it's very important that we are not setting a specific program for these spaces. Because the gallery boxes are so clearly defined, it was crucial, I felt, to leave the interstitial spaces undefined. As soon as you define a program, then it starts to impose architectural constraints. You might suggest, "We need an event space." But then the museum is going to say, "OK, great, so now we need this kind of lighting, this kind of acoustic performance, this kind of auditorium seating." And all of a sudden there are a lot of limits on what can happen there.

I think nowadays the success of the museum lies in the diversity of experiences it can provide. And it's so important for a museum to be able to show the community that it's dynamic and engaged. Whenever you go there, something new should be happening. And, of course, in the end this isn't completely up to the architect. It has to be collaborative. At the AKG I thought of these interstitial zones as improvisational spaces for the curators. It's up to them to make everything work.

JR – The shift from imposed space to found space is brilliant, and I can see how it would invite curatorial collaboration because it's more about pointing out areas of opportunity than prescribing solutions. But I'm curious to know if that's also an effective approach to collaborating with artists. Your AKG project includes a large permanent work by Olafur Eliasson, *Common Sky*. I'm especially interested to hear the story behind that work, because over the years some architects have complained that his works are so ambitious in scale that they overwhelm their architectural context. His 2003 project for Tate Modern's Turbine Hall, *The Weather Project*, came in for particularly heavy criticism because it seemed to be the leading edge of a whole genre of supersize installations that emerged in the first decade of the twenty-first century, maybe as a kind of attempted corrective to the Bilbao effect. As museums got bigger and more spectacular, artworks did, too, and not everyone was happy about that arms race.

SS – Sure, there was a period when the artist was becoming almost like a god, and Rem was one of the most vocal critics of that. But the collaboration at the AKG was very simple. Part of the Bunshaft design was to put a courtyard between the old building and the new one, and the space was not very well used. Initially we considered putting our building there, but it was clear that the historic preservationists would not allow it. Even after we chose the current site, we still had the ambition to somehow activate the courtyard, and we thought about adding a roof. But the historic preservationists argued that even a roof was too disrespectful to Bunshaft's building. So we thought, well, maybe the roof could be an artwork.

JR – That's interesting—rather than compete with the artist, you took advantage of the fact that they get to play by different rules.

SS – Right. And in the end, *Common Sky* is a kind of hybrid. It's a site-specific installation, but it also transforms the courtyard into an enclosed space, which can now be used year-round. In the existing building there is a staircase with a wall piece by Sol LeWitt, and to me this felt like a beautiful moment where art was integrated into the architecture. Continuing that kind of integration became a focus for me.

JR – I see the connection, but I have to admit I'm more struck by the distance between the two. The LeWitt is essentially a mural—one of the most ancient combinations of art and architecture. The Eliasson is a highly sophisticated steel-and-glass canopy, and that implies a way of working that's actually much closer to architecture than to a traditional artistic practice. This isn't Michelangelo up on the scaffold hand-painting the Sistine Chapel ceiling. I imagine Eliasson had to work with his own team of technical consultants, from engineers to fabricators, to realize this.

SS – Definitely. He founded an office called SOS, Studio Other Spaces, with an architect named Sebastian Behmann. That office is tasked with creating all Olafur's built works. Behmann was very involved in the logistics of realizing *Common Sky*, and he is credited as a coauthor of the piece.

JR – So you were collaborating with a collaboration, in a sense.

SS – Well, of course, I had many discussions with Olafur, and there was close structural coordination between us and SOS, but he took his own direction. I think there was a level of confidence on both sides of this collaboration that reflects a new level of capability among artists. If you think back to when Norman Foster designed the new roof for the Great Court of the British Museum, in 2000, I don't know if there were any artists in the world who could have built that structure at the time. But somehow, as you were saying, the expanded engagement of art and architecture in the first decade of the twenty-first century inspired a lot of artists to do architecture themselves, and I think Olafur's practice is a progression of that trend. So he is confident that he can take on a project like this, and we can be confident about commissioning him, because it's not like he's just a freewheeling artist. We know he's going to be able to create something within our framework, and what we get in the end is an architectural element—a roof—designed by an artist.

JR – That trajectory is very interesting because it seems counterintuitive. I might expect artists to become more competitive with architects as they become more capable of making architecture themselves, but you're suggesting that this actually makes them better collaborators.

SS – I think there was an older generation of artists who wanted to critique or attack architecture, and maybe an older generation of architects who were threatened by this, but those attitudes are shifting. The AKG was one of the first clients that commissioned me, specifically, as their architect. From the very beginning it was clear that it wasn't just an OMA project, it was a Shohei Shigematsu project. And when we first approached Olafur, I was worried that he might reject the offer because he wasn't going to be working with Rem. But then after we started working together, I realized that he actually liked that. It's a new generation of collaboration.

JR – I want to return to your idea that there are only two kinds of museums, the ones in the park and the ones in the city. The New Museum, for which you're currently designing an expansion, does seem to be almost the exact opposite of the AKG. Instead of sitting in an Olmsted-designed park, it's in the middle of a block on New York's Bowery. The urban museum comes with its own typological baggage, especially when it's for contemporary art. The site for your expansion is at 231 Bowery, next door to the 2007 building designed for the New Museum by SANAA. The existing structure at 231 was a classic industrial loft building, the kind that artists started using as studios—many in this same neighborhood—in the 1950s and 1960s. Spaces like this have also been used as museums and galleries at least since the 1980s, and some people argue that they're in fact the ideal spaces for exhibiting contemporary art because they echo the spaces in which that art was produced. My first question,

Shohei Shigematsu/OMA, rendering of the New Museum of Contemporary Art expansion, New York, New York, anticipated completion 2025

then, is why did you decide to demolish 231 Bowery and build something new in its place?

SS – When we got the competition brief, we were the first ones to understand the importance of that loft space, because the New Museum had been using the ground level of 231 Bowery as a gallery space for years. And in 2011 we actually did our *Cronocaos* exhibition there, which looked at the increasingly urgent topic of preservation in architecture and urbanism. Our show was one of the first in that space. One of the things we wanted to talk about was the gentrification of the Bowery, so we kept one side of the space exactly as it was—it had been a restaurant supply store—and the other side we renovated to basically make the typical loft gallery.

JR – And then less than ten years later you found yourself facing a much more extreme version of the same decision—do you tear the building down or completely renovate it?

SS – Exactly. And our first thought was to preserve this building. Even at the Whitney, in 2001, we had suggested keeping a historic brownstone owned by the museum, which, combined with our extension, would have created three different generations of architecture. We thought that the museum could gain a kind of authenticity from this diversity of spaces, because they could show prewar art in the brownstone, modern art in Marcel Breuer's modernist museum, and contemporary art in our contemporary building. For the New Museum, we thought of trying something similar, where we would partially preserve the building in its original state in the front, build new galleries in the back where they wouldn't be visible from the street, and then create a kind of interactive circulation that would connect these two with each other and with the SANAA building—stitching together the old, the recent, and the new.

But this is where I think we're more mature now. That's a very strong concept, but it's not really practical. The first problem was that the floor-to-floor height was low, so it was not compatible with the museum galleries next door. So we thought, OK, maybe we could preserve the facade and gut renovate the whole thing. But as we talked to engineers and contractors, we found out that, because of the site constraints, you'd need to remove most of the facade to access the space behind. And there's not enough room to store the dismantled facade on site, so you'd have to move it somewhere for safekeeping and then bring it back to rebuilt it. The cost kept going up as we were trying to plan, and eventually it was clear that trying to preserve the old building would be more expensive than building something new. And we decided that if we were going to completely change the interior space anyway, that kind of preservation would be cosmetic or superficial.

JR – How did you think about the relationship between your addition and the existing museum, then? In many museum expansions there's an obvious dichotomy between new and old, particularly when the original building is a neoclassical one. But you started designing your New Museum expansion barely a decade after the SANAA building opened, so the buildings are almost contemporaneous. And it's not like you could take clear cues from the art that's going to be exhibited inside. The New Museum is a non-collecting institution, and it's entirely devoted to contemporary art, so you couldn't try the kind of spatial-historical periodization that you had proposed at the Whitney.

ss – It was a challenge. But in a way, I was happy that we had to move beyond the kind of dichotomy you mention. I think that relationship tends to be too obvious, too easy—like the stone temple and the glass box we were dealing with at the AKG. We thought very hard about relationships between pairs. We did research in the studio, where we looked for images that expressed a complex relationship between two things that goes beyond a binary. One of my favorites was a photograph of one of Marina Abramović's early works, *Imponderabilia* [1977], where she's standing naked against one side of a doorframe and her then-husband is against the other side, and viewers have to squeeze between them. Another was a photograph of one of NASA's Saturn rockets with its launch tower. Those were both examples of interesting interconnections between two entities.

JR – I'm fascinated by the fact that this exercise seems entirely prespatial. It sounds like before you thought about making a drawing or a model, you wanted to undertake an almost philosophical inquiry into the nature of difference. These images aren't diagrams, in other words; they're concepts or metaphors.

ss – This kind of conceptual approach was very important to me. What I learned from the Whitney failure—if I can call it that—was that we had a good idea about providing spatial diversity, but the architectural forms we chose to communicate that idea created too much contrast. So somehow the translation of the idea into a design had been a little too abrupt, and before I thought too much about the form our extension to the New Museum should take, I wanted to ask, on a very abstract level, What is the relationship between these two buildings?

JR – But then how did that abstract thinking inform your approach to the concrete problem of providing more exhibition space?

ss – As we looked at the program it was clear that the museum almost wanted to clone their first building. The new program was almost exactly the same in terms of the amount of gallery space, office space, event space—everything. And that was the challenge. It's a contemporary art museum. How are we supposed to make another contemporary art museum right next to it? Our strategy was to match the floor-to-floor heights exactly so the spaces would be continuous in section, but then in plan our building has a very different footprint so we could introduce a different character into the space. In the SANAA building, for example, the largest space, on the second floor, has the lowest ceiling, and the smallest space, on the fourth floor, has the highest ceiling. And we felt that, proportionally, that produced a space that could be a little bit difficult to use. So in our building, the galleries get bigger as you go up; we've added a long gallery to the fourth floor, and we feel that the ceiling height is a little more convincing with these proportions. And I would like to believe that this ambiguity— two buildings that are super connected but somehow have different personalities—emerged through our initial exercise of collecting those images.

JR – Did you introduce any new spaces that weren't called for in the brief?

ss – In a way, yes. This is how our research works. We knew that the museum was becoming more and more popular, and the current lobby was not working. They also do a lot of public events, but sometimes these had been kind of clumsy because they didn't have the proper space. So we were thinking about how 231 Bowery is situated exactly at the eastern end of Prince Street, and we decided to create a kind of urban cutout that marks this terminus. This move also creates a kind of buffer zone of public space around the new entrance to the museum, along with a real lobby space. And that's why the elevation of our building is such a contrast to the SANAA building, because we pulled the facade back at an angle to create that open space.

JR – So again there's a kind of found space, analogous to what you did at the AKG. It also strikes me that both projects are expansions, as are most of the museum projects you've worked on, both built and unbuilt. Have we reached the point where continuous expansion has become part of what defines the typology of the museum?

SS – Definitely. That's been part of our research. We found that museums are growing at a historically unprecedented speed. Institutions are buying more and more art, art itself is becoming bigger and bigger, and the museum program itself is expanding. The museum used to be primarily about the collection, but community engagement is becoming more and more critical. So now these buildings need spaces for education and all kinds of public programming. But the speed of physical expansion is, of course, limited. The typical time frame for a museum expansion is fifty or sixty years—that's what you see at the AKG. But even the New Museum—which is very quick, relatively speaking—will be more than fifteen years between buildings. So often there's a discrepancy between the spaces called for in the brief and what the museum might need even five years in the future. And that's part of the reason I'm interested in interstitial, improvisational spaces that can house a diversity of activities.

JR – Is another way of dealing with this continual growth to shift from thinking about the museum as a large building to seeing it as a small city? In 2011, you designed a proposal for the National Art Museum of China, in Beijing, and that was the basic premise of your project.

SS – I think we've learned since then that the megamuseum is not viable. It's still happening in some places like the United Arab Emirates or Saudi Arabia, in new planned cities, but it's very difficult to incorporate a project like that into existing urban fabric. I think that the analogy between the city and the museum is more interesting to think about through the biennial or the art fair. These have a mothership, which is usually the convention center, but for their duration the entire city is activated with different exhibitions, installations, and events. Venice is a great example. If you go during the Biennale, the entire city is like a field of art. I think that's more plausible, and somehow more authentic, than a single institution trying to create a citylike museum, which is only going to be possible in a very small number of contexts.

JR – You mention the convention center, which is already a fairly generic building type, but in many cities, art fairs are housed in tents these days. In a sense, architecture is disappearing— are you concerned about that?

SS – I think it's quite fascinating. It's kind of the opposite of the Bilbao effect, right? Instead of an iconic museum transforming a city by drawing everyone to a central point, you have this decentralized network of events and installations that activates the entire city at once. And I think there are still many roles for architects in conceptualizing and executing this process. When I was teaching at Columbia University, I did a research project into what I called "perennialogy," which is the explosion of biennials, art fairs, and expos. The research started from a kind of skepticism about the so-called creative industry. We discovered, for example, that there's something called the UNESCO Creative Cities Network. When I first got interested in it, in 2016, there were 116 "creative cities" in the world. But we looked into the rate of growth, and it was exponential. To make a little fun of it, we did a projection and said that, by 2025, there will be 423 of these cities. The intention was to make these cities unique, but this idea of creativity is becoming totally standardized—it already seems obsolete. The same thing with the perennials. We found that, in any given month, there are twenty fairs and biennials happening simultaneously around the world. There's a flattening that results from the reduction of culture to an economic resource. We had a manual called *32 Ways to Activate Your Soft Power: Tips for Museums and Cities.*

JR – Wait, sorry—the manual was something you created as part of your parody of this trend?

SS – No, it's real! It was prepared in 2015 by a consulting firm [Gail Dexter Lord and Ngaire Blankenberg of Lord Cultural Resources] as a kind of textbook for municipalities to monetize their culture: if you do an event at this scale, the economic effect will be that. But, of course, the problem is that a lot of cities start doing these events without any particular cultural context or background, and they become cookie-cutter. They have no choice but to rely on the whole global ecology that has developed—you have the rock star curators, the rock star artists, the collectors flying in their jets from fair to fair. There's no specificity and no locality.

JR – **And do you see your role as an architect as somehow reestablishing a level of specificity, a connection to place?**

SS – Our role is to find the potential in these developments. The research started as a kind of provocation, but I do think that the fairs are part of a whole series of profound economic and cultural shifts, and we can't just dismiss them. The art market is becoming part of the global economy, and it's important to accept that reality, because it's quite powerful. And that reality does create new opportunities. Yes, the fairs are a marketplace for art, but they also allow people to see art in different ways than going to the museum. And they create platforms that museums can't, combining design, fashion, food, and all kinds of other cultural activities. But I don't think permanent art spaces are going to become irrelevant—I still think both museums and perennials are necessary for the success of a city in the twenty-first century, and they will continue to influence each other. In fact, new typologies are already emerging. If you think about Venice, for example, permanent institutions like the Pinault Collection or the Prada Foundation are clearly in dialogue with the Biennale. In Miami, I designed the Faena Forum, which opened in 2016. It's a kind of hybrid program—an event space and a cultural center—that is related to my thinking about the fairs. I realized that the fairs are mostly about visual art, so when they're in town there's a need for venues for performance art, too. But, of course, it's difficult to make money off performance art, so it makes sense to create a building that can be used commercially—for a fashion show or a wedding, too.

JR – For much of the twentieth century, the idea of radical innovation in both art and architecture—the dream of the avant-garde—has been linked to an idea of resistance, of maintaining some distance from both mass culture and commercialism. Is that connection no longer viable or, perhaps, no longer relevant?

SS – I think the hierarchy of the cultural over the commercial, the competition of the art fair versus the museum, is becoming less important. It's just about accepting the reality of the transactional dimension of contemporary art. Sometimes that even funds architecture now. We recently made another hybrid event space in LA, called the Audrey Irmas Pavilion, which opened in 2022. Audrey Irmas was an early collector of Cy Twombly. She sold one his paintings for $40 million, and that paid for our whole building.

JR – That's incredible. It actually reminds me of a story from a distant period of architectural history. In the thirteenth century, King Louis IX of France commissioned the Sainte-Chapelle in Paris to house his collection of relics from the passion of Christ. At the time, he paid substantially more for the relics than he spent to construct the building. Eight hundred years later, Sainte-Chapelle is considered one of the great treasures of Gothic architecture, and the relics (to most people, anyway) are just some pieces of very old wood. I'm not sure quite what the lesson is there, except that the relative values of different kinds of cultural artifacts are shifting all the time.

SS – And as value systems shift, opportunities will open up. That's why architects need to embrace the evolution of industry and typology and culture. The end of something always brings new potential.

KULAPAT

YANTRASAST

JULIAN ROSE – There's long been tension between museum architecture and exhibition design. Architects tend to look down on exhibitions because they're "only" temporary and assume that they play a less important role than a permanent building in establishing an institution's identity. Artists and curators, on the other hand, often embrace the ephemerality of exhibitions, using them as venues for radical experimentation that wouldn't be possible with permanent construction. And so, on the one hand, the history of art is full of revolutionary exhibitions that took place in totally unmemorable buildings, while, on the other hand, there are any number of museums that are highly praised for their architecture while also being notoriously hard to hang a show in. But your practice is unique in that, from the beginning of your career, you've pursued both museum architecture and exhibition design in parallel. One of your first projects was a new, ground-up building for the Grand Rapids Art Museum, which opened in 2007, and you've continued to construct museum buildings for almost two decades. Over that time you've also become known as something of an expert in designing or redesigning galleries in buildings by other architects, as you're currently doing in the Michael C. Rockefeller Wing of the Metropolitan Museum of Art, which was originally designed by Kevin Roche John Dinkeloo and Associates. How do you think about the relationship between these different dimensions of your work?

KULAPAT YANTRASAST – That's a very good question, and something that I think a lot about. Today, I'm not sure there's such a relevant binary between permanent and temporary. Most people assume that architecture's mission is timelessness. Architecture is supposed to last, and its power comes from that stability. And I think it's true that, traditionally, architecture has helped to anchor culture and society. If you go to the center of a European city and look at the cathedral, it's saying, "This is who we are as a people. Look how civilized we are." But today, more and more, architecture is also used as an agent of change, so people are looking to architecture to suggest what the future might look like. Museum architecture needs to address these diverse expectations.

JR – That's especially true of museums, which have moved from their original mission of collecting and preserving culture to creating it. A century ago, a museum of contemporary art was almost inconceivable, while today museums play a crucial role in the ecology of contemporary art.

KY – Exactly. A traditional museum was designed like a pair of gloves, tailor made to fit one unique pair of hands—the individual collection. But museums have changed so much. Today they respond not only to the collections—they expand to engage many activities outside of art. Museums become full sites of civic, social, and cultural engagement. They are now interactive hubs.

JR – It seems like that shift puts a lot of pressure on you, the architect, because the museum's program has become both more complex and more ambiguous. You can't just design the perfect glove anymore. How do you deal with that?

KY – The role of architects has to change along with the societies we engage and serve. There's still a very powerful cult of the genius architect, as seen in *The Fountainhead* [1943]. Howard Roark is a lone wolf whom no one understands. He does not need to engage his client or community; he only needs to express and serve his own vision, which everyone is expected to worship and cherish. Of course, that's a fictional illusion, but it's such a seductive vision of what an architect does. And, in a way, museums have exaggerated that illusion, as the museum is revered as the highest form of architecture, the most sculptural a building can be. Its function is seemingly just to be a beautiful temple of art. So I think a lot of architects who design museums come to see themselves as artists; museums are their expressive masterpieces. And people who make decisions about museum architecture might also have old-fashioned ways of thinking about architecture. They are looking for that sculpture to house artworks, so they organize design competitions, which—if not done with certain essential criteria—can turn into architectural beauty pageants: "I like that one, but this one has better curves." These oftentimes put architects in the simplistic role of form maker, starchitect, or prima donna, which limits what they can contribute toward positive social and cultural change. In reality, we architects need to be more like conductors than prima donnas. It's our job to bring everyone's voices together in synergy and to build a long-lasting architectural solution that serves the most people with the most sustainable processes.

JR – That sounds quite complicated, though, because not only do you have to reinvent your role, but you also have to convince your clients and perhaps even the public to accept this new vision of what the architect does.

KY – It's about understanding all the different stakeholders and communities involved in the project and integrating their voices. And I think my background has helped and even pushed me toward this. I was born in Thailand, and then I spent fifteen years studying and working in Japan. I got my MA and PhD from the University of Tokyo, and then I worked closely with Tadao Ando for eight years. So I was immersed and well versed in a world of refined Japanese minimalist architecture. But as I was practicing architecture with passion for precise Japanese aesthetics, I also missed and longed for a spirit of openness and malleability— the Thai tropical warmth and maximalism. I thought much about how these two disparate cultural ideals could thrive in concert. I dreamed about a new kind of architectural aesthetic where clarity of thought is enhanced with human touches and the richness of craft.

Then I thought about food, which is always my go-to for cultural references. I compare Japanese food and Thai food. Japanese food is about clarity and purity, minimal and singular, one strong ingredient at a time. Its strength lies in that purity and depth. Thai food is the opposite. It derives from rich mixtures of diverse influences and ingredients. The food incorporates a lot from China, from India, and from local practices and traditions, and, from this cultural mash-up, this small country has created one of the most unique cuisines in the world.

So I learned from these opposite food legacies. I deploy structure and clarity in ideas and planning, like Japanese food, but I also engage people's voices and forage new viewpoints and activities to enrich a project. I love to approach a new project that way. I never use a preconceived design or personal signature style. I love to engage in conversations with many people around a project and to allow these collective thoughts and aspirations to trigger and steer a specific vision. The design comes from inside of me, but it emerges through a process of immersive engagement with people.

JR – I certainly take your point that museum design requires a flexible approach, in part because, today, museums are expected to serve many different constituencies. But do you ever feel that there's a danger that architecture itself will get lost in all this collaborative discussion? After all, you, the architect, are bringing a specific expertise to the design process that the other stakeholders don't share, no matter how good their intentions or how invested they are in the project.

KY – Your point is well taken. It is very important that the cocreation process focuses on vision, strategy, and impact, and absolutely does not devolve into everyone ushering their preferences to a potluck design process. The rules of communal engagement are key in museum design. And the museum buildings we design are about interactivity of people and flexibility in usage, but they're also about a certain architectural excellence. We want architecture to inspire people. Historically museum buildings have done that. When you see a grand staircase leading up to a building or a beautiful exterior colonnade, you know you're going to have a special experience when you go inside.

JR – I'm fascinated by the fact that you're referring to explicitly neoclassical elements like the grand stair or the colonnade. Museum architecture is often criticized for being grandiose and alienating, and neoclassical museums come in for especially heavy criticism because they represent a very specific Western cultural tradition and are closely associated with European and American colonial expansion. The concern is that neoclassical architecture represents power in a way that makes some people feel unwelcome in the museum, and in some contexts that's clearly the case. But you're suggesting that there's nothing inherently wrong with powerful architecture, per se. It sounds like you see the colonnade and the stairway less as architectural symbols and more as experiential devices. They're techniques that you can use to engage visitors and get them excited about your building.

KY – But staircases and colonnades exist all over the world! I like the phrase you use, "experiential devices." These things are fundamental tools we have as architects. Similarly, if I am a filmmaker, I might use certain shots or camera angles to engage audiences with my story, and I might adopt these devices from the full history of world cinema. My message as an artist might be influenced by my cultural and social background, but the experiential devices I deploy could come from any place on Earth. You are right that Western museums used to be designed as temples of art, and many of them are therefore in neoclassical styles, with their colonial connotations and consequences. So we need to redesign architecture for new museums in a way that elevates art experiences and also engages and inspires all people.

Let me give you an example. I am very attuned to scale and proportion—they are two of the first things I notice in any space. The first time I visited the Alhambra in Spain as a young student, almost forty years ago, I was so struck by its beauty and proportions that I felt like I was hit by lightning. The Alhambra is so distant from my background—created in a different time for a different culture and belief system. But when I walked into that central courtyard, my body started to vibrate. I could really feel its power. The Alhambra was made as a palace for kings and leaders to impress and incite, but I could sense the uplifting human qualities from my own experience. I felt that my mission as an architect was to deeply mind how this undeniable place made me feel, and then to imagine and build new places that empower people to feel as profoundly, in their own ways.

Architecture unquestionably has the power to impress and inspire. People throughout history—kings or popes, dictators or patrons—have used this power so well. Today, I think it is crucial for museum architecture to wield this power in support of inclusive cultures and human flourishing. How could a museum building inspire a child to imagine their future? How should a museum empower a community to unite and to progress?

JR – I love the way you foreground ambitious architecture in the museum. But as you talk about architecture's power to connect with people across space and time, you're also implicitly raising the question of context, which is central to museums. I'm curious about that question in the context of your commission to redesign the Rockefeller Wing at the Met, which houses its collection of the art of sub-Saharan Africa, Oceania, and the ancient Americas. Cultural artifacts like these are very difficult to present in a Western museum. You're basically confronted with two options, both of which have serious problems. One is to aestheticize the objects by decontextualizing them—the most extreme vision of this is to place them in a white cube. Ironically, the intentions behind this approach are usually good. Before our conversation, I looked back at what Nelson Rockefeller, who donated the bulk of the collection, and Thomas Hoving, the Met's director at the time, said when the wing was being planned in the seventies. The conversation was all about "elevating" non-Western art to the same level as the Western canon; the idea was to take, say, a Mayan stela and show that it was just as much of a masterpiece as a Greek bust. But, of course, the very idea of a masterpiece is a Western construction; etymologically the term comes from the guild system in medieval Europe, where it referred to the piece that qualified a craftsman as a master maker. And it's indelibly associated with a certain romantic notion of artistic genius that's rooted in the Renaissance—it's just as much a cultural mythology as the Howard Roark–style genius architect you were critiquing earlier. All of which is to say it doesn't necessarily make much sense to take an artifact from another culture and treat it like a Western work of art.

But, in the second option, trying to recreate the context of that artifact in the museum often verges on problematic. I always think of the great anthropologist James Clifford's critique of the musée du quai Branly - Jacques Chirac in Paris, which was designed by Jean Nouvel to house Indigenous art from Africa, Asia, Oceania, and the Americas. The museum's architecture is conceived as a primordial forest—the lighting is very low, there are earth tones everywhere, the columns are shaped to evoke trees, and so on—and the idea is that visitors should feel like they're having some kind of natural encounter, as if they stumbled onto these objects in the jungle. Clifford was scathing—he pointed out that while the museum's ostensible goal is to contextualize the artifacts, really it ends up exoticizing and fetishizing them. He called this approach "ecstatic primitivism."

KY – Your description is spot on. I know the musée du quai Branly well. In fact, way back when, I was the project architect with Tadao Ando competing for the commission that Jean Nouvel won. So I know the vision, the collection, and the site. I think there were good intentions behind Nouvel's concept, and the design has interesting elements, but the way they all come together is arguably patronizing, almost like a cultural theme park. When you go through that building you feel equally entertained and manipulated—the presentation is very dramatic, but it's a one-sided way of experiencing the collection. Similarly, the storytelling is engaging, yet it's forced upon you.

JR – You're making two great points: first, that a museum like this has a responsibility to tell broader, more complete stories about its collections; second, that the museum's architecture should grant visitors the freedom to have different kinds of experiences and different kinds of encounters with the artifacts. Are these some of the goals of your design for the Met?

KY – One key goal of our work is to enhance and broaden the institution's impact and relevance. Museums come in all shapes and sizes, so no two experiences are going to be the same; in every project I want to make what can only be made at that given place.

When we began working on the Rockefeller Wing at the Met, we were also working on the Northwest Coast Hall at the American Museum of Natural History in New York, which is just across Central Park. And what's intriguing is that these museums are quite different in their missions, even though their collections have a lot of overlaps. For example, you might have a Mayan sculpture at the Met and perhaps a similar object at the Museum of Natural History. Yet how these two objects are installed and experienced in these two buildings could be extremely different, and perhaps rightly so.

JR – How would you describe that difference?

KY – Well, in a natural history museum or an anthropological museum, the focus is more on storytelling about the culture and the people behind the objects—their livelihood and belief systems. The objects are surely crucial, but in a sense they serve as symbols or illustrations of the culture they originated from. So at the Museum of Natural History, we brainstormed a lot about the stories that truly needed to be told. The Northwest Coast Hall was the very first gallery of that museum; it was conceived by the anthropologist Franz Boas in 1896. Boas did his fieldwork in the Pacific Northwest, and he acquired or commissioned the artworks he wanted to exhibit from the cultures he collaborated with and learned from. When the hall opened, it certainly offered a new way of understanding the Native cultures of Northwest Coast.

But now, more than a century later, our recognition of and engagement with the Native cultures have changed so drastically. Many representations of these Indigenous cultures from 1896 are obsolete and even offensive today. Because these are *living* cultures—people are still living and thriving in the communities that many of these artifacts came from. While I was working on the project, I spent three months living and working with First Nations and Native American communities, and so many of them said, "We don't want to be seen as a dead civilization. We're still here—we're still fighting for our way of life." So the comprehensive stories told through the art objects, via the voices of these people,

WHY, rendering of Michael C. Rockefeller Wing of the arts of sub-Saharan Africa, Oceania, and the ancient Americas, Metropolitan Museum of Art, New York, New York, anticipated completion 2025

WHY, Northwest Coast Hall, American Museum of Natural History, New York, New York, 2022

KULAPAT YANTRASAST   327

are diverse, engaging, and open for visitors to join and continue with their own thoughts.

JR – And how does that compare to your approach at the Met, where you're dealing with a much greater geographical and historical range?

KY – Well, an art museum has a very different approach. It's traditionally more focused on artistic lineage and achievements—artistic vision and innovations throughout history—with perhaps less emphasis on the life stories of the people the objects came from. At an encyclopedic museum like the Met or the Louvre or the British Museum, there is also a strong effort made to encourage visitors to experience artworks across place and time, to see artistic links that cross cultures and centuries. For example, in a single visit to the Met you could deeply appreciate a Cycladic carving in one gallery and then run over to compare it with a Constantin Brancusi sculpture in another.

But the irony is that it had taken Nelson Rockefeller, a very prominent art patron, a few decades to convince the Met to accept his collection of art from sub-Saharan Africa, Oceania, and the ancient Americas. Even though the collection housed in the Rockefeller Wing includes artworks from nations and cultures occupying 75 percent of the globe, they were seen as belonging outside the art museum. And even when Rockefeller succeeded in bringing these artworks to the Met, these objects from more than seven hundred cultures across three continents got lumped up together in this one wing, which people used to call Primitive Art. So in a way, our hope was to help people to really look more closely at and think more deeply about the collection. There are hundreds of diverse artistic traditions spanning thousands of years, and we want visitors to appreciate this incredible depth and range and to develop their own senses of curiosity and discovery.

JR – In architectural terms, how do you start to do that?

KY – The main idea is that we plan to organize the collection into three distinct zones that represent these three major continents, and each will have its own points of entry from other wings of the museum—as well as strong visual and content connections to neighboring cultures and crossovers between civilizations. We also strive to represent each individual culture in its own right so people can discern and appreciate their nuances and unique qualities.

In terms of architectural design, you brought up the choice between the white-cube museum and the quai Branly, and I think we offer a range of experiences in between these two poles. We deploy natural materials like wood and stone for the art installations and enclosures, so the gallery architecture is in dialogue with the artifacts. And we include rich colors. But instead of painting surfaces, we rely on the colors of the objects—textiles, sculptures, and decorative arts. Moreover, we design the wing to give visitors a sense of wholeness and clear orientation; they know where they are and what they can explore next. We want people to feel at ease while they move around but also to give them surprises and opportunities to discover unexpected things. We deploy strategic sightlines across cultures and give key objects primary positions to create landmarks for visitors moving through the space.

Another big change is that we bring in natural light and visual connections with Central Park through the south glass wall. The Rockefeller Wing is located on the south side of the Met, where sunlight is very strong and penetrating, yet most of the collections are very light sensitive; previously these windows were blocked. So we reengineered the glass wall to filter the light, and this allows people to enjoy the views and feel a connection to the park. The priceless art objects remain fully safe but also benefit from a new combination of direct and indirect illumination. The natural light also helps people feel refreshed and prevents museum fatigue.

I think of people moving through a museum like wind flowing through a space. If you want to get air moving through a room, you have to open two windows: one for it to enter and one for it to exit, right? People are similar; they want to have a clear exit strategy. If a space looks like a dead end, they don't want to go in. It's helpful to plan galleries so that when people enter, they know how to move around, and they know their options. They might say to themselves, "OK, I'm going to spend ten minutes here. I'm just going to look at that one sculpture and then I'm moving on." Or they could say, "I really want to see as much as I can here. I'm going to spend an hour browsing this gallery." Having that kind of awareness and choice is so important to visitors, especially in a museum like the Met, where the sizes of the collections are mind-boggling. What this all boils down to is that I want to empower visitors to plan and own their museum journeys.

JR – You mentioned earlier that flexibility is very important in your museum designs, but as you describe your work at the Met, I'm realizing that you're referring more to experiential flexibility than architectural flexibility. Or, rather, you're interested in a kind of experiential flexibility that is produced by the architecture. The architecture itself is not just expressing the cliches of flexibility in museums—the huge column-free space, or the system of moving partition walls.

KY – The architectural flexibility is key to the experiential flexibility. The architectural flexibility lives in all the ways in which the spaces could be freshly organized and the artworks variably installed. Most museums can only present a very small percentage of their collection at a given time, due to the difficulty of moving and reinstalling the objects, so our museum designs strive to change that. We design galleries, caseworks, and installations so it is easier to change objects around and easier to create things like pop-up exhibits without disrupting visitors' experiences or having to close galleries down for reinstallation.

JR – So it sounds like you have a kind of hybrid approach: if it's well designed, a single architectural configuration can offer a multiplicity of experiences, but you also want to be able to reconfigure the space to expand the experiential possibilities even further.

KY – Yes, one configuration can be experienced in multiple ways, but wouldn't it be great if that configuration also lent itself to adaptability? In a way, this goes back to the comparison I was making between Japanese and Thai food. Let me tell you about a lesson from my first museum, in Grand Rapids. It had been planned as the most sustainable museum imaginable; its ambition was to be a new cultural hub for the city, integrating art, science, and technology. As it was my first museum, I did not want to use concrete as the main material, since Tadao Ando was my mentor and I didn't want to be using a material so closely associated with his work. But because I had extensive experience working with concrete all over the world, I knew how to use it cost effectively, sustainably, and with high aesthetic quality. So in the end, due to our sustainability goals and strict limits in cost and time, I designed that museum with concrete and glass. That simply made the most sense in terms of durability, and in terms of our ability to use local materials and minimize transportation costs, and it also allowed us to bring ample natural light into the interior and connect the museum to its surroundings.

But when the building was completed, I was quite concerned about how people would perceive it. I didn't want the architectural community to think I was doing Ando in America, even though, of course, concrete had been used so well here by giants like Frank Lloyd Wright and Louis Kahn. When the museum was about to open, we commissioned Ellsworth Kelly to make a prominent artwork for the central space [Blue White, 2006]. At that point I had known Ellsworth for many years, since my Ando tenure—he had made an important piece for the Ando-designed Pulitzer Arts Foundation in St. Louis. I had gotten to know him working on that project, and after I moved to the US, Ellsworth and Jack Shear, his partner, had been very kind and supportive. So I was nervous for him to see the museum, as he, of course, knew Ando's work very well.

After we finished his installation, as we were at the dinner table having glasses of wine, I just had to ask him, "Ellsworth, do you think people will think I tried to make an Ando building here?" And he replied, "No. Not at all. Ando is Japanese, and his buildings

WHY, Grand Rapids Art Museum, Grand Rapids, Michigan, 2007

are all about precision and control. They're about one way of walking; he regulates how you move, what you see, and what you discover. But you are Thai; your museum is generous and totally open. You're allowing people to make their own journey: they can look this way or that, they can walk over here or turn over there." I was so surprised and happy hearing that—it felt like Ellsworth gave me license to fly! Deep down, I knew I left Japan because I had become frustrated with the control and conformity I witnessed, and I longed for the openness and warmth of my Thai roots. Ellsworth encouraged me to imagine how I could merge these two formative influences and integrate unique elements from both rich cultures—clarity and flexibility, refined abstraction and human interaction. I think my museum designs represent this creative fusion.

JR – I'm glad you brought up Kelly, because I want to talk more about your relationships with artists. You have a very compelling vision of museum architecture as a kind of open framework that produces experiential flexibility, but at the same time it strikes me that some of the artists that you're close to seem to need a different kind of architecture for their work. I'm thinking of someone like Gabriel Orozco, whose installations often hinge on the transposition of everyday objects into the gallery setting—his first show in New York caused quite a stir because he simply placed one yogurt lid on each of the four walls of Marian Goodman Gallery [*Yogurt Caps*, 1994]. Or Rirkrit Tiravanija, whose practice is rooted in introducing everyday social activities that wouldn't otherwise be particularly noteworthy—most famously, cooking pad thai—into the gallery or the museum. What I'm getting at is that this work is asking for a certain kind of institutional framework to push against, not only conceptually but spatially and aesthetically. Simply put, it works very well in the white cube, where the sudden appearance of an object or activity from everyday life is the most startling.

KY – I'm deeply inspired by this kind of artwork. There are different art terms for it; you might call it relational aesthetics or social practice. But, for me, it comes down to the relationship between art and life. In a way, the white cube was the previous generation's ideal. The idea was that art should exist outside of everyday life and that the museum should be like a neutral laboratory with the best conditions—perfect proportions, perfect light—so that you could almost objectively examine the artwork. But the reason I admire someone like Gabriel is that he reminds us that a work of art is perhaps just like a flower—the minute you cut it from the plant, it dies. I think his work is an important critique of the white cube, but I don't think it needs the white cube in order to make this statement.

JR – To play devil's advocate, though, I could argue that if your architecture brings too much life into the museum, then work like this will fall flat. If you, as the architect, have reinvented the museum so that it's a freewheeling, convivial space and no longer an isolated temple of art, does it still make sense for an artist to base their practice on bringing the everyday into the gallery?

KY – You are right that too much life introduced into the context could make it difficult to truly experience the message of some of these artworks, but I don't think it is an all-or-nothing dilemma. Artists also love repurposed buildings—warehouses, factories, or schools. These are definitely not white cubes; they have their own presences and stories. But the authenticity of the structure and the generosity of space make these buildings conducive as setting for artworks.

I also don't think the relationship between art and architecture has to be competitive. They could and should work together—they could both be well connected to life, and they could help each other make this connection, especially when an artist is working outside the museum. In 2016, Rirkrit was invited to make an artwork for the LA Public Art Biennial, and he gave me a call to collaborate. He had an idea that he wanted to explore, and of course I'm a big fan of his work, so I understood what he was trying to do, and I could help to expand and execute his concept. It ended up being a wonderful collaboration.

WHY, David Kordansky Gallery, Los Angeles, California, 2014

JR – In LA, you two produced a pavilion together, and I can see how that kind of project would be an ideal venue for collaboration, but does the relationship between art and architecture become more difficult to maintain when you're designing a more open-ended space that will exhibit the work of many different artists?

KY – Well, one case study might be my designs for David Kordansky Gallery in LA [2014 and 2020] and New York [2022]. These are commercial gallery spaces, so by nature they need to be fully flexible for all types of art and artists. But the spaces I designed are not neutral, abstract, white cubes. I worked hard to get a sense of specificity into the spaces—exposed structures, skylights in the ceilings, windows to gardens—and I planned their individual proportions very carefully. In the beginning, I was wondering if some artists would think my design was too strong and intentional; would they think the architectural character distracted from their work? But I learned from artist friends that they actually love to have something to react to. I remember at the opening event in LA, Mary Weatherford came to talk to me. She's a close friend now, but at the time I didn't know her well. She said to me, "This feels like a challenge. There's a tension in this space that makes me want to do something here."

JR – Would you say you want your spaces to be challenging to artists, then?

KY – I think a challenge is a way of showing respect. In 2014, we did the Studio Art Hall for Pomona College, and, while I was designing it, I went to visit dozens of art schools. I remember visiting Rob Storr at Yale, one of the most influential studio art programs in the country. I asked him, "What is the most important thing for an art school building?" And he said, "You have to give them stages. Every student in an art school is in touch with what they want to do, but they need a good stage to share that work."

So in our art building for Pomona, we didn't only think about designing the perfect studio spaces for making art. We intentionally added many in-between spaces where other things could happen. We made the corridors wider than normal, so they can function like intimate, casual galleries. We were careful with where we placed doors and windows, so there's not just good light and access but as much uninterrupted wall space as possible. The idea was to create different kinds of spaces that would inspire the students to express themselves in different ways. After the building opened, it was gratifying to see that the students immediately put their work in every place imaginable. Some of them told me they loved that I designed a building that they could hack.

I think as an architect you do have the power to create specific conditions that can help an artist express themself. Even if you take an extreme example, like a musician singing on a street corner— they don't just sing on any corner, right? There will always be certain street corners where they want to perform, where they feel welcome or even challenged. That's the synergy of place that I love.

WHY, Studio Art Hall, Pomona College, Claremont, California, 2014

JR – I appreciate how comfortable you are with the idea that you're creating the context for artists to do their thing. In a way, this gets back to one of the first points you made, which was about the problems with seeing the museum as a sculptural building. If architects think of themselves as artists, it's probably inevitable that the museum will become a site of conflict.

KY – Architecture is definitely an art form, but I like to think of it as a sheltering art form; architecture hosts and nurtures the other arts—it provides the frame for sculptures and paintings or the stage for music and performance or even the setting for enjoying food. We are providing the place where everything can and should come together. That is the power of architecture as art, and when we try to frame architecture as mere sculpture, we sacrifice so much of its intrinsic potential.

In the twenty-first century, art and architecture both need to compete for attention with phones, screens, and games. Time is limited, so a person could choose to stay home and play a game online rather than going out to experience art. We are all in the experience business, and our customers are very demanding and distractible. So the question is, how can art and museums in the physical world compete for time with virtual or augmented reality experiences that offer entertainment in the comfort of one's own home?

JR – That's a great point, if also a slightly scary one. So much of the discussion around museums in the last fifty years has been about art versus architecture, but whatever conflicts there are between the two fields, they're both on the side of embodied experience in physical space.

KY – But even that, I don't think, needs to be an either-or. Virtual reality, augmented reality, and now even AI-generated immersive experiences are becoming big parts of our culture, so it's important to explore how architecture can incorporate them or, to return to the metaphor I was using earlier, how architecture could host these new phenomena within its own languages and devices. My studio has been engaged in experimental design in VR, immersive AR, and the metaverse, which many architects might perceive as irrelevant.

There are currently big divides between the physical and the digital, and these have been exacerbated by the COVID-19 pandemic. It put physical experiences and places at a grave disadvantage and spurred a push for digital connections and place making. But as an architect who is interested in connecting people, I don't see the need to debate physical versus digital supremacy. I'm always curious about new ways to make new kinds of connections, and I'd like to focus on end results rather than getting too caught up in questions about what is or is not an authentic experience. There is no question that museums need to change and evolve with the societies they serve, and I think architects must play a big role in that evolution. If we see ourselves only as sculptors and we insist that making expressive forms is our raison d'être, our days of relevancy might be numbered. But architects could be crucial to the future if we deploy our skills in planning, design, communication, and organization toward creating a rich variety of newly integrated forms of human experience. And that's what I strive to do.

PETER

ZUMTHOR

JULIAN ROSE – I see an interesting tension in your background. Your education exposed you to different ways of understanding not only architecture's relationship to art but also the relationship of both practices to history. You studied at the Kunstgewerbeschule [School of Arts and Crafts] in Basel in the early 1960s, when its curriculum was still based on that of the Bauhaus, including the famous Vorkurs, a one-year preliminary course that taught the foundational skills supposedly common to all areas of art, architecture, and design. The Vorkurs was fundamentally interdisciplinary—a model of synthesis and continuity. But its historical paradigm was one of total discontinuity. It emphasized invention, innovation, originality—modernity.

PETER ZUMTHOR – Yes, it was almost antihistorical. Design was about finding new solutions and, in a sense, fighting history.

JR – But you arrived there after completing an apprenticeship as a cabinetmaker. That experience would seem to have emphasized the reverse: a profound connection to history, a sense of knowledge being passed down continuously across generations. And yet in the apprentice system each craft exists in isolation, with its own unique skill set—a carpenter does not make a cabinet, and a cabinetmaker does not build a house. How did these contradictions influence you?

PZ – In a good way. There were positive elements to both approaches. The Vorkurs was really good—a whole year of modest but very focused study, learning how to look carefully, how to draw precisely, and so on. (I didn't learn so much from the Fachklasse, the specialized courses that came after, which I did in industrial design.) My apprenticeship was also a very powerful experience, and from this I had already learned that everything I do is connected to the past. When I look back, I think this is how life happens.

JR – One of the great struggles of recent architecture has been to reconcile the lessons of modernism with a desire to reconnect with the past—yet you make it sound so simple! You also studied abroad, coming to the United States in the fall of 1966 to enroll at Pratt Institute. Did that help you synthesize your previous educational experiences?

PZ – The Kunstgewerbeschule did not grant an academic degree. It was a trade school, and I had applied with my certificate of apprenticeship, which in those days was accepted as a qualification. So I did not have even a high school diploma. I had no academic credentials, and I thought if I wanted to work outside Switzerland that would be a problem. I had been the youngest in my class, and I said to myself, This can't be the end of my studies—I have to do something else. So I went to New York.

JR – And that is where you began to study architecture?

PZ – No. I still didn't dare to do architecture. When I was in school in Basel, the architects did not take the industrial designers very seriously, because they knew most of us were craftsmen who would be going back to our small workshops after graduation. I had great respect for them, but I thought maybe architecture was something that I could not do.

JR – Which courses did you enroll in, then?

PZ – First I tried industrial design. But I went to the head of the department and showed him my work, and he said, "You shouldn't study here. You won't learn anything. You already know more than my students do when they finish their master's degree."

JR – I can imagine that the standards of craftsmanship were higher in Basel than in Brooklyn. Where did you go next?

PZ – I went to interior design, which I hated, although it opened me up to the possibilities of making big drawings, so it was a good experience in that way. Then I took courses in urban planning, but this was going from door to door with a questionnaire. I thought it was unbelievably boring.

JR – How did you finally get into architecture?

PZ – Everybody in the whole school went to Sibyl Moholy-Nagy's lectures on the history of modern architecture. She was *the* professor. The auditorium was always packed—it was an exciting atmosphere. I started going to the lectures, and then I enrolled in her course. I became close to her, and I asked her a lot of questions. I wrote two papers for her.

JR – What about? Do you remember?

PZ – Typical topics in modern architecture. One was about Louis Sullivan, and the other was about art nouveau. I think they weren't very good. But she gave me a good grade, and she encouraged me to look into the architecture department, and for the first time I started to think, Maybe I should do this. But that was the moment when my father came and took me back to Switzerland.

JR – After one year?

PZ – He would only pay for one year abroad, and then he told me I had to come home. That was the end of my university studies. I spent the next ten years working in the department of preservation in Switzerland. It was more than a decade before I did any architectural design.

JR – So in a sense Sibyl's lectures constituted your entire architecture education. That's fascinating because she herself was such a complex figure. She's a direct link to foundations of modern architecture—she played an important role in the German avant-garde of the 1920s and early 1930s, and her husband, László Moholy-Nagy, taught the original Vorkurs at the Bauhaus. But she was also one of the first people to begin looking for alternatives to modernism by taking vernacular architecture seriously. Her book *Native Genius in Anonymous Architecture* was published in 1957, years before Bernard Rudofsky's *Architecture without Architects* [1964], Robert Venturi's *Complexity and Contradiction in Architecture* [1966], or Aldo Rossi's *The Architecture of the City* [1966], even though those later volumes tend to be better remembered today as the pioneering challenges to modernist doctrine. Was that ambivalence part of what attracted you to her teaching?

PZ – I went to her lectures because she was not a historian— she was one of the key figures of modernism. She was part of all of it.

JR – You were hungry for a firsthand account?

PZ – Exactly. We students would provoke her with our questions. I remember once we asked, "Mrs. Moholy-Nagy, would you please tell us your opinion of Mies van der Rohe?" And she said, "No, I'm not going to talk about that now." And we said, "Please? Please?" And then all of a sudden she said, "OK, I'll tell you. Mies destroyed modern architecture!" She was captivating.

JR – She saw that by the 1960s the revolutionary ambitions of modern architecture had been reduced to an architectural fashion: the international style. Even through modernism was still being promoted by many of the same architects—people like Mies or Walter Gropius—they were now selling something quite different. I think it took most architects decades to recognize this trajectory, which is why so many of them were drawn into a protracted struggle with the legacy of modernism. The same is true of many critics and historians, for that matter. You heard this critique directly from one of modernism's protagonists, and I can't help but imagine that this is partly why you didn't get hung up on your Bauhaus-inflected training.

But I'm also curious to hear what else you took from your studies in the US. The late 1960s were a time of tremendous innovation in American art, marked by the emergence of everything from conceptual art and minimalism to land art and performance art. Did you encounter any of this during your year in New York?

PZ – No, because that work had not arrived in architecture schools. At Pratt the teachers were very sheltered, and I think they probably didn't even know about those artists. It was only later, when I got to know people like Walter De Maria personally, that I realized that they had been working right there at the time. I discovered this American art when it became really influential in Europe, and especially in Switzerland, of course.

JR – That was not a long delay—arguably radical American art from this period found a wide audience in Europe even before the United States. Did you go to *Live in Your Head: When Attitudes Become Form*, curated by Harald Szeemann at Kunsthalle Bern in the spring of 1969? That show has become legendary for introducing innovative artistic practices, both American and European, to the public.

PZ – I didn't go—I should have! But there were many reports about the show in the newspapers, and I read all of them. I was completely fascinated.

JR – Where did you finally see this kind of artwork in person?

PZ – Basel was a hot spot. The Kunstmuseum showed Donald Judd in the 1970s. There were great curators. They bought important works by Jackson Pollock, and Joseph Beuys showed there. There was a guy called Georg Schmidt who was the director of the museum for many years.

JR – He was an early advocate of modern art. He brought one of the first museum exhibitions of the Bauhaus to Basel in 1929—almost a decade before the Museum of Modern Art in New York had its famous *Bauhaus: 1919–1928* show in 1938.

PZ – Exactly. He was a communist—and his brother was an architect who had worked in the Soviet Union—so he was not allowed to teach at the university in Basel, but he gave lectures at the museum. I remember going to see him. I was a student; this was before I had gone to New York. He was talking about modern art, and I had the feeling that most of the artists he spoke about were people whom he had known personally. Up to that point I had no interest in art history—I cannot learn from people telling me,

"This is what this means, and this is what that means," and so on. But Schmidt spoke with such passion: "Look at this! Can you see that?"

JR – It sounds like there are parallels between Schmidt and Sibyl Moholy-Nagy. Whether they were discussing art or architecture, both of them presented you with a living practice rather than a historical subject. But I would like to speak in more detail about how specific encounters with contemporary art shaped your work. Over the years you have often spoken of your admiration for American art of the 1960s and 1970s.

PZ – Without those artists, my work would look completely different.

JR – Which artists, in particular?

PZ – We have already named two of them: Donald Judd and Walter De Maria. But also Michael Heizer, Richard Serra, Robert Ryman, and Bruce Nauman.

JR – You can't have seen all of them at Kunstmuseum Basel?

PZ – I also traveled to exhibitions: *Documenta 6* in Kassel in 1977 and *Skulptur Projekte Münster*, which started the same year. And then in 1983, the Hallen für Neue Kunst opened in Schaffhausen. They had a great collection with major works by most of those artists.

JR – The museum in Schaffhausen is an interesting example, because it was housed in an old textile factory—to my knowledge among the first art exhibition spaces to open in a renovated industrial structure. The gambit was that these works needed to be shown in a large space, not only because of their unprecedented scale but also because many of them explored a temporal, embodied experience. Viewers needed to move around and through them, so they relied on a fluid dynamic between artwork, body, and building. Was the way this work implicated architecture part of what appealed to you about that museum?

PZ – The impact wasn't so direct. I was fascinated by the whole approach. In Kassel in 1977, Walter embedded a one-kilometer-long [.62-mile-long] brass rod into the earth [*The Vertical Earth Kilometer*]. This was mind-blowing. It was a radical new way of making a sculpture. He was not asking, "Should I make the shape a bit like this or a bit like that?"

JR – Right, it's a total departure from the modernist approach to composition, which was all about balancing one form with another, establishing harmonious relationships between different parts, and so on. But I'm also intrigued because what you're describing is also not merely the kind of stripped-down anticomposition, based on seriality and repetition, that's associated with minimalism— as in Judd's famous mantra "one thing after another." Much ink has been spilled about the connections between minimalism and architecture, but it sounds as if, in your case, land art might have been more important. There's a raw ambition, something primordial and poetic, that you were responding to.

PZ – Look at the basics. Use elemental forms. That's what I took from this work. And I learned to look at the landscape like a land artist. When I went to see *The Lightning Field* [1977], I couldn't even believe someone had made it. It's so powerful. When I first met Walter, years later, he asked me very carefully, "Have you seen *The Lighting Field*?" And I said, "Yes, I've been there." And then he looked at me with a huge smile because he knew I understood his work. You must go there to understand it. There's no other way.

JR – I can see how discovering this work was a revelation, but I want to hear more about how it translates into architecture. I would argue that buildings are inherently complex and heterogeneous assemblies in a way that makes them resistant to the kind of elemental approach you're describing. Architects must deal with things like thermal breaks and expansion joints, and a building inevitably has a hierarchy, a kind of division of labor between its elements: some things hold other things up, some things let light in, some

Atelier Zumthor, Kunsthaus Bregenz, Bregenz, Austria, 1997

things keep water out. Whereas a piece like *The Vertical Earth Kilometer* or *The Lightning Field*…

PZ – It's not architecture.

JR – Exactly. Let's take one of your museums as an example. The Kunsthaus Bregenz is an extraordinarily sophisticated building. The gallery spaces are formed by a cast-in-place concrete core surrounded by a structurally independent steel framework, which in turn holds the etched glass panels of the facade. These three systems are interwoven in such a way that natural light is drawn in from the sides of the building and reflected down into each gallery through a translucent ceiling. The result feels impossible: a four-story museum in which every gallery space is lit with daylight, *from above*. This kind of interconnection is not a Walter De Maria idea or a Donald Judd idea. It's an architectural idea.

PZ – It's also an urban idea. I remember Judd being invited to make a small building in front of the Kunsthaus.

JR – This was the building across the plaza, which you ended up designing?

PZ – Yes. We needed a structure for the museum offices and the bookstore and café. It was a kind of political strategy of the museum's director at the time. He told me he had a big name he would like to get involved in the project and asked if I would mind. So it was not my idea, but I could imagine it working. I talked to Judd and explained the urban situation and asked if he could respond. But then he just brought in a building from the United States. It was a design that he had not been able to realize there, so he brought it to Bregenz and said, "I want to do this here." And when I tried to talk to him about the urban context, he wasn't interested. He was friendly, but he didn't want to engage. So I finally decided I had to do the building myself.

JR – I've seen his design, and you're exactly right. He was fascinated by vaulted structures: he added barrel vault roofs to the two artillery sheds he renovated in Marfa in the early 1980s, and he also tried, unsuccessfully, to build a group of vaulted concrete buildings on his property there. His proposal for Bregenz was almost identical to the unrealized concrete buildings in Marfa.

PZ – I'm not criticizing. A lot of great artists work like that. James Turrell puts his sky spaces all over—there must be fifty of them around the world. That's continuing a long tradition. An artist makes a painting, and then it goes somewhere to hang on a wall.

JR – You've had other collaborations with artists: for example, your work with Louise Bourgeois on the Steilneset Memorial to commemorate the victims of witchcraft trials in Norway, which opened in 2011. How did that project come about?

PZ – When Michael Govan was director at Dia, the foundation was given some works by Louise Bourgeois. Michael and Lynne Cooke—the brilliant curator who was also working for Dia at that time—asked me to design a space to exhibit those works. Louise saw this thing I designed, and she liked it. When the Norwegians asked her to do the memorial, she said, "OK, but I want to work with Peter Zumthor." I was very pleased that she wanted to involve me.

JR – I can imagine! How did the collaboration proceed?

PZ – I wrote to her and said, "Please tell me when you have an idea, and then I'll start my design." She wrote back to me and said, "*You* start!"

JR – Was that because she wanted an architectural setting to respond to? It's surprising, in a way—almost like hearing that a painter wants to have a frame picked out before they touch a brush to their canvas.

PZ – Well, she was too old to travel then. I think she wanted me to go and look and then design something that she could react to. The site was on a rocky stretch of coast with no trees. When I got there I had an idea overnight: a very simple, long volume stretching across the empty landscape. I made some watercolors and sent them to her in New York. I waited for ten days, then finally there came a small sketch, which was the floor plan for a simple square glass building, with her work in the center. I was disappointed because I had already envisioned the other design, but I wrote back to her and said, "OK, I'll give up my long building. I'll do your idea." Then she said, "No, I want both."

JR – This is an unusual collaboration because your architecture played a dual role. You designed a glass pavilion to house Bourgeois's sculpture *The Damned, the Possessed, and the Beloved,* which is a jet of gas flame rising from a steel chair, reflected in a ring of surrounding mirrors. In that sense the architecture is a frame. But your other structure is a long walkway lined with texts about the history of the trials and the lives of the victims. That is architecture as an experience.

PZ – It was a dialogue. I made this very melancholy thing, a place for you to go inside and walk and reflect. There was no aggression visible in my work. Her piece is full of aggression and intensity—it has a fire burning in it.

Atelier Zumthor, Steilneset Memorial, Vardø, Norway, 2011

JR – I'd like to keep discussing this question of architecture as a frame. You were also asked by Dia to design a pavilion for Walter De Maria.

PZ – Yes, it was for a single work, *360 ° I Ching/64 Sculptures* [1981]. The piece is based on the hexagrams of the I Ching, and it is a field of hexagonal rods laid out in squares surrounded by a circle. It needed a large, uninterrupted floor area and even light, so I designed a monolithic concrete shell with a deep grill for the roof to diffuse the daylight. Walter also wanted the piece to have a relationship to the landscape, so there was a large window on the east side. Talking with Walter was crucial for the design.

JR – I can see how, with the right artist, that kind of collaborative conversation could be very satisfying. But I wonder if it's a problem that art has come to rely more and more on this kind of architectural framing. Since we're already discussing De Maria, I'm thinking of his work *The New York Earth Room*, which is also from 1977, where a large space is filled with dirt. In a way, this piece is paradigmatic for an entire generation of artists whose work is defined by the space in which it is exhibited. There's a wonderful line in Rosalind Krauss's famous 1978 essay "Sculpture in the Expanded Field" where she says that, by the 1960s, sculpture had become simply "what is in the room that is not really the room."

PZ – Ah, that's good. It's true.

JR – But there's an irony here, no? Architecture becomes more crucial than ever—it's literally delimiting the work—but at the same time it is cast in an emphatically secondary role: it's the frame or the foil. I wonder how you feel about that, as the person who's designing the room. Is it ever frustrating to have to create the ideal envelope for a work of art?

PZ – Not at all. Recently I had a strange experience. I was at a university to give a lecture, and I stopped in the art museum, which has a very good collection. I started in the Oceanic galleries. There were all these beautiful artifacts, but I was shocked at how they were displayed. Everything was packed together, as if by a teenager decorating the walls of their bedroom. I'm thinking, All these things, they might be from the same island—or they might have nothing to do with each other! Then I went to the painting galleries. It was just one painting after another lined up in a row on the wall. It looked like a stamp collection! You don't do justice to art if you exhibit it this way. I got so mad that, after the lecture, when I met some friends for dinner, they asked me, "Peter, do you need a drink?"

JR – I hope they gave you one! But you're saying you would have liked to build an architectural framework for these things?

PZ – The objects felt helpless to me. I had the feeling that I would have liked to take just one of them and make a huge room for it. Then, all of a sudden, maybe in a mysterious way, it would start to tell me a story. I saw this done a long time ago in Paris at an exhibition of the small figures of Alberto Giacometti by the Swiss artist Rémy Zaugg. It was at the Musée d'Art Moderne in 1991, and they stood in this huge space—these tiny figures—and it worked. What I want to say is that there should be a sensitive shell or a skin that creates the possibility of understanding these alienated objects, and yes, architects should design it.

JR – I love the idea that a work of art doesn't have to be an enormous piece by Walter De Maria to deserve its own space. But I wonder if there is another irony here when it comes to art today. There are exceptions—we've been discussing many artists who make incredible site-specific pieces—but the base condition of modern and contemporary art is precisely that of alienation. Artworks are made to be homeless, because it's the fact that they can move from the studio to the art fair or the commercial gallery to the collector's house or the museum that allows them to function as commodities. The entire art market depends on alienation. Does this create an obstacle to building good museums by creating pressure to provide a neutral or interchangeable context?

PZ – None of that stops an architect from making a good home for art. Site specificity and permanent installation are not the only answers. A building that allows us to see the work of one artist in-depth works very well for modern and contemporary artists. I achieved this in Bregenz without really knowing what I was doing: because of the scale of the building it works perfectly for mono-thematic presentations. And my new building under construction for the Fondation Beyeler is exactly this idea. It's only three levels, three times five thousand square feet. They can dedicate the whole space to one or two artists and make a focused show that is more than a stamp collection.

JR – What strikes me about both the Kunsthaus Bregenz and your building for the Beyeler is that you're able to limit the program exclusively to spaces for art.

PZ – I push away all the other things.

JR – Which is an extremely effective approach, but does it only work for smaller institutions? Major museums today are expected to offer so much more than exhibition space—there are auditoriums, theaters, classrooms, conservation labs, offices.

PZ – Spaces for selling products, too!

JR – Right, we can't forget the bookstore and the gift shop, not to mention bars and cafés and restaurants. How do you deal with all this? In an ideal world, would you break apart the museum into a kind of campus?

PZ – There's always a different way to approach this problem. You saw what I did in Bregenz: the café, the bookstore, and the offices are in a separate building across the square. At LACMA [Los Angeles County Museum of Art], all the art is one floor up, on one continuous plane. The whole ground floor is open, and on this street level we also have an education center and a store and three restaurants. I think this will be very successful—LA will get a huge new public space.

Atelier Zumthor, rendering of Los Angeles County Museum of Art,
Los Angeles, California, expansion anticipated completion 2026

JR – When I first saw your design for LACMA, I thought of
Lina Bo Bardi's Museu de Arte de São Paulo, where the main gallery
is lifted to create a wonderfully vibrant plaza at street level. Did you
have that project in mind?

PZ – I wasn't thinking of that building specifically, but it's
related. There's a connection to Oscar Niemeyer's museums in São
Paulo's Ibirapuera Park, too: the idea of an elevated building that
becomes a big roof over the ground. I couldn't do this in Europe.
You need a big landscape.

JR – And a warm climate, and LA certainly has both. But I want
to get back to what happens inside the galleries for a moment. When
you were discussing your Bregenz museum in a recent lecture, you
said you told the director, "Bad art will look good in this building,
and good art will look even better."

PZ – That was sort of a joke, of course.

JR – Yet it struck me because, to be honest, I agree—and I have
mixed feelings about it. On the one hand, it's so nice to hear the
power of museum architecture openly acknowledged. It's almost the

opposite of something Yoshio Taniguchi supposedly said after he won the competition to design the Museum of Modern Art expansion in 1997: "Raise a lot of money, and I'll give you great architecture. Raise even more money, and I'll make the architecture disappear." So often we're presented with a false binary, as if the only possibilities are that museum architecture must either fade into the background or overwhelm the art. But, on the other hand, I wonder if a building like Bregenz is doing more than some art deserves, or more than some art is asking for.

PZ – What do you mean? Can you give an example?

JR – Well, I saw the Lawrence Weiner exhibition in Bregenz in 2016, and for me it was strange to see it in that space. I admire his work very much, so this is not a simple case of your architecture making bad art look good. But in a sense he spent his whole career trying to undermine the traditions of sculpture and of aesthetic contemplation—that motivated his turn to language in the first place. And then I see his wall texts against the richly textured concrete, under the perfect lighting, and the letters are just faintly reflected in the polished floor, and I feel like I'm looking at Bernini! Do you ever have reservations about how much work the building is doing to create a certain—undeniably powerful—kind of aesthetic experience?

PZ – No, no, no. I don't worry about that. I think the artists and the curators should do what they want. You can go there and have that kind of experience and think, Should his work be here? Maybe not. But that's not my decision. I'm the architect. I'm very happy that since the museum opened it's been one good artist after another. And I think the artists like it. I asked Thomas Demand what it was like when he was invited to show there, and he said, "It's like getting the gold card from the bank!"

JR – His metaphor of the gold card raises another question. Bregenz is constructed with an extraordinarily high level of crafts-manship. Unfortunately, at least in America, we're at a point where craftsmanship has become associated primarily with luxury products.

PZ – Yes, in Europe, too.

JR – You're in a unique position where you can take ten years to build a museum, and the building can be made largely by hand. And it may well be that this is how a museum *should* be done.

PZ – But it's hard.

JR – Right, even for you, it's hard! So is that approach of grounding architecture in craft no longer sustainable?

PZ – The conditions now are purely economic. The construction system is completely commercial. For example, on many projects, the general contractor will set a GMP—a guaranteed maximum price. From then on, the client can sleep well, because they know exactly how much the building will cost. But this also takes away all the responsibility from me and from the client. Now I'm at the mercy of the general contractor. I design something, and he can say, "This is how much it will cost." And maybe I know it should only cost 10 percent of what he's saying, so I tell him that. He says again, "This is how much it will cost." Poker face. There's nothing I can do.

JR – The problem with this kind of organizational structure is that it sets up an adversarial relationship between the architect and the contractor. Their incentives are at cross purposes. The contractor wants to inflate costs when setting the GMP, but then wants to build in the absolute cheapest way possible. And it's difficult for the construction process to evolve intelligently because any update becomes a change order, which both the architect and the contractor will try to blame each other for.

PZ – But there are other ways to build. My client for the Beyeler took responsibility for hiring the craftsmen, trade by trade, themselves. So they take on more liability, but we have much more freedom. We can find working methods to solve problems as they come up.

JR – So it's not about spending more money, it's about how you structure the project. You're arguing for a more collaborative approach.

PZ – Yes, and we need clients who understand how this works. But the other problem is that craftsmanship has almost died out. You outsource everything to the factory. They create standard products, and you just assemble them on-site. Everything that is done by hand in a building, like the primary structure, you never get to see. Because they clad everything! That's industrialization.

JR – But what can you do about it? Is the alternative for the architect to start working more like an artist?

PZ – You have to become a collaborator. Craftsmen like me because I am a good partner. At first, when I visit the construction site, they think, "Oh no, the architect is coming!" But then they find out that they can talk to me more easily than to the general contractor. Because I can ask, "What's the problem here?" And then either I have a solution for them or they say, "No, that doesn't work, but we can do it this other way." And I know when they are right because I listen to them. It's a direct relationship. Soon they're asking, "Can you come more often?"

JR – You're inviting the people who are actually putting the building together to participate more actively in the process.

PZ – In the LACMA building the concrete structure is exposed. I told one of the workers, "You're making this building. One day you can come back with your grandchildren and show them what you did." Normally you would have to go to the parking garage to see anything that was made by hand.

JR – Right, or a mechanical room—you'd have to go somewhere the client didn't bother to pay for a cladding product because they didn't think anyone would see it. But your comments have made me realize something else: the commercial pressures of the construction industry push museum architecture toward the same generic condition that we were discussing earlier as ideally suited to the homeless status of contemporary art. Sheetrock hides the building's structure at the same time that it creates the white cube.

PZ – That condition serves the encyclopedic museum, too, because it erases context and allows the museum to create any historical narrative it wants.

JR – It's a good point that the abstraction of the white cube isn't just about aesthetics; it's also about creating a blank slate for the schema of art history. The funny thing is that, on an experiential level, it's profoundly antihistorical. Take the Metropolitan Museum of Art. This is my hometown museum, and I love going there, but when I walk in I can look at an altarpiece in basically the same way I can look at an impressionist painting. That doesn't make any sense, because one was made for a church and the other was made for a bourgeois living room! Encyclopedic museums often suppress historical specificity by bringing everything to the same level of experience.

PZ – It's also a question of how you move through the museum. I think you will see that in Los Angeles. For LACMA we have created these meandering spaces around twenty-four cubic galleries. It's like a village. Each gallery is like a house on a street that you can visit. It has only one entrance, and it is important that you go in and out by the same opening, because this means that a complete, concentrated experience is possible. You don't just pass through. But then outside the galleries you can wander and find your own way. You can look out to the city all around, and you can turn whichever way you want.

JR – This kind of fluid circulation seems crucial for rethinking the ways in which museums present history, because, of course, the original encyclopedic museums were in converted palaces, or at least modeled on the palace, which meant that the galleries were organized in a strict enfilade—a very linear circulation for a very linear conception of history. But materials themselves can also provide a link to history. In your Kolumba Museum in Cologne [2007], you designed a brick (which was custom-made for the project) that related to the medieval stonework of the ruined chapel that already stood on the site. Or in your shelter for the Roman archaeological site in Chur [1986], you used steel and timber with a light touch that emphasizes the gravity of the ancient foundations. Do you think that some of what we might call the historical task of the museum could be accomplished in material terms?

PZ – That's a big question. I don't know. What I know is a small thing: it's good to have substantial architecture; it's good to work with material presence. Let's say it like that. Because if an object is worthy of being exhibited—if it is worthy of being kept— it deserves a material presence. It should not be put into a shiny, glittery world of alienation. We seem to share the idea that isolating objects is a terrible operation. They should have a chance to react to earth, or stone, or wood—to the material world. That's where they came from.

Atelier Zumthor, Shelter for Roman Ruins, Chur, Switzerland, 1986

Notes

page 9 "I don't like museums much": Paul Valéry, "The Problem of Museums" [1923], in *The Collected Works of Paul Valéry*, vol. 12, *Degas, Monet, Morisot*, ed. Jackson Mathews (New York: Pantheon Books, 1960), 202 (translation slightly modified).

page 9 "seen as jewels or diamonds": Quatremère de Quincy, fifth letter, quoted in Martin Gaier, "The Art of Civilization: Museum Enemies in the Nineteenth Century," in *Images of the Art Museum: Connecting Gaze and Discourse in the History of Museology*, ed. Melania Savino and Eva-Maria Troelenberg (Berlin, Boston: De Gruyter, 2017), 37.

page 9 "a necessarily unusable excess of capital": Valéry, "The Problem of Museums," 204.

page 9 "Their mother, Architecture, is dead.": Valéry, "The Problem of Museums," 206 (translation slightly modified).

page 20 "the precise identification": Tafuri's book was first published in Italy in 1973 as *Progetto e Utopia*. This quotation is from the preface Tafuri added to the first English edition, published in 1976. See: *Architecture and Utopia: Design and Capitalist Development* (Cambridge, MA: MIT Press, 1976), ix.

page 28 "the here and now": This essay, written by Benjamin in 1935 and originally published in 1936, was first translated into English under this title by Harry Zohn and published in the 1968 volume *Illuminations*. It has since been retranslated by Zohn and Edmund Jephcott as "The Work of Art in the Age of Its Technological Reproducibility" and published under this title in the anthology of Benjamin's writings published by Harvard University Press. All quotations here are taken from this version. See Walter Benjamin, "The Work of Art in the Age of Its Technological Reproducibility: Second Version," in *Walter Benjamin: Selected Writings*, Volume 3, 1935–1938 (Cambridge, MA: Harvard University Press, 2002), 103.

page 28 "decay of the aura": Benjamin, "The Work of Art," 104.

page 29 "From a photographic plate": Benjamin, "The Work of Art," 106.

page 30 "object of simultaneous collective reception": Benjamin, "The Work of Art," 116.

page 30 "You can be a museum": This remark has been repeated ad infinitum over the decades, often without citing a source, but it was not published by either Stein or Barr in their own writings and is possibly apocryphal. When a source is given, it is usually MoMA director John B. Hightower, who wrote in his foreword to a 1970 exhibition catalog: "'You can be a museum or you can be modern, but you can't be both,' Gertrude Stein once firmly told one of my predecessors as Director of The Museum of Modern Art." See: John B. Hightower, "Foreword," in *Four Americans in Paris: The Collection of Gertrude Stein and Her Family* (New York: Museum of Modern Art, 1970), 8. The first time the remark appeared in print seems to have been in a 1967 *New York Times* article by the paper's art critic, John Canaday, who asserted its veracity while being slightly more cautious: "The story goes (and rings true) that when Alfred H. Barr, Jr. approached Gertrude Stein on the subject of leaving her collection to the Museum of Modern Art, she replied that she was not interested, since 'You can be a museum or you can be modern, but you can't be both.'" See: John Canaday, "Can You Be a Museum and Modern Too?," *New York Times*, June 18, 1967, https://timesmachine.nytimes.com/timesmachine/1967/06/18/89671229.html?pageNumber=107.

page 34 "Is the department store a museum?" John Cotton Dana, *The Gloom of the Museum* (Woodstock, VT: Elm Tree Press, 1917), 23. With ambivalence, Dana was ready to answer his own question in the affirmative. In the same passage cited here, noting the liveliness and popularity of most American department stores, he admitted: "A great city department store of the first class is perhaps more like a good museum of art than are any of the museums we have yet established."

page 35 "there are relations": Walter Benjamin, *The Arcades Project* (Cambridge, MA: Harvard University Press, 1999), 415.

page 37 Studies at major museums: While internal studies of viewing habits conducted by museums are rarely made public given the sensitive nature of the subject, a 2017 academic study by a team of psychologists working with the Art Institute of Chicago supports this time frame, finding that visitors spent a mean of 28.63 seconds looking at paintings in the Art Institute's collection. See: Lisa F. Smith, Jeffrey K. Smith, and Pablo P. L. Tinio, "Time Spent Viewing Art and Reading Labels," *Psychology of Aesthetics, Creativity, and the Arts* 11, no. 1 (2017): 77–85, https://doi.org/10.1037/aca0000049.

page 37 "received in a state of distraction": Benjamin, "The Work of Art," 119.

page 57 "The citizen must appropriate the bridge." Frantz Fanon, *The Wretched of the Earth*, trans. Richard Philcox (New York: Grove Atlantic, 2007), 141. Originally published in French as *Les Damnés de la Terre*, 1961.

page 91 "Were we trying to find an 'alternative space'": Vito Acconci, "Text," in Alanna Heiss et al., *Rooms P.S. 1* (New York: Institute for Art and Urban Resources, 1977), 127.

page 95 "is essentially domestic in scale": Rubin made this remark to *New York Times* architecture critic Paul

Goldberger when Goldberger interviewed him for his review of Cesar Pelli's MoMA expansion, which opened in 1984. See: Paul Goldberger, "The New MoMA," *New York Times*, April 15, 1984, https://timesmachine.nytimes.com/timesmachine/1984/04/15/123681.html?pageNumber=648.

page 176 "There is no such thing as phenomenology": Ludwig Wittgenstein, *Remarks on Colour*, ed. G. E. M. Anscombe, trans. Linda L. McAlister and Margarete Schättle (Berkeley, CA: University of California Press, 1977), I §53.

page 194 "to reshape the old and the familiar": John Michael Vlach, *By the Work of Their Hands: Studies in Afro-American Folklife* (Charlottesville, VA: University Press of Virginia, 1991), 5.

page 258 "What is proposed is like a monstrous carbuncle": The then Prince of Wales made these remarks in a speech he gave at a gala celebrating the 150th anniversary of the Royal Institute of British Architects (RIBA). The full transcript is available on the website of the royal family: www.royal.uk/clarencehouse/speech/speech-hrh-prince-wales-150th-anniversary-royal-institute-british-architects-riba-royal-gala. The vivid phrasing lodged in the popular imagination and has been much repeated in the press. Eventually the British magazine *Building Design* even launched the Carbuncle Cup, a humorous award given annually to the ugliest building completed that year in the United Kingdom.

page 325 "ecstatic primitivism" James Clifford, "Quai Branly in Process," *October* 120 (Spring 2007), 5.

page 352 "what is in the room that is not really the room": Rosalind Krauss, "Sculpture in the Expanded Field," *October* 8 (Spring 1979), 36.

Biographies

David Adjaye was born in 1966, in Dar es Salaam, Tanzania. He studied architecture at the Royal College of Art in London before establishing Adjaye Associates in 2000. Adjaye was knighted in 2017 for services to architecture. He is the recipient of the 2021 Royal Gold Medal from the Royal Institute of British Architects, and he was appointed to the Order of Merit in 2022. His studio currently has offices in Accra, London, and New York, and has designed acclaimed museums worldwide, including the Museum of Contemporary Art Denver; the Aïshti Foundation, Beirut; and the Smithsonian National Museum of African American History and Culture, Washington, DC.

David Chipperfield was born in 1953, in London, England. He graduated from the Kingston School of Art in 1976 and remained in London to study at the Architectural Association, receiving his diploma the following year. In 1985 he founded David Chipperfield Architects, which currently has offices in London, Berlin, Milan, Shanghai, and Santiago de Compostela. In 2007 Chipperfield received the Royal Institute of British Architects Stirling Prize, and he was awarded the Pritzker Architecture Prize in 2023. The firm's notable museum projects include the Neues Museum and the complete renovation of Mies van der Rohe's iconic Neue Nationalgalerie, both in Berlin; Turner Contemporary, Margate, England; and the Museo Jumex, Mexico City.

Elizabeth Diller was born in 1954, in Łódź, Poland. She graduated from the Cooper Union School of Architecture in 1979, and two years later cofounded Diller Scofidio (now Diller Scofidio + Renfro) in New York. In 1999, Diller received the first MacArthur Foundation grant given in the field of architecture. Diller Scofidio + Renfro designed the Institute of Contemporary Art in Boston; the most recent expansion of the Museum of Modern Art, New York; and the Shed, a multidisciplinary exhibition and event space in New York.

Frank Gehry was born in 1929 in Toronto, Ontario, and studied architecture at the University of Southern California. In 1962 he established his practice in Los Angeles, which became Gehry Partners in 2001. He was awarded the Pritzker Architecture Prize in 1989 and received the Presidential Medal of Freedom in 2016. In addition to his renowned design for the Guggenheim Museum Bilbao, Spain, his other notable cultural projects include Fondation Louis Vuitton, Paris, and the Guggenheim Abu Dhabi, UAE.

Richard Gluckman was born in 1947, in Buffalo, New York. He received his bachelor and master of architecture degrees from Syracuse University and established his New York–based firm Stelle Gluckman (now Gluckman Tang) in 1977. Gluckman was the first architect to work for the Dia Art Foundation and designed exhibition spaces for Dia throughout New York. In addition to working and living spaces for many notable artists, Gluckman has executed a wide range of major institutional projects, including the renovation of the Whitney Museum of American Art, New York; the Andy Warhol Museum, Pittsburgh; and the Museo Picasso Málaga, Spain.

Jacques Herzog was born in 1950, in Basel, Switzerland, and studied architecture at the Swiss Federal Institute of Technology in Zurich. With his classmate Pierre de Meuron he cofounded the Basel-based firm Herzog & de Meuron in 1978. The firm was awarded the Pritzker Architecture Prize in 2001; two years later, they received the Royal Institute of British Architects Stirling Prize. In addition to their acclaimed design for London's Tate Modern, the partners have designed many other museums and cultural institutions, including the Perez Art Museum, Miami, and the Park Avenue Armory, New York.

Steven Holl was born in December 1947, in Bremerton, Washington. He studied architecture at the University of Washington, graduating in 1971. In 1977 he founded Steven Holl Architects; the firm currently has offices in New York City, New York's Hudson Valley, and Beijing. In 2012, Holl received the American Institute of Architects Gold Medal, and in 2014, he was awarded the Praemium Imperiale Prize for Architecture by the Imperial Family of Japan and the Japan Art Association. He designed the Museum of Contemporary Art Kiasma, Helsinki, Finland; the Bloch Building at the Nelson-Atkins Museum of Art, St. Louis; and the Nancy and Rich Kinder Building at the Museum of Fine Arts, Houston.

Walter Hood was born in 1958, in Charlotte, North Carolina. He studied landscape architecture at North Carolina A&T State University before earning graduate degrees in both architecture and landscape design from the University of California, Berkeley, in 1989 as well as an MFA from the School of the Art Institute of Chicago in 2013. In 1992 he founded Hood Design Studio, based in Oakland. Hood received the Cooper-Hewitt National Design Award for Landscape Design in 2009 and was awarded a Mac-Arthur Fellowship in 2019. Hood's projects include the de Young gardens in San Francisco, the grounds of the Oakland Museum of California, and the landscape design for the International African American Museum in Charleston, South Carolina.

Liu Yichun was born in 1969, in Haiyang, Shandong, China. He earned his master's degree in architecture at Tongji University in 1997, and for the next three years he served as chief architect at the university's Architectural Design and Research

Institute. In 2001 he founded Atelier Deshaus with Chen Yifeng and Zhuang Shen in Shanghai. Notable works by Atelier Deshaus include the Qintai Art Museum in Wuhan, China, and the Long Museum West Bund in Shanghai.

Renzo Piano was born September 14, 1937, in Genoa, Italy, and graduated from the Polytechnic University of Milan in 1964. He collaborated with British architect Richard Rogers and Irish structural engineer Peter Rice on the winning competition entry for the Pompidou Centre in Paris, completed in 1977, and established the Renzo Piano Building Workshop (RPBW), currently based in Genoa and Paris, in 1981. In 1998, Piano was awarded the Pritzker Architecture Prize. Among his many notable museum projects are Houston's Menil Collection and the new downtown building of New York's Whitney Museum of American Art.

Denise Scott Brown was born in 1931, in Nkana, Northern Rhodesia (now Zambia). She graduated in 1955 from the Architectural Association School of Architecture in London, later earning master's degrees in architecture and city planning from the University of Pennsylvania. In 1967, Scott Brown joined Robert Venturi's firm, Venturi and Rauch, in Philadelphia, which became Venturi, Scott Brown and Associates. Scott Brown's notable cultural projects include a major addition to Allen Memorial Art Museum at Oberlin College; the Seattle Art Museum; and the Sainsbury Wing of the National Gallery, London.

Kazuyo Sejima was born in 1956, in Mito, Japan, and studied architecture at Japan Women's University. In 1987 she established Kazuyo Sejima & Associates, and in 1995 she cofounded the Tokyo-based firm SANAA with Ryue Nishizawa. SANAA won the Pritzker Architecture Prize in 2010. The firm designed the New Museum of

Contemporary Art, New York, and the 21st Century Museum of Contemporary Art, Kanazawa, Japan.

Annabelle Selldorf was born in 1960, in Cologne, Germany. She holds a bachelor of architecture degree from Pratt Institute and a master of architecture degree from Syracuse University in Florence. In 1988 she founded Selldorf Architects, based in New York. In 2014, Selldorf received the Award in Architecture given by the American Academy of Arts and Letters, and in 2016 she was awarded the Medal of Honor from the American Institute of Architects New York Chapter. Selldorf has designed major renovations and expansions of museums across Europe and the United States, including the Museum of Contemporary Art San Diego, California; the Frick Collection, New York; and the Art Gallery of Ontario, Toronto.

Shohei Shigematsu was born in 1973, in Fukuoka, Japan. After graduating from Kyushu University in 1996, he studied at the Berlage Institute in Amsterdam. In 1998 he was hired by the Office of Metropolitan Architecture, where he is now a partner, working out of the firm's New York office. Shigematsu has directed many of OMA's museum projects, including the Pierre Lassonde Pavilion at MNBAQ, Québec City, and is currently overseeing the expansion of the New Museum of Contemporary Art, New York.

Kulapat Yantrasast was born in 1967, in Bangkok, Thailand, and holds advanced degrees in architecture from the University of Tokyo. Before establishing his own practice, he worked as a close associate to Japanese architect Tadao Ando, leading various museum projects. In 2004 he founded WHY, a multidisciplinary design practice with main offices in New York and Los Angeles. WHY's first major commission was the Grand Rapids Art Museum,

Michigan. The studio recently renovated the Northwest Coast Hall at the American Museum of Natural History, New York, and is currently renovating the Michael C. Rockefeller Wing of the arts of sub-Saharan Africa, Oceania, and the Americas at the Metropolitan Museum of Art, New York.

Peter Zumthor was born in 1943, in Basel, Switzerland, and studied at a vocational arts school in Basel before moving to the Pratt Institute in New York. In 1979 he established his eponymous practice in Chur, Switzerland. Zumthor was awarded the Praemium Imperiale in 2008, the Pritzker Architecture Prize in 2009, and the Royal Gold Medal from the Royal Institute of British Architects in 2012. Several of his best-known works are museums, including Kunsthaus Bregenz, Austria, and the Kolumba Art Museum of the Archdiocese of Cologne. Zumthor's design for the David Geffen Galleries, a new building for the Los Angeles County Museum of Art, is currently under construction.

Credits

About the Author

Julian Rose is a historian and critic of art and architecture. From 2012 to 2018, he was a senior editor at *Artforum*, and he regularly contributes to a wide range of publications, including *Aperture, Architectural Review, Artforum, Bookforum, Log, Perspecta,* and *October.* His work as a cofounder of the award-winning design studio Formlessfinder has been exhibited internationally at venues including the Museum of Modern Art, the Chicago Architecture Biennial, and the Venice Biennale of Architecture. Rose received a BA in the history of art and architecture from Harvard University and an MArch from Princeton University and has taught architectural design and history at Columbia University and Princeton University. He is currently completing a PhD at Princeton on the origin and evolution of museums of contemporary art.